THE EXCHANGE

THE EXCHANGE OF WORDS

Speech, Testimony, and Intersubjectivity

RICHARD MORAN

OXFORD
UNIVERSITY PRESS

OXFORD
UNIVERSITY PRESS

Oxford University Press is a department of the University of Oxford. It furthers
the University's objective of excellence in research, scholarship, and education
by publishing worldwide. Oxford is a registered trade mark of Oxford University
Press in the UK and certain other countries.

Published in the United States of America by Oxford University Press
198 Madison Avenue, New York, NY 10016, United States of America.

© Oxford University Press 2018

CIP data is on file at the Library of Congress
ISBN 978–0–19–088290–7 (Pbk.)
ISBN 978–0–19–087332–5 (Hbk.)

To my friends in the Harvard Department of Philosophy:
Colleagues, Students, and Staff

And once more, to Borgna

Contents

Preface   ix
Acknowledgments   xiii

1. Speech, Intersubjectivity, and Social Acts   1
   1.1 Reid and the Social Acts of Mind   1
   1.2 The Speaking Subject and the Political Subject   5
   1.3 The Epistemological Perspective and the Participants'
        Perspective   16
   1.4 Speech as Indicative Sign   22
   1.5 The Self-Understanding of the Social Act of Mind   30

2. Getting Told and Being Believed   36
   2.1 The Realm of Testimony   36
   2.2 Evidential Relations and the A Priori   39
   2.3 Perversity, Dependence, and Risk   42
   2.4 Assertion as Assurance   44
   2.5 Photographs and Statements   49
   2.6 The Importance of Being Non-Natural   52
   2.7 The Speaker's Conferral: Having Your Say, Giving Your Word   63
   2.8 Evidence and Disharmony   68

3. The Meaning of Sincerity and Self-Expression   76
   3.1 Sincerity and the Telepathic Ideal   76
   3.2 Williams on the Norm of Sincerity   78
   3.3 Two Forms of the Expression of Belief   83
   3.4 Sincerity and the Speaker's Guarantee   89

4. The Claim and the Encounter   96
   4.1 Grice: The Production of Belief (in Others) through the
        Revelation of (One's Own) Belief   96

4.2 Verbal Communication and Perception   100
4.3 Sincerity, Self-Understanding, and Self-Manifestation   105
4.4 Two Forms of Knowing What One Is Doing   110
4.5 Moore's Paradox and the Meaning of Overtness in Assertion   112

5. Illocution and Interlocution   122
  5.1 Addressing, Claiming, and the Second Person   122
  5.2 Theoretical Reasons and Their Transmission   124
  5.3 Perlocution, Illocution, and the Idea of a Normative Power 127
  5.4 Recognition and Reciprocity   135
  5.5 The Observer's Perspective and the Perspective of the
       Interlocutors   137

6. The Social Act and Its Self-Consciousness   145
  6.1 The Bearing of the Agent's Understanding on the
       Description of What She Does   145
  6.2 The Illocutionary, the First Person, and "Hereby"   152
  6.3 Speech as Production and Speech as Social Act   158
  6.4 The Meaning of Mutuality   166
  6.5 Grice's Third Clause and the Role of Overtness   170
  6.6 Strawson and Avowability   177
  6.7 The Perspective of the Conversation   183

7. The Self and Its Society   190
  7.1 Thinking as the "Soul's Conversation with Itself"   190
  7.2 Talking to Oneself, to Others, to No One   197
  7.3 Supplying the Missing Interlocutor   205
  7.4 And Who Shall I Say Is Calling?   213
  7.5 Last Words   218

Bibliography   221
Index of Names   229
Index of Subjects   231

Preface

My own relation to my words is wholly different from other people's.
—Wittgenstein, *Philosophical Investigations* (1956)

This book is an exploration of what is distinctive about the forms of human intersubjectivity that are exemplified in acts of speech, primarily the act of one person *addressing* another, and aims to give a philosophical account of the relations between various dimensions of this basic human phenomenon. Human beings may be said to communicate in a multitude of ways: consciously and unconsciously, explicitly and implicitly, individually and collectively, and both verbally and nonverbally. Language makes possible a specific way in which one person can address a particular other person and explicitly claim something as true and make herself accountable to her addressee for its truth, and by making *herself* thus accountable provide her addressee with a reason to believe *what* she has said.[1] In one way or another this form of human interaction has been explored by philosophers as various as Augustine, Grotius, Hobbes, and Hume, as well as by contemporary philosophers of language, of ethics, and in epistemology. The capacity to take oaths and bind oneself with words has been located at the origins of the idea of a social contract and the very notion of political authority, and the capacity to verbally attest to some fact and have that count for one's audience is central to the most basic forms of self-presentation and social recognition. At the same time this capacity is manifest in the most ordinary and transitory of acts, as with any time one person tells someone something in response to a casual question. From a philosophical perspective this is a phenomenon with multiple aspects, whose relations to each other remain relatively unexplored. The focus of this book is a phenomenon of

---

1 Except where the context would make it confusing, I will tend to use feminine pronouns to refer to the first speaker and masculine ones for second speaker and interlocutor. This will both help keep straight the distinctness of the two parties and also underscore that "speaker" and "hearer" are names for the roles they alternate between in the course of a conversation.

language, and in particular the speech act of telling. It is also a phenomenon of moral psychology in that speaker and audience are in a complex normative relation with each other. At the same time it is a phenomenon in the philosophy of mind in that what is in question here is a specific form of intersubjective understanding, one that is dependent on certain specific capacities studied by developmental psychologists and others, and is also a form of intersubjectivity whose philosophical description poses a special challenge to traditional models for thinking about the nature of understanding another person and the "problem of other minds." And it is also of course a phenomenon of epistemology, one that is central to the nature of rationality, since in the ordinary course of things, in having been *told* something by another person one will take oneself to have been given a *reason* to believe something, and indeed (often enough) to *know* the thing in question. The project of this book is to understand how the different dimensions of this phenomenon and the human capacities it expresses are implicated with each other and depend upon each other, and in this way to understand better the social dimension of speech, of knowledge, and of the mind.

A guiding question throughout is, What is distinctive about the way that a speaker provides a reason to believe something for her hearer when she tells him something? And what is the nature of the intersubjective act when a speaker asserts something as true to her audience, and that person believes her? There are two broad ways in which a speaker's words can provide her audience with a reason to believe something. In one of these ways, we may learn something from the speaker's utterance in the same way we learn from her blushing, or the way the sound of her speech reveals her accent and her origins. Here the event of the speaker's utterance is functioning in the same way as ordinary evidence, an indication from which we infer something. But when we do attend to someone's speech in this way, the knowledge we acquire (e.g., about her origins) may have nothing to do with the content of her statement, with what she means to *say*. Nor is it the case that we believe *the speaker* herself when we arrive at a conclusion by attending to her voice in this way. In another way of relating to the speaker, one that is more at home in the situation of ordinary dialogue, the audience believes *what* the speaker says (i.e., the very thing asserted by her) because he believes *her*, and he believes her because she has addressed a particular claim or assertion *to him*, and presented it as true, worthy of belief. In the former situation, where the hearer adopts an inferential or "symptomatic" relation to the speaker's utterance, it need not matter to the soundness of his conclusion that the speaker *means* for him to draw that conclusion, or indeed is addressing her words to anyone at all. If her accent reveals something about her, it does not make any epistemic difference to the audience whether the speaker intends to communicate anything by her utterance or whether she is aware of what conclusions are being drawn from it. By contrast, in the ordinary dialogic situation of explicit communication it makes all the difference in the world whether the speaker *understands* what she is saying, whether she *means* her utterance as a committed assertion of the facts or as something else, and whether *she herself* is to be believed or not. In the absence of these assumptions about how the speaker understands her own utterance and how she is addressing her audience (i.e., in the mode of assertion, or question, or exercise, etc.), the audience will have no reason for belief at all, or not one connected with the content of what the speaker has said.

What this contrast suggests is that what I am calling the ordinary situation of verbal communication, insofar as this centers on acts like that of one person telling something to another, is an intersubjective act in which the status of the utterance as a reason to believe what is said depends on the speaker and her audience being related in a way with a particular structure. The speaker affirms or attests to some *fact*, and does so toward her *addressee*, and the success of the act consists in the addressee understanding the speaker, and either believing the fact in question by way of believing the speaker herself, or responding by way of challenge or question to the speaker. Unlike the situation where a listener draws conclusions from the quality of the speaker's voice, here the speaker addresses her audience directly and explicitly presents her act as having a particular epistemic significance, that of being a reason to believe the content of what she asserts. A speaker's assertion is not merely the *occasion* for believing something (as the sound of her voice may be); rather the content of her assertion itself is *what is believed* (or disbelieved). Unlike a mere phenomenon (a sound, a sight), what a speaker asserts is a possible *direct* object of belief, and in the ordinary case the content asserted is believed by way of believing the speaker herself. The epistemology itself is irreducibly social and intersubjective.

Although I don't emphasize them in what follows, there are several overlapping themes between this book and my previous book, *Authority and Estrangement*, and in fact I had originally conceived of them together, although I worked on them quite separately. In both there is a critique of the dominance of a certain observer's perspective on the phenomenon in question (thought, action, speech), and an account of the agent's perspective and practical knowledge in constituting the domain to be understood. In both the appeal to a notion of "mind reading" comes under question, and the criticism in *Authority and Estrangement* of appeal to "higher-order states" to describe self-consciousness is of a piece with the criticism here of the "higher order" picture of mutual recognition between participants in a conversation. In both, the limits of the observer's perspective are explored in terms of something like an "ideal symptomatic stance," and toward the end of this book the discussion of Peter Strawson's early work on speech acts brings in the idea of "avowability," which appears in a different guise in the earlier book. Some of these thematic connections only became evident to me fairly late in the process.

I take the distinctiveness of the first-person perspective to be basic to the ideas of human thought and action, and to have a scope beyond the question of first-person privilege or authority, extending to systematic restrictions on the possibilities of self-relations. The domains of thought, action, and speech are marked by asymmetries in the perspective and capacities of the first person and those of others, and in the previous book the perspective of the other person was mostly represented from the third-person, or observer's, position. In this book, however, the relevant other person is not an observer but a participant in the conversation, and the speaker's understanding of her own role must incorporate the perspective of the interlocutor, as the two people in dialogue alternate between the role of speaker and audience in the course of the conversation. The act of making a claim or a promise is an exercise of self-consciousness by the speaker, an act whose reality depends on the speaker knowing in a first-person manner how she means her utterance to count for the other person. But this self-understanding of the nature of her act must also be shared by her interlocutor if her act is to amount to anything. Speech, and in particular the act of claiming something as true, is in a way emblematic of something that is in one sense an act of self-assertion, and also, in its solicitation of the recognition of an audience and participation in the wider public institution of language, an acknowledgment of dependence or deferral. Hence in the story presented here I am just as concerned to emphasize the forms of relation and types of act that are reserved for our relations with *other* people, and which are not possible, or are not the same possibilities, with respect to oneself.

Acknowledgments

This work has taken so long to complete and has benefited from so many conversations throughout the years that I want to begin by thanking all those whose contributions I cannot recall today. It will come to me later.

I was fortunate to present chapters from this as work in progress at a number of seminars and departmental talks. These include the Humanities Center at Johns Hopkins University in 1999, a conference on my work at the University of Valencia, hosted by Joseph Corbi in 2006, the University of Siena hosted by Carla Bagnoli in 2007, a Sawyer Seminar on the second person hosted by James Conant and Sebastian Rödl in 2011, and the Berlin Conference on Reciprocity and Social Cognition hosted by Richard Moore in 2015. I am grateful to all the participants at these occasions.

An especially valuable opportunity was provided to me when Adam Leite and the Department of Philosophy at the University of Indiana, Bloomington, invited me for a week as the Nelson Distinguished Visitor in 2015. It was a great occasion to present and discuss this work with faculty and students over several days, and I benefited in particular from the responses of Adam, Gary Ebbs, Kate Abramson, and Kirk Ludwig. Adam has been a "critical supporter" of this project for a long time, and I have relied on his judgment in countless ways.

In recent years I have benefited from the conversation and friendship of several philosophers in France, who provided occasions for me to present portions of this work in contexts that were always challenging and encouraging. In particular, I'm grateful to Vincent Descombes and to Sandra Laugier for making it possible for me to visit the École des hautes études en sciences sociales, Paris, in 2013, and Paris 1 Panthéon-Sorbonne in 2016. I'm grateful to Sandra for arranging a workshop on a draft of the full manuscript, where I received valuable responses from Vincent himself, Jocelyn Benoit, Daniele Lorenzini, Elise Marrou, Pierre Fasula, and David Zapero-Maier. On other occasions I learned much from conversations on these topics with Bruno Ambroise, Valérie Aucouturier, Rémi Clot-Goudard, Sophie Djigo, Jean-Philippe Narboux, Denis Perrin, and Denis Vernant.

During the years I have been occupied with this project I have received generous support from the Princeton Center for Human Values in 1998–99 and the American Council for Learned Societies in 2014–15, and been supported throughout by Harvard University and the Department of Philosophy, not least by our administrator Ruth Kolodney.

The people whose comments and encouragement I have benefited from over the years are too numerous to mention, but I want to thank Jonas Ahlskog, Kent Bach, Carla Bagnoli, Byron Davies, Kate Elgin, Paul Faulkner, Luca Ferrero, Anton Ford, Elizabeth Fricker, Miranda Fricker, Amy Gutmann, Matthias Hasse, Paul Harris, Jane Heal, Pamela Hieronymi, Karen Jones, Christine Korsgaard, Jonathan Lear, Béatrice Longuenesse, John MacFarlane, Ben McMyler, Richard Moore, Fred Neuhouser, David Owens, Angus Ross, Tim Scanlon, Eleonore Stump, David Sussman, Michael Thompson, David Velleman, Jonathan Vogel, Jennifer Whiting, and George Wilson.

Berislav Marušić, Jed Lewinsohn, and Jeremy Wanderer provided comments and conversation on nearly the whole manuscript, without which it would be a poorer thing. I am grateful for their companionship and intellectual passion.

What I owe to the years of continuous conversation with Matt Boyle, Doug Lavin, and Martin Stone goes well beyond this book, but was surely present to me throughout the writing of it.

Peter Ohlin at Oxford University Press has been a great support from the beginning, and I want to thank him for commissioning two excellent reader's reports, and to thank Lucy O'Brien and Elizabeth Fricker for identifying themselves and being the impetus to many late improvements in the manuscript.

Sandy Diehl has been an indispensable help to me in preparing this for publication, as well as advising on many last revisions.

Three articles which are part of this project have been published earlier: "Problems of Sincerity," *Proceedings of the Aristotelian Society* 105 (December 2005): 341–61; "Getting Told and Being Believed," *Philosopher's Imprint* 5, no. 5 (2006); and "Testimony, Illocution, and the Second Person," *Aristotelian Society Supplementary Volume* 87, no. 1 (2013): 115–35. I am grateful to the original publishers for the inclusion of these articles in this work. In the course of incorporating them here I have tried to keep changes to a minimum while at the same time eliminating repetition across the chapters. In the years that I've been working on this topic, the nature and structure of intersubjectivity has arisen in widely separated areas of philosophy and related disciplines, and the topic of testimony has attracted a great deal of attention. The profit I have gained from this literature in the years it has taken me to finish this book goes well beyond the explicit references in the text.

THE EXCHANGE OF WORDS

I

Speech, Intersubjectivity, and Social Acts

1.1 Reid and the Social Acts of Mind

I call those operations social, which necessarily imply social intercourse with some other intelligent being who bears a part in them. A man may see, and hear, and remember, and judge, and reason; he may deliberate and form purposes, and execute them, without the intervention of any other intelligent being. They are solitary acts. But when he asks a question for information, when he testifies a fact, when he gives a command to his servant, when he makes a promise, or enters into a contract, these are social acts of mind, and can have no existence without the intervention of some other intelligent being, who acts a part in them. Between the operations of the mind, which, for want of a more proper name, I have called solitary, and those I have called social, there is this very remarkable distinction that, in the solitary, the expression of them by words, or any other sensible sign, is accidental. They may exist, and be complete, without being expressed, without being known to any other person. But, in the social operations, the expression is essential. They cannot exist without being expressed by words or signs, and known to the other party.

—Thomas Reid[1]

In the passage above, Reid distinguishes between "solitary" and "social" operations of the mind, or, as he goes on to call the latter, "social *acts* of mind." While Reid's distinction is well known, it fits uneasily within contemporary thinking about the mind and its powers, and I think the consequences of

---

1 *Essays on the Active Powers of Man*, Essay 5, "Of Morals," chap. 6, "Of the Nature and Obligation of a Contract."

taking it seriously are more revisionary for our picture of the mind than have commonly been appreciated. The first group he mentions includes such phenomena familiar to philosophy of mind and moral psychology as seeing, hearing, remembering, and judging. These he calls "solitary" in that their completion does not involve what he calls "the intervention of any other intelligent being." He contrasts these with what he calls "social acts of the mind," which include testifying to some fact, commanding, and promising. From a contemporary perspective, it might be objected that there is only a false contrast here, because the items on the two lists do not belong to a more general category within which they are different species. Seeing, remembering, and judging, it will be said, are genuine mental phenomena (even if many today might resist calling some of them, such as seeing, *acts* of mind), but testifying, promising, and commanding are only the *effects*, the external expressions, of genuine mental phenomena such as believing, intending, or desiring. It might be thought that, contrary to his intent, Reid is not marking a difference between two kinds of mental operation, one solitary and one social, but is rather displaying the difference between the genuinely mental operations, which are all solitary, intrinsic to the individual, and the various activities, some of them involving other people, to which these mental phenomena can give rise. On this view, any genuinely mental operation originates within the individual, and if it manifests itself outwardly at all this will either be by something that the individual does (e.g., speaking as the expression of belief or desire), or directly, without the mediation of any action (e.g., blushing as the expression of embarrassment). Reid, however, says that testifying, commanding, and promising are themselves acts of mind, and not just the byproduct or external sign of acts of mind in the individual or internal sense. In addition, he says that for these other "social" acts of mind their expression is *essential* and not accidental to them.

This is a further way in which he seems to be employing a conception of the mental different from the one familiar in contemporary philosophy, for on the current view it will be hard to understand how it could be *essential* to a given mental operation that it gains expression. Insofar as mental life is understood either introspectively, or computationally or neurologically, it will be a contingent matter whether a given mental operation gains external expression in the behavior of the individual, or indeed whether the mental operation is embodied in a living individual at all (and not, e.g., a machine state, or a brain in a vat). Reid, however, believes there is a class of mental operations which are not contingently related to their external expression, but which only exist as expressed. This raises a question not only about the notion of the "mental" being employed, and how it could be correctly applied to an operation that is not internal to the individual, but equally about the relevant notion of expression. For it is clear that by "expression" Reid does not simply mean whatever may make some internal happening visible or otherwise discernible on the outside. Rather, he claims that what is essential to these operations of mind is that their expression take a certain form, viz., in an *act* of expression on the part of the person as such, rather than the passive manifestation of some internal state in a person's face or voice. The act of expression that realizes or completes such operations of the mind is primarily a verbal act. What is distinctive about this notion of expression is not simply its medium (speech, language), but that it is expression that is *directed* in a certain way. These operations of the mind are said to be such that they only exist and are complete insofar as they are expressed in words to another intelligent being; in short, they exist in being addressed to another person, and understood and taken up by that person in a certain way. The claim is not simply that these mental operations must be realized or embodied in some external medium, but that they exist insofar as they are expressed *to* another intelligent being. In principle, these are two distinct requirements, that the medium of expression be linguistic and that the form of expression be expression *to* another person, but Reid clearly sees these as very closely related requirements. We cannot understand his claim that these social operations of the mind are such that expression is essential and not accidental to them unless we bear in mind the particular *form* of expression he has in mind, and to which the medium of *speech* is, if not strictly necessary, then nonetheless paradigmatic. It is expression to another intelligent being that is said to be essential to this class of mental operations, the act of expression to another speaker.

The social nature of these mental operations is not, however, exhausted in their form or in the fact that they are, as it were, aimed in a certain direction. Reid's challenge to the standard, individual notion of genuine mental operations is more thoroughgoing than that, for in this passage he insists that the acts of mind he is describing "have no existence without the intervention of some other intelligent being, who acts a part in them." It is thus not only that it is essential to these acts of mind that they be expressed, and expressed to another intelligent being, but that other being must *know* them, and "act a part" in their realization. In this way, the mental operation is described as social not only in its aim and context, but in the actual involvement of another person, who must not only be aware of what the first person is expressing with respect to him, but who must also do something himself, who has his own role to play in the completion of the act of mind. The very notion of completion may seem obscure here, for what could the mental operation itself be such that *it* has "no existence" except insofar as it is expressed to and known by some other person? It is difficult to see how something described this way could *be* a possible object of expression or knowledge, if it has no existence prior to being expressed or known. No one will doubt that there are social acts that require two or more people in some kind of relation to each other, but it may be doubted that there are acts of *mind* which essentially involve more than one person in this way, such that the mental act is only completed insofar as it is expressed toward another person who plays his own part. The so-called "social acts of mind," it may be thought, must always be decomposed into a properly "mental" part, followed by the various possible ways a person may either act upon or give expression to this properly mental state of hers and gain the understanding and cooperation of another person. Reid notes the "common opinion of Philosophers" that "the social operations of the mind are not specifically different from the solitary, and that they are only various modifications or compositions of our solitary operations, and may be resolved into them." Such a "resolution," however, he believes to be "extremely difficult, if not impossible."

Along with commanding, promising, and asking a question or a favor, Reid includes "testifying a fact," that is, telling someone something, as one of the social acts of the mind. Hence the transmission of knowledge from one person to another is included along with other acts with a more explicitly social meaning, in that they consist in the negotiation and adjustment of the normative statuses among people, often within certain defined social roles. As a group, these are among the most basic human expressions of intersubjectivity, and yet "testifying a fact," when it is conceded to belong to this group in the first place, raises its own distinct set of issues. Unlike commanding, there is normally no special role that a person must occupy with respect to another person to tell him what she knows. Unlike promising, what the successful act of testifying a fact accomplishes is not just an alteration in the obligations and entitlements between the two people themselves, but also and centrally a relation to something beyond the two parties themselves and their relation to each other, namely, the fact itself that is testified, whose truth is independent of the social act of mind itself.

This is related to another difference, for if testifying a fact necessarily looks *outward* beyond the social relationship itself toward the independent truth being claimed, the language of "transmission of knowledge" suggests the role of an *inward* perspective as well, in the idea of the conveyance of something, the knowledge in question, from one mind to another. If we begin with the picture of some knowledge contained in one mind which is to be transmitted or made accessible to another mind, it would seem that the role of "expression" could only be the contingent one of making outwardly apparent something possessed by one person that would otherwise remain private or invisible to the other person, and there is nothing essentially social in that, not in the way we can see commanding and promising as being acts which essentially consist in transforming the normative relations between persons. In thinking about intersubjectivity generally, what Reid's formulation provides is an emphasis on the *acts* of intersubjectivity, acts like telling or testifying, rather than conceiving of it as a condition of access of one mind to another or as overcoming the boundaries between one mind and another. From this perspective, social acts of mind are achieved through the joint participation in intersubjective acts which relate a distinct subjectivity to another one, and these acts take place out in the open, in the overt expression that is essential and not accidental to them. The idea of an act of mind to which expression is essential would seem to require a different notion of "expression" in relation to mental phenomena, for we cannot think of expression in this context as the manifestation of something which is complete in itself but hidden in another medium. From this other perspective, speaking and testifying to some fact are not to be understood as providing a window to an otherwise inaccessible mental state, but as acts which require two distinct parties for their completion, each with their own role to play.

1.2 The Speaking Subject and the Political Subject

This book is an exploration of what a picture of speaking and telling looks like that concentrates on the fact of the social-relational nature of the act of telling, the fact that in its primary instances, one speaker addresses another and thereby purports to give the other person a reason to believe what she said. I call this situation the primary instance, and indeed much of the discussion to follow will concern two people in each other's presence, but I do not mean for that focus to suggest the denial of the institutional, indeed impersonal, character of language itself, or the fact that the sources of the words we hear and see in daily life are often far removed from us in space and time, or indeed not locatable at all. Our everyday encounters with language, even with what we might think of as *testimonial* uses of language, do not always involve encounters with persons. A familiar and inescapable fact of the contemporary scene is the confrontation with words, statements, claims, demands, solicitations, and warnings whose origins are not available to us. Like proverbs and other sayings, these are in an important sense phenomena of speech without authors, certainly not authors we could confront or question, and often enough "utterances" we have no reason to think anyone believes or has the standing to claim. Even in those cases where we rely on written signs to guide us in matters of life or death, these messages are often anonymous in their origins and circulation. We don't imagine there is any specific *speaker* to complain to when a road sign is ambiguous or leads us astray, let alone with regard to the inscriptions whose authors, if they ever had any, are long gone.

There is, in addition, the enormous variety of "uses" and contexts of speech, both spoken and written, which lie outside the picture of one person speaking or telling something to another. Words are recited and preserved, performed in songs and incantations, practiced and repeated by rote, issued forth in cries of pain or surprise, and carried along in stories, jokes, and curses. In none of these is anyone being asked to believe anything. And yet for all that, much is expressed, communicated, and circulated in such verbal activities. In many such contexts, the speaker may think of herself as alone, apart from the fact that language itself is a social phenomenon. One's operations with words may be as solitary as playing with the items in a coin collection, even though money is also a social phenomenon. Many operations with words, then, do not immediately involve another person at all, and many of those that do address themselves to another person do not involve any attempt to convey information to another person. The category of meaningful speech is far wider than that of the communicative, and the category of the communicative is itself wider than the case of conveying information from one person to another. And yet, it is natural for philosophers and others concerned with the act of speaking and communication to take as central the case of one person telling something to another person. What does it mean to consider this as the primary case, when it is hardly the universal case?

Part of what it means lies in the idea that for a speaker to be in a position to *say* anything, her words have to be seen to *count* for other people in certain ways. At a general level, the sounds or marks she makes must be *accepted* by others as instances of the same words and sentences which they employ on other occasions, as belonging to a language which they share.[2] More specifically, the speaker must be credited with the ability to make what she says count as a claim *about* something, something concerning the world she shares with other speakers. Without that, the sounds produced could not progress beyond the status of mere cries or other manifestations of her state. If being a speaker means at a minimum the ability to say, assert, or claim something, then there is a further way, beyond the complexities of sharing a language, in which this capacity involves the social recognition of a certain status, which in turn means that the speaker's ability to say something depends on other speakers. The idea of status and recognition here has several dimensions, including semantic competence and epistemological standing, but also dimensions associated with practical life, that is, moral, political, and a certain sense of the economic, and I want to begin by placing the discussion to follow in some of these contexts.

The political dimension of the capacity for speech has several aspects, and finds expression in the relation between the very notion of *saying* something and such acts as making a *claim*, an assertion of oneself (along with the fact asserted), as well as the explicitly political acts of contracting, entitling, or revoking. The very language of authority and political rights describes these relations in terms of the exercise of the specific capacities of a speaking animal. Joel Feinberg, for instance, in a classic discussion of the notion of rights, links the very notion of rights to their *assertion*, to their embodiment in a claim of one party on another, and the recognition of that claim.

> Even if there are conceivable circumstances in which one would admit rights
> diffidently, there is no doubt that their characteristic use and that for which

---

2 In the context of an extended reading of Wittgenstein, Stanley Cavell puts it the following way: "If I am to have a native tongue, I have to accept what 'my elders' say and do as consequential; and they have to accept, even have to applaud, what I say and do as what they say and do. We do not know in advance what the content of our mutual acceptance is, how far we may be in agreement. . . . But if I am to have my own voice in it, I must be speaking for others and allow others to speak for me" (1979, 28).

they are distinctively well-suited, is to be claimed, demanded, affirmed, insisted upon. (Feinberg 1970, 252)

The language linking rights with claims and assertions is familiar enough, but what is worth emphasizing here is that the notion of political right is being related not to a particular *content* of what is claimed or asserted, but rather, the stance of the speaking subject itself. The very capacity to say, assert, make claims, is described as having a political dimension in that it is a power essentially addressed to others, and internally related to and "completed by" their recognition. As Feinberg puts it later in the essay, "To respect a person then, or to think of him as possessed of human dignity, simply *is* to think of him as a potential maker of claims" (252). A political subject is a speaking subject, but also conversely: to be a speaking subject is to claim a certain authority, not just to "give voice" to oneself, but to make a claim upon others, and to be recognized as exercising the capacity to commit oneself publicly, to bind oneself or to refuse to be bound to specific others in specific ways. A person may have full command of the vocabulary, syntax, and grammar of a language and not be credited with the authority to *tell* anyone anything at all. Before a certain age, for instance, a young child is not in a position to promise, congratulate, or perhaps even announce an intention, despite having the verbal forms available to her, just as a full-grown adult speaker may not be credited with the authority to perform the speech act of casting a vote or hiring someone. The simplest acts of speech take place within the social practices of speech, involving the distinction of roles, the shared understanding of the acts in question, and the dependence on the recognition of others for their accomplishment.[3]

The idea of an internal relation between the very notion of the political and the capacity for speech has a much longer history, however, than the modern discourse of political rights. A classical tradition that goes back as far as Aristotle makes the capacities of the speaker a condition on political

---

3 In a formal legal context the status of being in a position to give testimony can be very strictly delimited, for example excluding children, or women, or noncitizens. Notoriously, slave societies frequently exclude slaves from giving formal testimony, even when a slave is assumed to be in possession of information relevant to the court. "A special rule governed the testimony of slaves: they could not appear in court, but a statement which a slave, male or female, had made under torture [*basanos*] could be produced in court as evidence" (MacDowell 1986, p. 245). For discussion of the less explicit ways in the contemporary world in which the testimonial authority of certain people is denied or diminished, see Miranda Fricker's book *Epistemic Injustice* (2007).

life. In the *Politics*, Aristotle relates the idea of what distinguishes "man" as the *zoon politikon* to the human being as the animal who speaks, in terms which distinguish the merely expressive capacities which we share with the other animals (including vocal expression) from the claim-making capacities distinctive of speakers.

> It is also clear why a human being is more of a political animal than a bee or any other gregarious animal. Nature makes nothing pointlessly, as we say, and no animal has speech except a human being. A voice is a signifier of what is pleasant or painful, which is why it is also possessed by the other animals (for their nature goes this far: they not only perceive what is pleasant or painful but signify it to each other). But speech is for making clear what is beneficial or harmful, and hence also what is just or unjust. For it is peculiar to human beings, in comparison to the other animals, that they alone have perception of what is good or bad, just or unjust, and the rest. (Aristotle, *Politics* 1253a10ff.)

The other gregarious animals, who live together in flocks, or schools, or herds, express themselves in various ways, and may even be said to communicate in various ways. The "gift of speech," however, is said to make something else possible, which goes beyond "mere voice," the expression of pleasure and pain, and presumably beyond even the strategic display of states of fear or postures of threat. Aristotle does not explain here what it is about mere voice that falls short of the ability to "make clear what is beneficial or harmful, and hence also what is just or unjust," or what it is in the human capacity for speech that enables it. But the contrast with the expression of states of pleasure and pain suggests that speaking, in the sense that is relevant to political life, must go beyond the indication or registration of states of the creature, and lay claim to standards of the beneficial or the harmful, the just and the unjust, and in that way relate itself to the responses of others.

It is in the modern period, and with Hobbes in particular, that the very idea of the political, that is, the possibility of a commonwealth, is tied to the status and capacities of the speaking subject.[4] For Hobbes it is only a creature with the power of speech who will then have the ability to *bind* herself to others and thus exercise the ability to form covenants, and in this way separate herself from the chaos of the state of nature. The very notion of a

---

4 Two recent studies which have illuminated this connection in Hobbes are Anat Biletzki's *Talking Wolves: Thomas Hobbes on the Language of Politics and the Politics of Language* (1997), and Philip Pettit's *Made from Words: Hobbes on Language, Mind and Politics* (2008).

person for Hobbes is tied to the capacities most characteristically expressed in speech. Chapter 16 of *Leviathan* is entitled "Of Persons, Authors, and Things Personated" and begins with the following definition.

> A person is he whose words or actions are considered, either as his own, or as representing the words or actions of another man, or of any other thing to whom they are attributed, whether truly or by fiction.
>
> When they are considered as his own, then is he called a natural person: and when they are considered as representing the words and actions of another, then is he a feigned or artificial person.

In this passage, speech is seen as something that is essentially "one's own," defining one as a person, but at the same time as something that is essentially transferrable to another, and this in two related ways. A person's very speech may be transferred to an artificial person who may then be said to speak in her place, to speak for her; and speech is the privileged medium (though not the only one) by which a person transfers what is hers to another person, whether it be property, or a right, or, as above, her place to speak itself. A person is an Author, which means both an origin of something which derives from and expresses the person as such (as her solitary actions do), and is also, as a speaker, someone exercising the capacity to *authorize*, where that means to delegate or transfer something of one's own outside of oneself, to another person or agency. Hence the connection of the notion of the Person with the notion of Author describes a movement in two different directions: from the words back to their origin in the person, as expressive of her (much as an animal's cry emanates from and is expressive of its internal state), and outward from the speaker as origin, to other persons toward whom she exercises the authority to transfer or delegate her voice. Hence the internal connection in Hobbes between speech as authoring (originating) and speech as covenanting, that is, voluntarily *binding* oneself to others.

> Signs of contract are either express or by inference. Express are words spoken with understanding of what they signify: and such words are either of the time present or past; as, I give, I grant, I have given, I have granted, I will that this be yours: or of the future; as, I will give, I will grant, which words of the future are called promise. (*Lev.*, chap. 14, p. 82)

Or as he puts it later in the same chapter, "all contract is mutual translation": the words must be "spoken with understanding of what they signify," and that understanding cannot be private to the speaker (that is, in *one* sense of something's being "one's own") but must be shared by the other party to the contract for any contracting to take place. Again the specifically human capacity of "authoring" must be understood as a relational power which in its very nature involves more than one person; that is, a capacity to originate something, a kind of utterance, which is nonetheless dependent for its completion on the understanding of someone other than the speaker. It is for this reason that Hobbes takes covenanting to be the exercise of a capacity proper to creatures with speech:

> To make covenant with brute beasts is impossible, because not understanding our speech, they understand not, nor accept any translation of right, nor can translate any right to another: and without mutual acceptation, there is no covenant. (*Lev.*, chap. 14, p. 85)

There may be animals other than the human, either here in our world or elsewhere, who can contract with each other, but Hobbes's point would be that if they can, then they must have an expressive capacity that is not *merely* expressive (Aristotle's "mere voice"), but which includes the capacity to "personate," to delegate one's voice, and thereby not only give voice to one's own sentiments, but engage with and be dependent upon the understanding of another, and thereby "translate" something of one's own to another. One way to put the thought would be that being a speaker means being credited with the sense that the words that one "authors" are "one's own," and that this entails being credited with the capacity to transfer one's word to another and have that count.

The possibility of such transfer, where that means "giving one's word" to another person, includes both the possibility of direct quotation by one's interlocutor and the necessity of going beyond direct quotation. To have given one's word to another means that one's interlocutor is now in a position to repeat those very words back to the original speaker, with the expectation that this repetition, these very words, will be acknowledged by her as being the very words she spoke. Without the possibility of such agreement and acceptance of the identity of the words in the mouths of two different speakers, no transfer can take place. The speaker's words are "her own," for purposes of saying something, only insofar as she can recognize them as hers (as "what you said" or "what she said") when spoken by another. The possibility of verbatim repetition of words by someone other than their original speaker is distinct from, more abstract than, the acoustic (or graphic) reproduction of the individual performance or token, and the agreement between speakers regarding acoustically distinct tokens as nonetheless instances of the same type is itself an expression of the social aspect of language.

At the same time, as various philosophers and others have pointed out, to ascend to the level of *saying* something with one's words, as opposed to mere repetition of an identifiable word or phrase, requires a further level of social dependence in the licensing of paraphrase and *indirect* quotation of one's words. Zeno Vendler makes this the hallmark of the use of words to perform the simplest speech acts of saying something in conversation: "indirect reproduction does not and cannot consist in a mere repetition of the speaker's words. It follows, therefore, that to perform an illocutionary act is to license the reproduction of what one says in a way in which the fidelity to words is superseded by a concern to preserve something else." The insistence on mere or verbatim repetition of one's words, and the refusal to recognize one's utterance in any paraphrase or indirect reproduction by another speaker (with the corresponding alterations in grammatical person and tense) would be to treat them as "one's own" in a way that precluded transfer to another altogether, and with that the possibility of saying something with one's words (Vendler 1972, 62). Without the possibility of direct quotation, there would be no such thing as holding someone to her word; but without the speaker acknowledging "what she said" in words *other* than the very ones she spoke, she won't count as having said anything at all. In a further way then, transfer to and translatability by another person is part of the ability to assert oneself in speech.

This very language of ownership, counting, crediting, claiming, and accepting takes us to what might be called the political economy of speech. Philosophers and others have long remarked on the extensive figurative relations between language, speech, and money and the forms of exchange they make possible, and it can easily seem that the connections between the systems of language and money are pervasive enough, and the two systems themselves are abstract enough, that the sense of one discourse being *metaphorical* for the other becomes quite unclear.[5] That is, for instance, is it

---

5 The theme itself can be traced back to antiquity. See Shell 1978, and the remarks by Cavell (1979, 94–95). Certain limitations to the comparison are just as important, in particular the fact that, while the difference between the real and the counterfeit is important to money exchange, this is not the same as the dependence on the speaker's understanding or the assumption of sincerity that governs speech acts.

any more or less metaphorical to say that we "credit" someone's account when it is a story she has told us rather than a promise to pay for her groceries at the end of the month? Which domain, the linguistic or the economic, is being used to illuminate the other when we speak of "giving one's word" or "accepting (or refusing to accept) a claim at face value"? Both the realms of property and everyday conversation are constituted by claims, counterclaims, and the negotiation of different forms of entitlement.[6] Words, like money, function as a medium of exchange; not only circulating among people (since viruses do that too), but specifically functioning as *signs*, that is, something perceptible which points to something *else*, something beyond the perceptible sign itself. Both conversational exchanges and monetary exchanges are made possible by the fact that the tokens themselves have their meaning and value as parts of an *institution*; that is, a transpersonal structure that precedes the individuals in the particular exchange itself. The institution makes possible a certain encounter between the parties to the exchange, but at the same time it relates them to others who are not present on the scene, but are removed from them in both time and space. Though the other parties to the institutions of either speech or money are not physically present in the encounter of any two persons on the street or marketplace, these transpersonal others must nonetheless make their presence felt. For the very meaning of the words and the value of the currency exchanged are constituted by their being *taken* to have that meaning or value. The entire structure is constituted by the mutually sustaining *acceptance* of the forms of value by the participants in the institution itself, without which the tokens themselves become worthless. And since what distinguishes money from barter, and speech from spontaneous gesture, is that the value of the token is tied to its continued convertibility with other parties beyond the two people in the initial exchange, this structure of acceptance must be assumed by the two parties to extend to other anonymous parties, whom they will never meet.

This institutional character of the economic and the realm of speech can give rise to a set of related anxieties: ontological, epistemological, and what we may call proprietary. The value of money and the weight of words

---

6 The idea of a system of entitlements and commitments is, of course, central to Robert Brandom's vision of language and other "social operations of the mind." For an elaboration and revision of this perspective see Kukla and Lance 2009 and the critical notice by Wanderer (2010).

may be as real and consequential as an act of war or a credit crisis, but
such phenomena themselves illustrate how the reality of such things is itself
constituted by appearance, by a mutually supporting network of congruent
appearances and the acceptance of those appearances (and the anticipa-
tion of further such acceptings, on various counterfactual or idealized
assumptions). In a sense, they are no more and no less than what they are
taken to be. This extends to the realm of social power quite generally, for as
Hobbes says, "Reputation of power is power" (*Lev.*, chap. 10, p. 51).[7] This
general form of fact can seem by turns either metaphysically impossible (the
inversion of the metaphysical hierarchy between Reality and Appearance),
or a structure of folly and illusion and therefore inherently unstable. Pascal,
on the other hand, anticipates certain modern thinkers in seeing this as a
structure of folly and illusion which is for that very reason as stable as can
be.[8] In this book, I will not be addressing the ontological issues concerning
the constitution of social institutions, but beginning in chapter 3, the importance of *manifest appearance* to the understanding of speech will begin
to come into focus. For now, what I have in mind by the epistemological
anxiety stemming from the institutional character of money or language
is just the fact that the parties to either form of exchange know that the
meaning and value of their different currencies are dependent on a structure of appearance and acceptance that involves not just the two of them,
but also an undefined group of others who are participants in the same institution, the same language, and who must be assumed to be playing their
role for the action the two of them are performing to mean what they take
it to mean. But they will never meet these other parties to the convention,
even though their relational activities implicate them with each other, and
for this reason it can be hard to see how the two speakers can *know* what
it seems they need to know in order to be entitled to the confidence that
they are performing the acts they take themselves to be performing. The
connection of the capacity to speak with the political ability to make claims
and assert oneself that we began with naturally suggests a picture of speaking
as the expression of a form of authority, but the social-relational character
of a particular speech act and the institutional character of language itself

7 In the *Behemoth*, Hobbes goes further and says, "The power of the mighty hath no foundation
  but in the opinion and belief of the people." This is quoted by Pettit (2008, 94).
8 "The power of kings is founded on the reason and the folly of the people, but especially on
  their folly. The greatest and most important thing in the world is founded on weakness. This is
  a remarkably sure foundation, for nothing is surer than that the people will be weak. Anything
  founded on sound reason is ill-founded, like respect for reason" (Pascal 1995, 26).

together highlight the constitutive and epistemic dependence of the act it-self on the context outside the two interlocutors.

The "proprietary" aspect of words relates the economic to the expres-sive. Hobbes and others characterize a speaker's words as "her own" in a fundamental sense, but as with the fact that the very reality of property and currency depends on a transpersonal system of recognition and accept-ance, it may be asked in what sense one's words can ever be "one's own." In what sense can I make them count for what I want them to count for, and in what sense can something I do ensure that they will be *accepted* by the other person at the value I mean to give them? As with the currency in my pocket, if the other person does not do his part in the exchange, refuses to take them at face value, then the words I pronounce are worthless, not simply devalued. Hobbes's description of the person as "authoring" her words and her actions is meant, of course, to be cognate with the notion of "authority," and at the same time to suggest the idea of expressing a power by being the *origin* of what is authored. This is the speaker's relation to the utterance she produces, the aspect of language as *parole* rather than *langue*. However, even at the level of the speaker's production of her own utterance, the connection of this notion of authority to an idea of power is complicated by the fact that, as we have seen, for Hobbes himself as well as others in this tradition, an assertion of power of this kind must at the same time be an expression of dependency, for political power, as opposed to brute force, depends on the recognition and acceptance of others for its very reality. Whatever the speaker's utterance may be said to authorize or to make happen cannot be a matter of the speaker's individual power, like that of her physical strength, but requires the recognition and cooperation of others in her speech community. And the relation of this notion of "au-thoring" one's words with being their *originator* is likewise complicated by the fact that the words one speaks and the language they belong to all pre-cede the speaker and are not her creation. Doubtless, a speaker's utterance is in an important sense her own production, but not the words themselves or the institution of language within which they have their meaning. The words she speaks are not "hers," and she is not their origin, in the way that her nonverbal, non-relational actions are "hers," and originate from her, and therefore "express" her.[9] A person may be said to be the origin of any of her

---

9   One theme to be explored in later chapters is the contrast between social-relational and non-relational notions of "expression."

overt actions, which "belong" to her simply in virtue of being "her" actions, and many of these may be said to "express" her in a way that is describable by reference to her alone. By contrast, the speaker's relation to the words she speaks is in the first instance a relation to a system which precedes her and which is not at her disposal. How then are the words she speaks to be thought to "express" her when they don't belong to her in the first place, and how does a speaker *make* them her own, especially when in her very production of speech she must make her performance of the words conform to the expectations of others if she is to make herself understood?[10] A person's speaking some words is an instance of an ordinary action, and we can presume some antecedent clarity to the notion of a person's actions being "her own" and, therefore, expressing that person, but for the reasons just mentioned this family of notions of authority, origin, and expression must be understood differently in the case of verbal acts. Exchange, transfer, and delegation, everything that goes into what Hobbes calls "personating," are intrinsic to acts of speech and the powers they express, whereas they are not intrinsic to actions generally or what Reid calls "solitary acts of mind." A theme to follow up here is that the very complexities and ambiguities in the proprietary notion of a person's words as "her own," as contrasted with other actions of hers, are what make possible the forms of commitment and entitlement that belong to ordinary speech acts like one person's telling another person something.

1.3 The Epistemological Perspective and the Participants' Perspective

The story developed here concerns how a speaker's assertion to another person comes to count a reason for that person to believe what he is told. It is an account of what is distinctive about this kind of act, and how this act must be understood by its participants. In this sense, rather than being concerned directly with epistemological questions, I am concerned here with the preconditions for there being an epistemic question of believing

---

10 For an excellent discussion, both diagnostic and analytic, of the "proprietary anxiety" described here, and its relation to the impersonal, institutional status of a shared language, see Descombes 2014a, chap. 10, "Objective Mind."

or disbelieving what one has been told. Of course, that very description of the project is already committed to the epistemological claim that people do commonly come to know things through being told by others; as well as the further claim that the speaker's act of asserting or claiming something, and its acceptance by the person she is addressing, is part of the reason for belief the addressee takes himself to have been given, and that the speaker and her addressee are not wrong in this understanding of their action and belief. I mean for this to sound platitudinous, but it is hardly beyond controversy in philosophy. Philosophical interest in testimony is often inspired by very general epistemological concerns that tend to downplay or displace the social character of the act of telling that interests me here. As mentioned at the beginning, it is undeniable that much of what we pick up from the speech of others, and what we reliably infer from the spectrum of verbal behavior around us, is not dependent on the forms of commitment that are part of *telling* someone something. There are three ways in particular in which the idea of speech, including testimonial speech, as a "social act of mind" seems to drop out of consideration in recent discussions of testimony. We may instead think of the interaction with the speech of other people as akin to ordinary sense perception, as something we relate to much as we do to natural signs. In this comparison, the role of the human interlocutor and her relation to her words and her addressee is rendered incidental to the phenomenon. As Quine and Ullian (1970) put it,

> When we hear an observation sentence that reports something beyond our own experience, we gain evidence that the speaker has the stimulation appropriate for its utterance, even though that stimulation did not reach us. Such, in principle, is the mechanism of testimony as an extension of our senses. (50-51)

More recently Ruth Millikan (2004) makes the comparison more explicit:

> Coming to believe something by being told it is so, in the typical case, is the formation of a direct perceptual belief. Forming a belief about where Johnny is on the basis of being told where he is is just as direct a process (and just as indirect) as forming a belief about where Johnny is on the basis of seeing him there. (120)

What we believe through direct perceptual access, as when we look out a window, is not addressed to us or to anyone at all. Nor do the beliefs we gain in this way depend on understanding what the scene before us is trying to get across or the assumption that our source of belief here is knowledgeable or trustworthy. These obvious differences between testimony and direct perception are not, of course, denied by philosophers favoring the comparison with perception, but are thought to be irrelevant to the more abstract story of how they can both function as reliable sources of knowledge.[11] Second, other accounts bring the speaker back into the picture, but only, as it were, as a psychological source, rather than as an informant or interlocutor: the audience needs access to the speaker's *beliefs*, because it is these that will, in fortunate circumstances, enable him to infer to some truth about the world. Here the speaker is present in the picture, but primarily as a believer rather than as a speaker, and the specific nature of her *act* of addressing and telling is incidental to the epistemological story. If access to the other person's state of belief were available apart from her having actually said anything, this would make no difference to the epistemic situation.

And finally, we may think of the broad class of utterances as simply a set of phenomena, available for epistemic assessment apart from their character as assertions or claims addressed by one person to another. From a broadly reliabilist perspective, the hearing of an utterance of any sort (a sudden cry, the recitation of some lines in a play) can, in the right circumstances, be the occasion for learning something, either learning something that is congruent with the semantic content of the words uttered, or something true that is wholly independent of that content. The epistemology of testimony can be conducted at a level of generality from which an utterance is treated as a perceptible phenomenon in the world, and the problem for the epistemologist is to determine under what circumstances the experience of such a phenomenon can be seen to yield true beliefs for an observer. And it is indeed true that at *that* level of description, for a range of interesting cases it need not matter to the reliability of the result that the hearer encounters an utterance that is believed or even understood by its speaker, or presented as an assertion at all.

In this connection, Edward Craig makes an important distinction between two different ways in which one person may obtain knowledge or true belief from another person.

---

11 Tyler Burge's (1993) comparison of the entitlement of testimony and that of preservative memory similarly downplays the role of the interlocutor in testimony, for there is nothing in preservative memory corresponding to the role of the speaker in expressing commitment to some proposition or giving her word.

There are informants, and there are sources of information. Or, to arrange the terminology differently, among the various sources of information there are on the one hand *informants who give information*; and on the other there are *states of affairs*, some of which involve states of human beings and their behavior, which have evidential value: information can be gleaned from them. Roughly the distinction is that between a person's telling me something and my being able to tell something from observation of him. (Craig 1990, 35; emphasis added)

It is only when regarding another person as a potential informant, rather than a mere source, that there is a question of believing or disbelieving that person. The verbal act of telling is one in which the speaker presents herself as an informant with respect to the truth being told, and in the case when the interlocutor is indeed informed by the speaker, and comes to know this truth, the interlocutor's knowledge comes by way of believing the speaker. By contrast, with respect to the various other ways in which true beliefs may be gleaned from the behavior of others, it is the state of affairs (of her behavior, or of her state of mind) that is the focus of attention and that is relied on, not the person as such. When relating to another's action as a potential source of information rather than relating to the person as an informant, the other person may be a perfectly unwitting source, having no knowledge or awareness either of the truth for which she is a source or of the fact that her behavior is an indicator of this truth. In the absence of the speaker's knowledge or understanding of the significance of her act, none of the information gleaned in this way will involve believing *her*. Certain epistemological projects can incline the philosopher to abstract the topic of testimony from the basic situation of telling and being believed, but I think that to do so risks losing touch with a distinctive philosophical topic altogether. Jennifer Lackey's influential book *Learning from Words* (2008) is a particularly forthright version of such an approach. Through a set of ingenious examples she develops a view of testimony which doesn't necessarily involve the transmission of knowledge from one person to another, since the speaker need not believe (and hence need not know) the truth which she nonetheless conveys by her remarks. It is possible that from a suitably abstract perspective we can describe cases where knowledge can be acquired from a speaker's words apart from her knowing what she is saying or meaning what she says, and to this extent the topic of testimony can be divorced from the phenomenon of communication altogether, a conclusion she seems willing to draw at the conclusion of her final chapter when she says, "there is no reason to suppose that true communication is needed for the acquisition of testimonially justified or warranted beliefs" (249). However, insofar as a philosophical account of human testimony distances itself from the context of communication, less importance will be given to the difference between relating to another as an informant and relating to another as a mere source of true beliefs, and with that the less reason there will be to think of the special cases as cases of testimony in the first place, rather than cases of the many ways in which a person's behavior, including verbal behavior, can be another person's source of knowledge.

The abstraction from the social act of speaking shared by such approaches is encouraged by the purely epistemological focus of recent philosophical interest in testimony. The topics and problems of classical epistemology orient themselves from the position of an inquirer confronting a state of affairs and seeking to determine what inferences may be drawn from it, or approaching a range of ambiguous phenomena and seeking a unifying explanation, or considering a set of propositions and investigating their relations of justificational support. Epistemological questions begin with an inquirer seeking to understand what would have to be true of the relations among our beliefs, and of our cognitive and perceptual capacities, for our beliefs to be justified, and thus to determine the conditions for knowledge of the world we confront. Accordingly, the epistemologist typically approaches the question of testimony together with the question of the reliability of perception, memory, or other potentially knowledge-conveying sources of information. This has the consequence that when we come to the topic of testimony, most contemporary epistemological discussions situate themselves exclusively from the consumer's point of view on the phenomenon, rather than as fellow participants in the practice of telling, being told, believing or disbelieving, asking and replying.[12] The epistemological focus, that is, is an external, unilateral one that aims to understand the potential of testimony as a source of knowledge purely from the point of view of an observer or recipient of the speech of others, with the account remaining open to the possibility of reaching a thoroughly skeptical conclusion about human testimony as a genuine source of knowledge. We are

---

12 Again, a notable exception here is Craig (1990), although the attention there is brief and not focused on the verbal act. See his subtle discussion of the first-person point of view of the provider of testimony in connection with "internalist" vs. "externalist" conceptions of knowledge (63–68).

not, however, only responders to the testimony of others but are producers of testimony ourselves, and any speaker (and any philosopher) thus has a participant's perspective on the act of claiming something as true with the aim of informing someone. If the speaker in a testimonial exchange did not have a particular understanding of the nature of her own act and how it provides a way for her interlocutor to come to know something, her action would not provide her audience with a testimonial reason for belief. The status of the utterance as a reason to believe what it says depends on the speaker's seeing her role as that of an informant, understanding her verbal act as reason-providing, and both parties to the exchange (producer and consumer) sharing in this understanding of the speaker's perspective. There is nothing parallel to this dependence in the more familiar topics of epistemology, where the source of epistemic significance (e.g., some visual evidence, a correlation of observations) is an aspect of the impersonal world, something with no perspective on itself or an understanding of the epistemic significance of its forms of self-presentation. We cannot understand how the testimony of others can be a source of knowledge for us from an exclusively consumer's point of view but must approach the problem as fellow participants in the practice who have an understanding of their own role as potential informants in determining how their own words are to count for another. For the liar as well as the truth-teller, the speaker must understand her verbal act as the kind of thing that she herself could understand and accept as a reason to believe something. The way in which one's words can provide another person with a reason to believe what is said has to be understood from the first-person perspective of the speaker as well, and the two roles of "speaker" and "hearer" must be understood in relation to each other and in the context of the practice as a whole.

In the ordinary act of telling someone that there is still some milk in the refrigerator, a speaker says some words and presents them to her audience as a reason to believe that he will find some milk there. For the speaker to succeed in this action, the other person has to *understand her*, must understand what she is doing with these words. This understanding, however, must take a special form. In some cases we may be able to understand what someone is doing better than she does herself. I observe someone trying and failing to fix something and come to the conclusion that it is in fact beyond repair for some specific reason and that her efforts will be fruitless. I learn this by understanding what the person is doing, though my understanding of the agent's action is in important ways different from her own. What I learn in this way is not dependent on an understanding I share with the other person. But what the speaker needs when reporting from the refrigerator is to be understood by her audience *as she understands herself*, in terms of the act she takes herself to be performing. In telling her audience something, the speaker seeks for her act to be understood as she understands it herself, and the person she is addressing needs to apprehend and share the speaker's self-understanding of her action if he, the audience, is to gain the relevant reason to believe that there is still milk in the refrigerator. If the speaker does not succeed in communicating her self-understanding of her action in speaking, she will not have told her audience anything (though her audience might well have still learned something from her performance). Specifically, the speaker needs to be understood as saying something, and as making a particular claim in doing so if what she is doing is to provide her audience with a reason to believe the thing in question. Likewise the audience needs to understand what speech act the speaker means to be performing for him to understand his own role in the exchange, to understand himself as having been *told* something, and hence as being in a position to believe or disbelieve this person and what she asserts. Every hearer is a speaker as well, and the complementarity of these roles is also part of their understanding of the acts of asking, telling, doubting, believing, and questioning.

1.4 Speech as Indicative Sign

> It is not to the point that another person may interpret our involuntary manifestations, e.g., our "expressive movements," and that he may thereby become deeply acquainted with our inner thoughts and emotions. They [these manifestations or "utterances"] *mean* something to him in so far as he interprets them, but even for him they are without meaning in the special sense in which verbal signs have meaning: they only mean in the sense of indicating. (Husserl 1970, 188)

In several ways it can be natural for philosophers to think about speech and communication in the light of the "problem of other minds." Person A wishes Person B to know something that she knows, and hence needs to convey that information to B. Or perhaps she wishes to *mislead* B into believing something that isn't true at all. In either case A needs to *do* something, either to bring this knowledge out into the open where B can find it, or to produce an external sign that will act upon the beliefs of B, altering them in some desired direction. And here may already begin the influence of a certain picture of what she needs to do and why she needs to do it. In the case of the communication of *knowledge* that she possesses, she needs to externalize it somehow so that B may become aware of it, since B cannot see into A's mind, where the knowledge is presently located. If B could read her mind, there would be no need for A to do or say anything. From *B's* point of view, when he desires to know what A knows, he needs this knowledge of A's to be made visible or audible somehow. Since B may not always trust A's expertise on various subjects, and hence may not credit her with *knowledge*, B sees his concern as one of gaining access to A's *beliefs* about some matter, and once in possession of these B can then make up his own mind as to whether these beliefs are to be trusted (and thus count as knowledge after all). In either case, A's knowledge or A's beliefs are inaccessible to B unless something in A's behavior makes them evident.

Naturally, there are many different ways for a person's knowledge or beliefs to be evident in her behavior. As in a well-worn example, someone grabbing an umbrella on her way out probably believes it may rain today, and someone else observing this behavior may both learn of this belief of hers and gain a reason of his own to take an umbrella. We may thus think of the umbrella-grabbing as an "indicative sign" of the person's state of mind, revealing to an observer her probable *belief* that it may rain (and yes, also her *desire* to stay dry, and not the one without the other). Here it is an intentional *act* of the person that serves as an indication of her attitude, but that is not really essential to the general picture. For someone's inadvertent acts and unconscious reactions can just as easily serve as signs of a person's state of mind, even as signs of a person's *knowledge*, and detectives and others make a regular practice of noticing and interpreting such signs. If their status as indications required their always being deliberate or intentional acts (let alone: intentional with respect to the specific aim of indicating something about themselves), a detective like Sherlock Holmes would have little opportunity for displaying his ingenuity.

But speech is special in various ways, or at least speech that is part of the family of acts such as asserting, *telling*, asking, or promising. Speech of *these* forms is both necessarily an intentional act (and not, e.g., a mere reaction like blushing), and intentional with respect to the aim of communicating something. It is speech within this family of acts that is our focus here, and I will sometimes use the word "speech" and its cognates without qualification to refer to this family. This is not to deny that there are other forms of talk, other verbal phenomena, which are not communicative acts or not even actions at all. Talking in one's sleep is arguably not an action at all, and the words that may be produced by stimulation of some region of the brain are not actions of the person (not accidental or inadvertent actions either). Speaking in tongues, or the processes involved in "automatic writing," if seen as actions at all, are only so in a qualified sense (and indeed the idea that the source is *not* in the agent but somewhere beyond or beneath is normally important to the practitioners who go in for these sorts of activities). Any of these may also be indicatively revealing, however, and may enable one to conclude something about the state of mind of the person in question. More familiarly, ordinary speech can be as spontaneous as a cry of pain or surprise, and manifest the state of mind of the person apart from any intent to do so. In a broad sense, then, we may see all these as forms of making visible (or audible) something about the mind of the person in question, but these forms of making visible do not depend on the indicative verbal sign being produced with any communicative intent, or even being part of an action of the person at all. In a given case, the epistemic value of the sign as indication may indeed only be enhanced by the assumption that it was *not* part of a deliberate action of the person, communicative or otherwise. These are the types of indication that the detective's mode of intelligence will be particularly interested in, being removed from all the motives people can have for concealing or disguising their thoughts.

Verbal behavior that is part of the family of telling and asserting, however, *must* be seen as an intentional act of the person for it to be the kind of thing it is, and for it to have the distinctive epistemic role that it has. It is essential to the way that someone's assertion provides a reason to believe something (whether about the speaker's beliefs, or about the topic of her assertion) that it be seen as an intentional act of the person. Someone may pronounce the same words in her sleep, or under hypnosis, or as a result of stimulation of the brain, and these words will not count as her asserting or telling anything. If we were at first mistaken about this, and assumed that what we just heard was someone's assertion, and then learn our mistake about the actual provenance of the words we just heard, we see that we don't after all have the kind of reason for believing something that we thought we had. We might then have a *different* kind of reason (the sort that might be the conclusion of the reasoning of the doctor or detective), but we don't have the kind of reason that is presented as being on offer when someone tells us something, makes a declaration to us.

So, when communicative speech does provide its audience with a reason to believe something (viz., the content of what is asserted, in the case of assertion), it does so in a way that is dependent on the assumption that the utterance is part of an intentional act of the person, and specifically a *communicative* intentional act. That is, the verbal behavior must not only be intentional (as talking in one's sleep is not), but must be intentional "under the description" of a communicative act of some sort.[13] That is, a piece of verbal behavior might be fully intentional, as when someone reads aloud from a list of French verb conjugations, without being intentional with respect to any communicative aim of hers. This distinction matters as well to a more precise characterization of just *how* an utterance must be intentional in order to be the kind of reason for belief that telling and asserting provide. That is, a person may indeed accidentally or inadvertently tell someone something, and in that sense the telling is not intentional, or not fully so. But for the utterance to be even an inadvertent act of telling someone something (letting it slip out in the course of talking about something else, not realizing who one is talking to), it must still be seen to be intentional *as an assertion* (and not, that is, as either "automatic" as in hypnosis, or intentional in the manner of reading out a list of verbs with no significance as a speech act).

When we turn out to have been wrong in either of these assumptions (it was not an act of the person at all, it was not a communicative act), the person's utterance loses the epistemic import for us that we thought it had. We thought someone had asserted, threatened, or promised something, but we now see that she had done no such thing, and so we don't have the reason to believe or to fear that we thought we had. Naturally, as above, we may retain another kind of reason to believe something, a reason proceeding from the broad class of indicative signs stemming from things people do, but we lack the kind of reason associated with being told something and believing that person. There turned out to be nothing of that sort on offer here after all.

---

13 The phrase is from Anscombe (1976) and has become a familiar point about the concept of intentional action since the monograph's original 1957 publication. Something that a person *does* (like grabbing an umbrella) is an intentional act only as described in certain ways and not others (e.g., when the thing done is also "grabbing someone else's umbrella by mistake").

How can what I have called the "epistemic status" of a piece of speech depend in this way on the assumption that it is part of an intentional action of the person, and indeed intentional as a specifically *communicative* act? How can there be this kind of epistemic dependence at all? That is, if some phenomenon (a symptom, an utterance) is genuinely a reason to believe something, then (it may seem) this must be an objective fact about it, independent of *anyone's* beliefs or intentions with respect to it, including the person who produced the sign. If the specific epistemic import of an act of telling or asserting is dependent on its character *as* act and as communicative act, how then does the exercise of agency contribute positively to this epistemic import?

The picture of speech from the point of view of the traditional problem of "other minds" suggested that the import of speech is to make manifest our internal states of belief, intention, desire, etc. Without speech we would have nothing but our natural gestures to reveal to each other what is in our minds. This picture encourages assigning a restricted importance to the idea of intentional action in this context: an *act* of the person is required in order to *produce* a visible or audible sign of her state of mind, for the other person to see or hear. *Something* must make one's state of mind manifest to the other person, but this picture suggests that a *passively* produced sign will often be just as good as, and in many cases a more reliable sign than, the one produced with communicative intent (as with the deductions of a detective). So the intentional character appears as external to the nature of the sign as indication, and may even interfere with its reliability.

This picture also suggests that the verbal sign, once produced, is as it were left behind as a phenomenon in the world, like a footprint or any other trace that a person might either deliberately or inadvertently leave behind in the course of her comings and goings. Whatever its epistemic status might be does not depend on the producer's *retaining* any special relation to it after it is produced. Later we will have occasion to discuss how if this were so, then the speaker's relation to the epistemic import of her own words would be the same as anyone else's (as it is, for example, with respect to her own footprints). This would follow from the idea that the epistemic import of the speaker's words is an objective fact, independent of anyone's beliefs or intentions with respect to them. Here as elsewhere thinking doesn't make it so, and genuine evidential value isn't something that can be breathed into one's words by an arbitrary act of will. As an objective fact then, the epistemic import of the speaker's words would be something that she herself might speculate about, inquire into, or report on, just as she might inspect the footprint she inadvertently left behind for what it may reveal. But the words someone speaks, when it is a question of believing *her* or not, only count as a potential reason for belief insofar as the speaker is presenting them in a certain way, in particular, when presented in the mode of assertion rather than as part of some other speech act or as mere recitation. It is the status of her utterance as committed act rather than as phenomenon or found object that makes it a matter of belief or disbelief for another person, and this status is not for the speaker herself a matter of theoretical speculation.

The assumption that the epistemic import of the sign as phenomenon must be a fully objective fact, independent of anyone's wishes or other attitudes with respect to it, suggests not only a certain picture of the nature of the sign in question (i.e., a monadic picture of an object or phenomenon one encounters), but also a certain view of the character of the *act* in question, that makes the utterance what it is. For on this view it can only be a notion of agency as *production* that is in question: the speaker produces a phenomenon (a sound, a sign), which then has an independent existence in the world, with certain consequences for the epistemic states of other people. Later we will see the need to invoke a different conception of agency to account for the epistemic status of the utterance, and the role of the speaker in constituting that status. If a passively or inadvertently produced sign will be just as good as an indication of someone's state of mind, and if an *intentionally* produced sign involves an additional risk for the person encountering that sign, since it may after all be produced with *deceptive* intent, this suggests that the ideal situation would be that in which one could dispense with all such mediation by the person altogether. Any of these external signs, intentional or not, communicative or not, are on this view simply forms of mediation between one person and the state of mind of another person. Whether I wish to know the mind of another because that gives me access to her beliefs and thus potentially to knowledge of the world I am interested in, or whether I am interested in her states of mind because I wish to know *her*, in either case it seems that her words can only be for me a second-best, as compared to an ideal of transparent, unmediated access to the contents of this mind. In this way the conception of the relevant agency in terms of *production* intersects with the picture of the relevant notion of sign to be that of a thing or *phenomenon*, an indication of some sort. The sign, then, is the thing produced, which is then subject to epistemic assessment like any other phenomenon we encounter.

The importance of the verbal sign on this view was always only its visibility, its audibility, as the indication of something not itself visible or audible. Hence ideally it should be seen as a *dispensable* means of access to something else, presumably something relating to the mind of the speaker. And yet this does not always seem to be so, not even ideally. This is part of what is contained in Reid's thought that for the social acts of mind, their overt expression to another person is essential to them: "They cannot exist without being expressed by words or signs, and known to the other party." We may think of contracts or apologies, for instance. They too require some overt enactment, embodied in something like a signed piece of paper, a gesture, or an explicit declaration. One person has not contracted with another even if she is gifted with the ability to read minds, and knows with certainty the facts of the other person's conditional intent. Nor have the two parties contracted if *each* of them is similarly gifted. Rather, they must each *do* something, an act is required, and what they do must take the form of relating each of them to something manifest, public, like a document or an overt act. Similarly, A may know with perfect certainty that B is aware with perfect certainty of A's remorse for her behavior the night before, but for neither of them need this knowledge mean that an apology could only be superfluous. We might say, in such cases, that a *token* needs to be produced and shown and accepted, but the point of the token isn't simply to be proof of either the other person's state of remorse or conditional intent, since the parties in question might have no doubts on these scores without that obviating the need for an open declaration of some kind.

So, sometimes at least, the overt act is not treated as merely a dispensable mode of access to something else. In these acts, the point of the visible sign is not that of something standing between one person and his epistemic goal: knowledge of another person's state of mind. The importance of the document or the gesture does not lie in being a visible, indicative sign for something else that is not visible. (Or not entirely anyway: the person's sincerity has its own importance, of course, and chapter 3 will take up the meaning of the assumption of sincerity in such cases.) Rather, in cases like that of contract or apology, the document or overt act is important not as a dispensable indication of something *else*, but rather as a constituent element in an act the two people perform, an act that is of its very nature visible and overt. They are not phenomena left behind like clues (pointing beyond themselves), but rather constituent elements in an act that relates the two people to each other.

In thinking about the role of speech in the context of *testimony*, that is, speech that purports to present a reason to *believe* something, these very considerations may suggest that this dimension of communicative speech, and the contrasts that have been drawn between acts of speech and indicative signs, cannot really be relevant to the topic. One thought would be: If mutual mind-reading could not in principle substitute for the role of the overt speech, and what matters instead in these cases is the performance by two people of an act that relates them in a certain way, this must mean that these more specifically relational aspects of communicative speech have nothing to do with knowledge or with the specifically *epistemic* role of speech. If certainty (*epistemic* certainty, that is) about either the remorse or the conditional intentions of another person still does not provide what is accomplished by an overt act involving words or other symbols, that can only mean that the overt act has nothing to do with the knowledge-conveying function of speech, indeed nothing to do with the *communicative* function of speech, at least as far as that is narrowly conceived.

That would be a hasty conclusion, however. For one thing, when person A does say the words or sign the document, person B *does* learn something about A; he learns, for instance, that she has *contracted* with him. This is a genuine piece of knowledge which, by hypothesis anyway, could *not* have been available to B in any other way. So, I am suggesting, the Indicative picture of speech that we began with already starts with an artificially restricted sense of what the properly *epistemic* interests of speech might be. That is, these interests are seen as confined to knowledge of the state of mind of the other person, which in fortunate, ordinary cases of true beliefs and honest intentions allows us to conclude reliably to some fact in the world. But in fact the relevance of the act in question, and the fact that the act must be *overt* in a special sense, can still be a properly epistemic one, without that meaning that its relevance is that of the indication of a psychological state. The difference is that here the "making visible," or what I will later call being "manifest," is, in Reid's terms, essential rather than accidental to the particular epistemic role it plays. Second, it would be hasty to conclude from the fact that this dimension of speech focuses on the establishment of a specific form of relation between persons, rather than a relation of indication between a sign and what it indicates (this indicated object at the other end being the epistemic *goal*, it would seem),

that we are therefore dealing with a dimension of speech that is not part
of its role as a conveyor of knowledge. It will be argued later that the specific form of agency exercised overtly in these verbal acts of relation is the
very form of agency that constitutes an utterance as any kind of assertion
or other illocution in the first place, and thus as so much as a candidate for
belief or disbelief.

1.5 The Self-Understanding of the Social Act of Mind

We have briefly seen how the Indicative picture suggests a wrong answer
to the question why it should matter to the status of the verbal sign that it
was produced intentionally. It suggests either that it shouldn't matter at all,
or that it may just as often have negative rather than positive import that
the sign was produced intentionally (the unguarded, inadvertent gesture
being more revealing, less subject to suspicion). From the perspective of
speech as a social act, by contrast, the relevant agency in question is seen
to be one's participation in a practice involving the exercise of a normative
power rather than the production of an effect, and this perspective seeks to
describe this agency as a constitutive element of the status of the utterance
as a reason to believe something, rather than the production of something
(a trace, like a footprint) which then *has* some epistemic import on its
own, independent of any agent's comprehending relation to it. The claim
will be that we need to see this agency in social-relational terms in order
to account for how the speaker's exercise of a form of agency could be a
constituent element in the epistemic status of the utterance, rather than as
something extrinsic to it (bearing some causal, productive relation to the
utterance as phenomenon).

Just as any account must say something about the importance of the fact
that a piece of verbal behavior must be seen as intentional for it to have
the status of an assertion or testimony, any account must also say something
about the fact mentioned earlier that a piece of verbal behavior must be
seen as done with awareness and understanding for it to have the status
of an assertion. The brief discussion of the Indicative picture has already
suggested a tendency to downplay the importance of agency and awareness
in the probative value of verbal signs. (In this way, the Indicative picture is

the empiricist version of the "hermeneutics of suspicion," and the role of "signs" and their decipherment in that discourse.)[14] But the point here is not the denial that, e.g., the inadvertent gasp can be more reliable or more revealing than the carefully composed speech, but rather that the basic phenomena of asserting and telling present a distinctive form of reason for belief, and that *these* acts depend for their very being on having been done intentionally and with awareness and understanding of their meaning. Once an act of assertion is granted to have taken place, then of course it may be profitably reflected upon for what it may reveal of the person unconsciously and inadvertently. But even those "external" interpretive reflections must begin with the assumption that an assertion about something has been made, which requires that it be made intentionally and with awareness, though not, of course, intentional under every possible description of it.

There are, of course, forms of interpretation, forms of symptomatic epistemic import sufficiently general to apply to *any* verbal behavior or verbal reaction at all (i.e., whether intentional, or "automatic," "hypnotic"). What is potentially revealing in what a person says and does is hardly restricted to what she may wish to reveal, is aware of revealing, or may be seeking to get across. Nothing in *that* thought, however, provides any reason to deny that the speech acts of telling and the like are such that they must be done intentionally and with understanding to be done at all. Hence if our topic is the way knowledge is communicated from speaker to speaker through acts of telling and informing, we need to account for how the distinctive kind of reason to believe which acts of assertion present themselves as carrying is dependent on the forms of knowledge and understanding that are intrinsic to these acts themselves, and not simply enabling conditions for the production of results understood independently. So the claim to be developed here will be that we need a social-relational story, one which distances itself from the Indicative picture, to account for the importance that the speaker's awareness and understanding of what she is doing has to the story of telling, along with a corresponding awareness and understanding on the part of her interlocutor.

The role of understanding here stems from seeing acts of telling, claiming, and the like as belonging to what Austin calls the "illocutionary" dimension of speech, as distinct from what he calls the "locutionary" and the

---

14 The phrase originates with Paul Ricoeur's 1970 book on Freud, but it has taken on a life of its own since then.

"perlocutionary."[15] In saying a certain meaningful sentence, a speaker has performed a *locution*, the sort of thing which may be done in the basic lessons and drills in learning a new language. The speaker performs an *illocutionary* act when she produces an utterance to do something such as apologizing, ordering, claiming, or telling her interlocutor something. Here the act in question is said to be accomplished *in* the saying itself, subject to various conditions of context and what Austin calls the "uptake" on the part of the audience. The two dimensions stand in a relation of dependence to each other in that the accomplishment of an illocutionary act typically requires the utterance of some locution. Further, either of these acts by the speaker may have various consequences for the audience, such as surprising, alarming, or persuading him. These consequences may be intended or unintended, known or unknown to the speaker. Austin refers to these as *perlocutionary* acts, and these he says are results produced *by* the utterance rather than acts accomplished *in* the saying itself. Like many ordinary actions, the perlocutionary act of surprising or alarming someone may be what is aimed at by the speaker or may be something done wholly unintentionally and without any understanding of the consequences of her utterance. In this they are different from illocutionary acts like ordering, apologizing, or telling someone something, for acts of this type are such as to be done intentionally, knowingly, and with understanding of the meaning of what one is doing. This condition of awareness and understanding has several dimensions. For the speaker's utterance to be an act of telling her audience something, the speaker has to be credited with knowledge of at least the following kinds.

- She must know what she is doing, in the most basic sense of knowing that she is saying something.

- She must know *what* she is saying. She must understand the language she is speaking, and the content asserted; otherwise no words she speaks can amount to an act of telling.

- She must know that she is saying these words specifically to *tell* her interlocutor something, and not simply reciting some lines, or paraphrasing someone else. She must know in general which illocution she is performing with these words.

---

15 Austin (1962), Lecture 9. Further discussion of the relations between these dimensions of speech is taken up in chapter 5 here (5.3).

- If she is telling her interlocutor that P, she must know that she is presenting her utterance as a reason for that person to *believe* something; specifically to believe the content of what she is saying. Hence she must take herself to be in a position to (thereby) provide another person with such a reason for belief.

Two aspects in particular of this knowledge that the speaker must be assumed to have will come up for attention later (chapters 5 and 6). One is that to make sense of this assumption of knowledge, and the role this assumption plays in constituting one's utterance as a potential reason to believe its content, we must understand the speaker's knowledge as a form of *practical* knowledge, rather than theoretical or observational knowledge. We said earlier that, unlike a footprint or other evidence, the speaker's utterance counts as reason to believe its content only insofar as the speaker is presenting that content in a certain mode, viz., the mode of assertion or claim. This will be a matter of the speaker's illocutionary knowledge of what speech act she is performing with her words. The point will be elaborated further in subsequent chapters, but the claim is that this speaker's knowledge of her illocution, which is a condition for it being the speech act it is, is not for her a matter of discovery or a matter of her best opinion about what she is doing. We can begin to see this if we reflect on the fact that, for example, a speaker's *uncertainty* about whether she is indeed asserting something with her words (rather than, e.g., speculating, guessing, asking) will normally be part of what compromises the characterization of the act *as* an assertion. To be uncertain here is to hedge on how one intends one's utterance to be taken up. A speaker may waver between claiming outright that the cat is on the mat, and merely supposing, speculating, surmising, or imagining the same state of affairs, and the wavering in question is at one and the same time a matter of how she means to commit herself and what illocution she means to be performing. For the speaker to claim outright that the cat is on the mat is for her to commit herself outright to that proposition, and she knows her illocution in knowing her commitment. This is one dimension of the practical nature of the knowledge a speaker must be presumed to have in performing ordinary actions of assertion and telling.

At the same time, while the speaker's practical knowledge is necessary for the determination of the identity of the particular illocution that is at issue, this knowledge must be shared with and taken up by her interlocutor if she is actually to perform the illocution of telling, asking, or denying.

The simple act of telling involves an interlocking system of authority and dependence on, or deferral to, the role played by the other person. As Reid says, social acts of mind are distinctive in that they "can have no existence without the intervention of some other intelligent being, *who acts a part in them*" (emphasis added). It is not simply that expression is essential to them in the sense that they must be broadcast or externalized, but they must be expressed *to* another party who recognizes them for what they are and "acts a part" in their "completion." The speaker has not managed to perform the act of telling or promising if there is no recognition of what she is up to by the person she is addressing, as it would be if the telephone connection went dead in the middle of speaking, or if she were speaking a language the other person cannot understand. The proper understanding of Austin's "uptake conditions" for ordinary speech acts will occupy us in chapters 5 and 6, and something that emerges from that is that the understanding of illocution generally requires an understanding of practical knowledge that involves two parties and not just one, and what they know together rather than just what they know about each other. For the speaker to be able to say, "I promise," "I claim," etc., her reflective understanding of her action must incorporate the point of view of her interlocutor and assume that he is indeed playing his part for the completion of the speech act, just as her interlocutor's uptake must incorporate her own understanding of the meaning of her utterance. The speaker's knowledge of what she is doing in speech depends on this very knowledge being taken up and shared by her interlocutor; otherwise she will not in fact be doing what she announces in saying, "I apologize, accept, refuse, tell . . ." These are social acts which consist in overtly assuming or declining to assume certain responsibilities toward another, and the ability to do so in speech is a basic capacity of any speaker, as basic as the ability to say yes or no and have that count in the conversation.

It is this essentially public and relational nature of the act itself that makes for the possibility of the speaker's knowledge expressed in saying, "I accept," "I refuse," etc., to be knowledge that is understood to be shared with her interlocutor, incorporating the other party's perspective, if it is indeed to be knowledge of what she is thereby doing in speech. For an illocutionary act is accomplished in a certain act of self-presentation being recognized and taken up by its addressee. The act is not the sign of something whose genuine reality takes place offstage. If a speaker presents herself to another as assuming the commitments of a promise or an act of telling and this is taken up by her interlocutor, then she has well and truly done that thing, whatever mental reservations she may harbor. Nothing about a difference between what she presented herself as doing (in the right context, etc.) and what she privately intended at the time cancels the fact that she did indeed promise or tell, and that, of course, will be her interlocutor's complaint should she fail to come through or be as good as her word. This aspect of the illocutionary, the sense in which the presentation counts as the deed itself, and its role in making an utterance count as an assertion and hence as potentially the kind of reason provided by testimony, will be hard to make sense of on the Indicative model. The story developed here aims to show how understanding the possibility of believing or denying what someone has said, that is, claimed or told someone, requires an understanding of informative communication in acts whose reality is overt and intersubjective in this way. These are social operations of the mind for which expression is essential rather than accidental, as Reid puts it, and for which the notion of "expression" itself is a specifically social one, meaning that the reality of the acts themselves is constituted by relations of recognition among the participants in the practice.

2

Getting Told and Being Believed

2.1 The Realm of Testimony

Recent interest in the epistemology of testimony has focused attention on what justification we may commonly have in the vast areas of life where we are dependent on what other people tell us. This dependence is not restricted to what we are told in face-to-face encounters, for we also take ourselves to know all sorts of things that only reached us through a long chain of utterances and documents, whose evidential status we have never investigated for ourselves and which we will never be in a position to investigate. And the content of such knowledge is not confined to the arcana of specialized studies, but includes such mundane matters as the facts of one's own birth and parentage, the geographical and institutional facts of one's immediate environment, and the general facts that make up one's basic sense of what the world is like.

In part it is the enormity of this dependence that makes for the interest in the subject of testimony, combined with the apparent clash between the kind of epistemic relations involved here and the classic empiricist picture of genuine knowledge basing itself either on direct experience of the facts or on working out conclusions for oneself.[1] It isn't just that the bulk of what we take ourselves to know is so highly *mediated*, as even

---

1 Cf. Locke: "For, I think, we may as rationally hope to see with other Men's Eyes, as to know by other Men's Understandings. So much as we ourselves consider and comprehend of Truth and Reason, so much we possess of real and true Knowledge. The floating of other Men's Opinions in our brains makes us not a jot more knowing, though they happen to be true" (*Essay Concerning Human Understanding*, 1, 4, 23).

knowledge gained through a microscope or other scientific instrument must be; rather it is that the vehicle of mediation here—what other people say—seems so flimsy, unregulated, and is known in plenty of cases to be unreliable, even deliberately so. People do lie, get things wrong, and speak carelessly. And while we may realistically hope for continued improvement in the various technical means of epistemic mediation (advances in scientific instrumentation are part of the history of scientific progress, after all), there is little reason to expect that the fallibility and mendacity associated with human testimony will one day be overcome. So in this light, reflecting on just how much we rely on the word of others, we may conclude that either we are very careless believers indeed, with no right to claim to know more than a fraction of what we think we know, or some great reductionist program must be in the offing, tracing this chain back to something resembling the classic picture of knowledge by acquaintance.[2]

Hume's (1977) famous discussion of the believability of reports of miracles is the locus classicus for attempts to understand the epistemic status of testimony as ultimately the same as any other reliable evidence. And part of what is meant by this claim is that the basis we may have in any given case for believing what we hear can only be an a posteriori judgment to the effect that in this case there is a reliable evidential correlation between the statement we are being offered and the facts themselves. Several recent writers, most notably C. A. J. Coady in his book *Testimony* (1992), have argued that the Humean picture cannot succeed in reconstructing our actual basis for believing what people say, and that our entitlement to believe what we are told must have, in part, an a priori basis. Somewhat lost in much recent discussion, however, is attention to the basic *relationship* between people when one person tells a second person something, and the second person believes him. This is the primary everyday occurrence, and it is the basic way knowledge gets around. Or at least, so we say. For normally (though not without exception) we take it to be sufficient for bringing someone to know that P that he was *told* by someone who knew, and he believed her. And now, of course, if this second person is taken to *know* that P, he may tell another person, and so on. This may seem absurdly simple and unreflective,

---

2 Or back to observation sentences: cf. Quine and Ullian 1970, 33–35, which makes explicit comparison of testimony with the "extension of the senses" provided by telescopes and radar.

and to be at odds with an earlier picture of genuine *knowledge* as being more of an achievement lying at the end of an arduous path from belief or opinion. My concern in this chapter, however, is not so much with the conditions for knowledge as with the nature of the two sides of the relationship described here. One person *tells* the other person something, and this other person *believes her*. I want to understand what "telling" is, especially as this contrasts with other things done in (assertoric) speech such as persuading, arguing, or demonstrating; activities which may also lead to belief or knowledge for the interlocutor, but in importantly different ways. And primarily I want to examine the relation of believing where its direct object is not a proposition but a person. For in the basic case described above, it is the speaker who is believed, and belief in the proposition asserted follows from this. These are different epistemic phenomena. For the hearer might not believe the speaker at all, taking her for a con artist, but yet believe that what she has said is in fact true. Whereas when the hearer believes the speaker, he not only believes what is said but does so on the basis of taking the speaker's word for it. I don't mean to suggest that this distinction has been wholly ignored in the literature of testimony, and I will soon come to discuss what I think is one of the best recent discussions of it. But both it and the distinction between the speech act of "telling" and other things done with assertion have not been given a central place in the discussion of what is distinctive about the epistemic dependence on testimony. Specifically, I wish to argue that any account of testimony that seeks to resist the (Humean) assimilation of its epistemic status to that of an evidence-like correlation between one set of phenomena and another will have to give a central place to the distinctive relation of believing another person.[3] Only in this way can we account for what is distinctive about acquiring beliefs from what people *say*, as opposed to learning from other expressive or revealing behavior of theirs. The hope is to show that the paradigmatic situations of telling cannot be thought of as the presentation or acceptance of evidence at all, and that this is connected with the specifically *linguistic* nature of the transfer of knowledge through testimony (which will take us through an epistemological reading of Grice's original account of non-natural meaning).

---

3 I follow other recent writers in characterizing this as a Humean position, but I don't argue for the attribution. For a dissenting view, see Saul Traiger (1993).

2.2 Evidential Relations and the A Priori

In part due to the epistemological context of recent discussion of testimony, that argument has focused on the question of the a priori or a posteriori status of our justification for beliefs acquired in this way. In recent work, both C. A. J. Coady (1992) and Tyler Burge (1993) have argued against a broadly Humean picture, by attacking the idea that we could only have a posteriori justification for believing what others tell us. Coady presents more than one argument against the Humean idea, but several of them begin with the following strategy. If we can only have a posteriori grounds for taking what people say to be a reliable guide to the facts, then on such a view it must be conceivable for there to be a community of speakers whose assertions bear *no* reliable relation to the facts. If we are to be in a position to deploy an a posteriori argument for the existence of such a correlation, it must be possible for us to begin confronting the linguistic evidence without begging that very question. Coady presents a powerful and connected set of arguments for the conclusion that this is not, in fact, a coherent possibility. Not only would the practice within the community of making or accepting assertions soon break down on such assumptions, but from a perspective outside the community, there are deeper reasons connected with the interpretation of speech which prevent the Humean scenario from being realizable. For assigning *content* to the utterances of the hypothetical speakers requires, for familiar reasons, regular correlation between assertive utterances and the conditions under which they would be true. Massive disparity between the content we assign to utterances and their truth or rationality would oblige us as interpreters to revise our original assignments of content to them. So there is, in fact, no genuine possibility of a community of speakers whose assertions failed, as a general rule, to correlate with the facts. And thus, contrary to the Humean picture, our general justification for believing what people say cannot be a purely empirical, a posteriori one.[4]

4 Tyler Burge's argument is very different, and I will not be examining its details here. In particular, unlike Coady as we will see, his account does not appeal to a principle of charity in the situation of radical interpretation. What it shares with Coady's argument is the aim of providing some a priori warrant for believing what is said. Burge argues for what he calls the Acceptance Principle, which states that "a person is entitled to accept as true something that is presented as true and that is intelligible to him, unless there are stronger reasons not to do so" (1993, 467). He states that this is not an empirical principle (469). And the general form of justification associated with it is meant to apply equally to our epistemic dependence on other *people* ("rational

Both arguments direct themselves against the idea that we have, at best, empirical, inductive grounds for believing what people say. I don't dispute this general point or the particular way it is argued for in these two instances, but I do want to point out that this general form of argument describes no particular role for the notions either of a speaker *telling* someone something, or of *believing* that speaker. What the generality of such arguments provides is a defeasible a priori warrant for believing that what other people say will normally be true. But any argument pitched at that level of generality will leave untouched the question of whether believing the person (as opposed to believing the truth of what is said) is a legitimate, and perhaps basic, source of new beliefs. For we might well have an a priori defeasible warrant for accepting the beliefs we gain through observing the behavior of others (verbal and otherwise) without this warrant involving the concepts of "saying" or "telling" at all. By itself, such a justification is no different from the presumptive right we may have (ceteris paribus) to rely on the deliverances of the senses or of memory. At this level of argument, the speech of other people could still be something which is treated as *evidence* for the truth of various claims about the world; the difference would only be that here we may have some nonempirical warrant for treating this phenomenon as evidence, perhaps even very good evidence.[5] This general line of thought begins, then, to look more like a nonskeptical *version* of the basic Humean view, and less like a vindication of testimony as a distinct source of beliefs, one not reducible to a form of evidence. And yet it is the special relations of telling someone, being told, and accepting or refusing another's word that are the home of the network of beliefs we acquire through human testimony. And these relations, I hope to show, provide a kind of reason for belief that is categorically different from that provided by evidence.

Another way of putting this criticism would be to say that arguments of the generality of Coady's do not address the question of what is distinctive

sources") and to our dependence on certain *capacities*, what he calls "resources for reason," such as memory and perception (469–70). By contrast, for my purposes the difference between our dependence on memory and perception and our dependence on other people and their overt acts of informing is all-important for the understanding of testimony.

5 Summarizing his line of criticism of one version of the reductionist thesis associated with Hume, Coady says, "The difficulty consists in the fact that the whole enterprise of RT' in its present form requires that we understand what testimony is independently of knowing that it is, in any degree, a reliable form of evidence" (1992, 85).

about acquiring beliefs from what people *say*, as compared with other things people do. At bottom, the epistemological role of communicative speech is not seen as essentially different from that of other behavior. But the observable behavior of other people may be a source of true beliefs in all sorts of ways, which need not have anything to do with believing the other person. I may look out my window on a sunny day and see people bundled up against the cold, and then reliably conclude from this that it must be colder outside than it otherwise looks. This transition in thought is not essentially different from the picture according to which I observe the verbal behavior of some exotic community, and in seeking to understand what it means, I necessarily rely on various assumptions about their rationality and general awareness. And here one could point out that the same "rationalizing" or charitable constraint on understanding what these people say also provides a defeasible warrant for taking *what* we understand them to say to be *true*. This is because we take their speech normally to express their beliefs, and we take their beliefs (as interpreted by us) normally to be true. This familiar, general scheme applies in the same way to the behavior of the people I see bundled up against the cold, and to the verbal behavior observed by the radical interpreter. Pictured in this way, one's relation to the exotic speech community does not involve being *told* anything at all, or believing *them*, any more than it does in the case of the people observed from the window. In both cases it is just a matter of an inference from behavior which is seen as rational to some conclusion about the state of the world. So nothing along these lines, justifying the beliefs we acquire from other people, can count as a vindication of our reliance on *testimony*, since it is not a vindication of what we learn through believing other people.

This is, of course, the familiar role of speech and its relation to belief in contemporary philosophy of mind, and it should not be surprising to see it exerting a degree of control over the recent discussion of testimony. Within this discourse, speech is seen as a kind of interpretable human behavior like any other. When we interpret such behavior, we seek to make it understandable within the rational categories of what is called "folk psychology," and ascribe beliefs and other attitudes which will be reasonable approximations to the True and the Good. And this picture of our relation to the speech of other people leads almost imperceptibly into a view about testimony. For we can argue from here: when we interpret the speech of another we do not only learn about the speaker, we also learn about the world. Most obviously, when someone makes an assertion, we may not only learn about what she believes, but if the assertion is *true*, we may also learn the truth of what is asserted. And if our interpretation is guided by principles of charity, we will indeed take most of what people say to be true, even in cases where we have no independent reason for thinking it true. In this way, the fact of the other person's belief (as interpreted by us) may function as *our* reason for believing the same thing. We thus gain true beliefs about persons as well as about the world they are talking about.

2.3 Perversity, Dependence, and Risk

What this general scheme provides us with is a presumptive warrant for sharing the beliefs we take the speaker to have. But, other things being equal, we would have the very same right *however* we learned of that person's beliefs.[6] This epistemic warrant described in this scheme need not involve a dependence on speech any more than it did when I learned about the weather by seeing how people outside were dressed. Speech, of course, can be an especially revealing and fine-grained basis for belief-ascription, but from this perspective it is but a particular instance of the more general scheme of interpreting behavior.

Since it is knowledge of the other person's beliefs that is doing all the epistemic work in this picture, we should note that while speech is in some obvious ways a privileged route to such knowledge, it is also one which subjects the interpreter to special risks which are not shared by other possible ways of coming to this same knowledge. When I learn of someone's beliefs through what she *tells* me, I am dependent on such things as her discretion, sincerity, good intentions—in short, on how she deliberately presents herself to me—in a way that I am not dependent when I infer her beliefs in other ways. People are known to lie, exaggerate, and otherwise speak in ways that do not express their genuine beliefs. Thus, in relying on what a person says, I am incurring an additional risk that the behavior she is manifesting may be deliberately calculated to mislead me as to what she believes. I am here dependent on *her*, and her intentions with respect to me, and not just on my own abilities as an interpreter of the evidence.

---

6 With some obvious exceptions; for instance, if I learned of someone's beliefs from the bragging admission of the person who deceived him. But these sorts of cases are just what is taken to be excluded by speaking of "other things being equal."

This source of error is a much more remote possibility in the case of inferences drawn from the private observation of someone's behavior. The people bundled up against the cold *could* be dressed up like that just so as to fool me, but this is hardly the everyday occurrence that lying and misrepresentation is. And that risk of error is not a possibility at all for those ways, real or imaginary, of learning someone's beliefs directly and without the mediation of voluntary expression or behavior at all (i.e., whatever is imagined in imagining the effects of truth-serum, hypnotism, or brain scans). If the epistemic import of what people say is at bottom that of an indication of what they believe, it would seem perverse for us to give any privileged status to the vehicle of knowledge (speech and assertion) where we are most vulnerable, because most dependent on the free disposal of the other person. And if we are considering speech as evidence, we will have eventually to face the question of how recognition of its intentional character could ever *enhance* rather than detract from its epistemic value for an audience. Ordinarily, if I confront something as evidence (the telltale footprint, the cigarette butt left in the ashtray) and then learn that it was left there deliberately, and even with the intention of bringing me to a particular belief, this will only discredit it as evidence in my eyes. It won't seem *better* evidence, or even just as good, but instead like something fraudulent, or tainted evidence.

Insofar as speech does occupy a privileged place in what we learn from other people, this sort of view seems to picture us as perversely preferring to increase our epistemic exposure, by placing ourselves at the mercy of the free disposition of another person, according a privileged place to human speech, which is here construed as a kind of evidence that has been deliberately tampered with. On the "evidential" reconstruction of testimony, speech functions as no more than a very possibly misleading way of learning the speaker's beliefs. Other things being equal, some more direct way of learning would be better; and *in particular* we should prefer any way of learning the speaker's beliefs that was not wholly dependent on the speaker's overt, deliberate revelation of them. Anything that necessarily involved her free action in this way, and thus brought with it the possibility of deliberate deceit, could only be a *less* reliable way of learning her beliefs than some otherwise comparable way that involved going behind her back (mind reading, brain scans, private observation of her behavior). If speech is seen as a form of *evidence*, then once its intentional character is recognized (that is, not just as intentional behavior, but intentional with respect to inducing a particular belief), we need an account of how it could count as anything more than *doctored* evidence.

2.4 Assertion as Assurance

Let us contrast this view with another picture of how what another person tells me may contribute to my belief, a picture that *will* give central place to the act of saying something and the response of believing or disbelieving the person. On a genuinely non-Humean account, when someone tells me it's cold out, I don't simply gain an awareness of her beliefs, I am also given her *assurance* that it's cold out.[7] This is something I could not have gained by the private observation of her behavior. When someone gives me her assurance that it's cold out, she explicitly assumes a certain responsibility for what I believe. What this provides me with is different in kind, though not necessarily in degree of certainty, from beliefs I might have read off from her behavior, just as what I gain from a declaration of intention differs from the firm expectation I may form from knowing someone's habits. On the evidential picture, by contrast, the speaker's assurance as such just clouds the issue, since all the verbal expression of assurance can do is interpose an additional piece of (possibly misleading) evidence between me and what I really want to know. I now have some more behavior to interpret, verbal this time, which brings with it special new possibilities for being misled. From my role as interpreter of others, my ultimate destination is the truth about the world, but often I must pass through the beliefs of another person as my only (fallible) access to this truth. And now relying on what this person deliberately *says* provides me with at best a distinctively fallible way of learning what those beliefs *are*.

On both views, when I take someone's word for something, I am peculiarly dependent on the will or discretion of the speaker, in a way that I would not be in the situation of interpreting the evidence of the person's behavior. But they look at this dependence differently. On the assurance

---

7 Since writing the paper that forms the basis of this chapter, the term "assurance" has been employed in a few different ways in philosophical discussions of speech and testimony. Krista Lawlor (2013) in particular makes a strong case for assurance as a distinct speech act from plain assertion, and while her usage is not the same as mine, in subsequent chapters I stress the distinction between assertion and the speech act of telling.

view, going behind the person's back to learn her beliefs would not be better, or even just as good. Rather, it is essential to the distinctive reason for belief that I get from being told that it proceeds from something freely undertaken by the other person. Only as a free declaration does it have that value for me. Evidence, by contrast, is not dependent on presentation in this way. A phenomenon will count as evidence however it came about, whether by natural causes or by someone's deliberate action, or just as easily by inadvertence or carelessness. But nothing can count as someone's assurance that was not freely presented as such, just as talking in one's sleep cannot count as making an assertion or a promise.[8] The two views, then, oppose each other most directly over this issue of the role of the speaker's freedom and the hearer's dependence on it. On the evidential view, dependence on the freedom of the other person just saddles us with an additional set of risks; now we have to worry not only about possibly misleading (natural) evidence, but deliberate distortion as well. On the assurance view, dependence on someone's freely assuming responsibility for the truth of P, presenting herself as a kind of guarantor, provides me with a characteristic reason to believe, different in kind from anything provided by impersonal evidence alone.

In the remainder of this chapter, I want to sketch out a defense of the alternative picture above and explore the case for denying that human testimony should be thought of as providing the same sort of reason for belief that ordinary evidence does. A guiding question will be this: As hearers faced with the question of believing what we are told, how are we to understand the nature of our dependence on the free assertion of the speaker, and how does this dependence affect the question of whether our epistemic relation to what is said is ultimately an evidential one?

In a groundbreaking paper on the central questions of testimony, Angus Ross (1986) begins by raising the question of whether it makes sense in general to treat what people say as a form of evidence, and he explicitly relates this question to the fact that speaking is a voluntary act. I have some

---

8 When in the course of a discussion of Moore's Paradox and the idea of "two people speaking through my mouth," Wittgenstein asks, "Where is it said in logic that an assertion [*Behauptung*] cannot be made in a trance?" I understand him roughly to be saying: Logic (on some conception of it) may well say nothing about the speaker's awareness of what he is doing in making an assertion, just as the same conception of logic permits statements of the form "P, but I don't believe it," but both possibilities are contrary to the point and hence the meaning of assertions (Wittgenstein 1980, § 818).

differences with how he understands this relation, but the general line of
thought seems to me deeply right and worth developing. Let me begin
with a moderately lengthy quotation from the early pages of Ross's article.[9]

> The main problem with the idea that the hearer views the speaker's words as
> evidence arises from the fact that, unlike the examples of natural signs which
> spring most readily to mind, saying something is a deliberate act under the
> speaker's conscious control and the hearer is aware that this is the case. The
> problem is not that of whether the hearer can in these circumstances see
> the speaker's words as *good* evidence; it is a question of whether the notion
> of evidence is appropriate here at all. There is, of course, nothing odd about
> the idea of deliberately presenting an audience with evidence in order to
> get them to draw a desired conclusion, as when a photograph is produced in
> court. But in such a case what is presented is, or is presented as being, evi-
> dence independently of the fact of the presenter having chosen to present it.
> If a speaker's words are evidence of anything, they have that status only be-
> cause he has chosen to use them. Speaking is not like allowing someone to
> see you are blushing. The problem is not, however, that the fact of our having
> chosen to use certain words *cannot* be evidence for some further conclusion.
> Our choices can certainly be revealing. The difficulty lies in supposing that
> the speaker himself sees his choice of words in this light, which in turn makes
> it difficult to suppose that this is how the hearer is intended to see his choice.
> (Ross 1986, 72)

First of all, it should be noted that Ross's target, like mine, is not the class of
all speech acts, not even the class of all *assertoric* speech acts. Not everything
done in speech, not even everything done with sentences in the declarative
mood, involves the specific relations of telling and being believed. Assertions
are also made in the context of argument and demonstration, for instance,
where there is no assumption within the discourse that the speaker is to
be believed on her say-so.[10] In such a situation the speaker is not aiming to
be *believed*, but is attempting to provide independently convincing reasons

---

9 I should add that I'll only be discussing a part of Ross's argument, focusing on his criticism of an
   evidential view of testimony, and not his positive account of how assertion contributes to belief. Michael Welbourne's account of testimony in his monograph *The Community of Knowledge*
   (1986) has various affinities with Ross's, including the denial that an act of telling is presented
   by the speaker as evidence, and an emphasis on believing the speaker as the target notion for
   an understanding of testimony (and the concept of knowledge itself, on Welbourne's view).

10 And if we take it that assertions are made in the course of following out a proof, or in ad
   hominem argument, then it's clear that their role in providing reason for belief needn't even
   depend on the assumption that the speaker believes what she says. This is taken up in the
   following chapter.

for the truth of the view in question, or laying out the steps of a proof. *Telling* someone something is not simply giving expression to what's on your mind, but is also making a statement with the understanding that here it is your word that is to be relied on. It is a common enough understanding, and commonly justified, but it is not one in place in such contexts as persuasion, argumentation, or demonstration. For different reasons it is also not the understanding of the speech of a person in the context of therapeutic treatment, in the oral examination of a pupil, or in the police interrogation of a suspect. Such discourses will contain *statements* of various kinds, but they may be received by the interlocutor in a very different spirit, as evidence for truth of a very different kind from the overt subject of the subject's statement. This again is quite different from the exchange of information through telling and being told in everyday life. (And on the picture of speech to be developed here, these other discourses emerge as ultimately dependent on the central discourse of telling.)

Having said that, however, how is seeing one's own utterance as evidence supposed to be incompatible with seeing my utterance as a voluntary act of mine, in Ross's words, seeing it as "up to me what I shall say"? He notes that there is nothing in the idea of evidence itself which is inconsistent with a person's deliberately presenting something as such, as when a photograph is introduced as evidence. And, it should also be noted, an item like a photograph can serve as good evidence even when it was not only deliberately *presented*, but also deliberately *produced* so as to lead one to a particular conclusion. So why cannot the speaker have essentially the same relation to her own words, as something she deliberately produces and presents to serve as evidence for some conclusion (and hence to bring the hearer to some desired belief)? Part of the answer Ross gives lies in the following view. Seeing the utterance as evidence would involve seeing it as the outcome of some general empirical law, the sort of "reliable correlation" Hume has in mind, connecting the making of the statement with the obtaining of the facts in question. Ross acknowledges that I may see the words of others or my own *past* words in this light, but

> What I cannot do is see the words I now choose to utter in that light, for I cannot at one and the same time see it as up to *me* what I shall say and see my choice . . . as determined or constrained by facts about my own nature. (73)

Such a stance toward one's own utterances may be barely possible, he says, but "it is hardly compatible with taking responsibility for those acts." While the emphasis on responsibility is important, I don't think this part of Ross's response leads in the right direction. For, as far as "reliable correlations" go, why could I not see my own utterance as securely linked with the truth, not in virtue of my being determined by the facts of my own nature, but in virtue of my own free but unswerving commitment to the truth? The sort of reliability my Humean interlocutor wants to count on does not abolish my freedom. I can present myself to myself and others as *reliable* in various ways, without that meaning that my reliability is a *constraint* to which I am passively subject. My utterance is a voluntary act of mine, something I take responsibility for, and *part* of what I take responsibility for is its correlation with the truth. So it seems it cannot be because I see my utterance as freely chosen that it cannot be taken by either myself or my audience as evidence for the truth.

However there is another strand in what Ross is saying here that clarifies the role of the speaker's freedom and its clash with the idea of evidence. In the first passage quoted he says that something like a photograph will be evidence "independently of the fact of the presenter having chosen to present it"; whereas by contrast,

> If a speaker's words are evidence of anything, they have that status only because he has chosen to use them.

Strictly speaking, this last statement is not quite right, as we've already briefly seen. If we've agreed that in various contexts a person's words *can* be treated as evidence, then this need not be dependent on the speaker's having *chosen* to use them. If my analyst can adopt a symptomatic stance toward my more conscious and deliberate statements, then he may make similar revealing inferences from my botched utterances and slips of the tongue, as well as the words I may utter under hypnosis. Speaking *is* a form of behavior, after all, and human behavior is infinitely interpretable, infinitely revealing, in ways that are not at the disposal of the person to determine their meaning. One's words can be evidence when not *chosen* at all, revealing like a cry of pain; or they can be evidence against one's intent, as when someone's tone of voice reveals that she's lying. What *is* true, however, but still in need of defense here, is that a statement only provides the kind of reason for belief that *testimony* does if it is understood to be something freely and consciously undertaken by the speaker. It is with respect to *this* sort of reason for belief that we, as hearers or readers, are *essentially* dependent on the free disposal of the speaker or writer. Thus, if the idea is that something is evidence, or is being treated as evidence, when it is a reason for belief independently of whether it was intentionally produced or presented as such, we need a fuller characterization of the kind of "independence" that pertains to the category of evidence, and a defense of the idea that testimony as such provides reason for belief that is *not* independent of assumptions involving the freedom of the speaker.

2.5 Photographs and Statements

It is here that Ross's passing contrast between our epistemic relations to photographs and speakers is worth developing in some detail. There are many ways in which what we see and what we believe may be dependent on what others do, say, or show to us. In my direct experience of a footprint, I may be dependent not only on the person who made it, but also perhaps on someone who drew it to my attention. And when my epistemic relation to it is mediated by another person in these ways, I am subject to the ordinary risks of distortion, since in principle any evidence may be tampered with. But even with these particular risks and dependencies, my relation to the footprint is still a perceptual one and does not involve me in the specific relation of believing another person. And this is so even if my perception of it is technologically mediated in ways that involve the doings and expertise of other people. In discussing the nature of photographic realism, Kendall Walton (1984) compares what we see in photographs with what we see through a microscope or in a mirror, to argue for the claim that in all three cases we actually *see* the thing in question, even though this seeing is mediated in various ways, and even though photographs can be doctored in various ways.[11] Real *experience* of a thing may also be mediated or subject to various epistemic risks, without that abolishing the difference between being told about it and experiencing it oneself. As Walton points out, what I see directly when someone points out the window may also be altered in various ways to deceive, but that doesn't transform the situation from one of perception to one of depiction. In Walton's terms, a photograph can be

11 For purposes of the account of testimony developed here, we need not of course follow Walton in his claim that the object itself is in fact seen in the photograph, for it is precisely the differences between photographs and assertions that concern me here.

"transparent" to the scene it depicts in part because, unlike in the case of a drawing, what we see here is not essentially dependent on what the photographer thinks is there in the photograph. As with a telescope, we may "see through" the photograph to the scene itself.

In this regard, consider the case of the photographer in Antonioni's movie *Blow Up* (1966). He takes some pictures in the park of a woman and a man, and then later discovers that one of his shots apparently shows the man's corpse lying in the bushes. This is not what he saw or believed at the time, but it is what he sees now. Still, the photograph he took is evidence, of the most ordinary kind, for the fact that this man has been killed. And it is evidence for this regardless of the photographer's beliefs about the matter. That is, it would be evidence even if he positively *dis*believed what it shows, or even if he took the photograph and showed it to someone with the deliberate intent to deceive. Its status as evidence is wholly independent of his beliefs or intentions. And it is for that reason that his *own* relation to the photograph can be an evidential one, like a detective or other investigator. When he gets home he crops and enlarges and studies his photograph in order to see more deeply into what it shows, to convince himself that the corpse on the grass is really there. In this way his own epistemic relation to the photograph he took is the same as that of the friend he shows it to later. They can both learn from it or doubt what it shows. The situation would be quite different if he were to have made a sketch of what he saw in the park, or taken some notes on what he observed there. It would be absurd for him to take his sketch home and blow up *it* to examine more closely what it shows about the man in the park. And were he to show his sketch or his notes to another person to convince him about the man in the park, he would be offering him a very different kind of reason to believe what happened. If he shows his friend a sketch of a corpse lying in the grass, and this is to be a reason for him to believe there *was* such a corpse, his friend has to assume such things as that the sketch was not made with an intent to deceive, that the person who made it was observing things accurately and not liable to error, and even that the aim of the sketch was an accurate picture and not an imaginary scene, etc. In short, the beliefs and intentions of the person who made the sketch are crucial for its status as a reason to believe anything about what was there in the park. Without those assumptions, the sketch does not become *poorer* evidence; it ceases to be evidence of any kind, or any other reason to believe. It's just a piece of paper, and any correlation with the facts in the park could only be by the merest chance.

So how does the issue of freedom figure in here, in a way that distinguishes the case of verbal testimony? After all, the photographer freely takes his picture, and then may freely present it to another person as a reason for believing a man has been killed. How is this different from his friend's relation to his verbal report of what he saw? So far we have seen the following difference. The status of the photograph as a reason to believe something does not depend on the photographer's own attitude toward it as evidence. It depends only on the camera's ability to record the scene, which need not involve any choice or consciousness on the part of the photographer at all. (The exposure could have been made by a remote timing device.) As such the photograph can serve for him as an independent correction of his impression of the scene, in a way that his drawing cannot. It is for this reason that when he looks at his photograph with his friend, they both stand in the same epistemic relation to it; confronting it as independent, public evidence, and trying to discern its import.

By contrast, the *speaker's* choice enters in essentially to the fact that her utterance counts at all as a reason for belief. The point is not that the utterance is voluntarily produced, for that in itself has no epistemic significance, and does not distinguish the case from that of the photographer. Rather the point is that the speaker, in presenting her utterance as an *assertion*, one with the force of *telling* the audience something, presents herself as *accountable* for the truth of what she says, and in doing so offers a kind of guarantee for this truth. This shows up in the fact that if we are inclined to believe what the speaker says, but then learn that she is *not*, in fact, presenting her utterance as an assertion whose truth she stands behind, then what remains is just words, not a reason to believe anything relevant to their content. We misunderstood the intent of Professor Higgins when we heard him say something about the rain in Spain, and now upon realizing this, the utterance as phenomenon loses the epistemic import we thought it had (whatever knowledge we may indeed take him to have about such matters). By contrast, if we learn that the photographer is not, in fact, presenting his photograph as true record of what occurred in the park, the photograph as document retains all the epistemic value for us it ever had.

2.6 The Importance of Being Non-Natural

Still, one might ask, why speak of the audience's dependence on the freedom of the speaker, rather than simply refer to his dependence on what the speaker has (freely) *done*? The reason is that the relevant speaker's responsibility is not simply her responsibility for the *existence* of some phenomenon, in the sense that she is the one who deliberately produced these spoken words. Rather, she is more centrally responsible for those words *having* any particular epistemic status. What is the difference, then, between the speaker's role in *providing* something (her utterance) with a particular epistemic status, and the role of someone like a photographer who *produces* something that *has* a certain epistemic import?

It is here, I think, that a consideration of Paul Grice's original 1957 paper "Meaning" proves helpful. The relation of evidence, one phenomenon's being an indication of something else, is the central form of what Grice calls "natural meaning." Natural meaning is not something at the disposal of the speaker to confer or revoke, but is a matter of the independent obtaining of causal relations in the world (e.g., the way smoke means fire, or doesn't). Nonetheless, persons belong to this same natural world and may thus produce or exhibit various evidential phenomena and employ them to get some point across (e.g., pointing to the smoke pouring out of the oven). But spoken words typically bear a different relation to the facts. In his 1957 article, Grice is primarily concerned to delineate the conditions for something he calls "non-natural meaning," or MeaningNN. This project famously evolved into an attempt to ground the notion of the meaning of an expression in a language in the complex intentions had by utterers of expressions on occasions of use; and, presented as a noncircular account of either word-meaning or sentence-meaning, it was progressively refined into baroque complexity under the pressure of counterexamples. However, the interest and importance of the original account of non-natural meaning is not exhausted by the prospects for an intention-based semantics of the sort he proposed. What he isolates under the title of "non-natural meaning" is a central form of intersubjective dependence, one that is indeed paradigmatically linguistic, but not restricted to linguistic communication.

A striking thing about the essay is how the technical notion of non-natural meaning is introduced by contrast with natural meaning, as if the former were an antecedently intuitive notion, one whose definition we could progressively refine by consulting our intuitions about a series of well-crafted cases and asking ourselves whether we should call *that* a case of non-natural meaning. We are given hints, of course, by way of both similarity and contrast with more familiar notions like that of conventional meaning, but Grice's target notion only emerges through the consideration of the cases devised and presented. The cases themselves all have a similar form in that in all of them one person does something which either succeeds or not in inducing another person to some belief P. This common telos to the cases invites two related questions. Since the endpoint of each of these encounters is that one person ends up with a new belief, we might look at the progression of cases from an epistemological point of view and ask what it is that brings the person at the receiving end to this new belief, what reason he may take himself to have been given for adopting it, and why the particular kind of reason Grice's account of non-natural meaning zeroes in on should be of special significance, either epistemologically or otherwise. It is not, of course, as if the other ways of inducing belief, disqualified as candidates for the non-natural, are thought to be insufficiently grounded as reasons for belief. Salome, for instance, certainly acquired justified belief about the fate of John the Baptist by seeing his head presented on a charger, however this may fall short as a case of non-natural meaning. Rather, the target notion of non-natural meaning is meant to capture a *way* of gaining a reason to believe something that is importantly different from others and that we have special reason to be concerned with, both as purveyors and receivers of such reasons. So the first question is: what is special about the reason for belief associated with non-natural meaning? And second, as the proposed definition of non-natural meaning is progressively refined in Grice's essay, what pretheoretical notion is supposed to be guiding our intuitions along the way, so that we can feel conviction about a range of cases that seem to fall more or less squarely in the category? Here Grice is more explicit, since by way of explaining the distinction that matters to him, and why something like the case of Herod's presentation to Salome does *not* count as non-natural meaning, he says, "What we want to find is the difference between, for example, 'deliberately and openly letting someone know' and 'telling' and between 'getting someone to think' and 'telling'" (1967, 44). So it is the ordinary notion of *telling* someone something, *that* way of inducing belief, that is to play a guiding role in determining which cases satisfy the philosophical notion of non-natural meaning, and Grice's distinction between natural and non-natural meaning can be seen as motivated by a concern with the difference between *telling* a person that P and other ways of bringing him to that same knowledge, such as providing him with evidence for P (evidence that may be accidental or contrived, openly displayed or inadvertently revealed).

As examples of "deliberately and openly letting someone know" some fact, Grice cites such cases as that of showing someone a compromising photograph, or "leaving the china my daughter has broken lying around for my wife to see."[12] In these cases, the phenomenon in question has some independent evidential significance, even though the person may be responsible either for drawing attention to it (the broken china) or for actually producing it (the photograph). Its independent significance shows up in the fact that the photograph or the china would have functioned as a reason for the belief in question without anyone's intervention or presentation, even if only stumbled upon accidentally. By contrast, in cases of "telling" or "non-natural meaning," the person (hereafter the "speaker") plays quite a different role in bringing her audience to believe something. Here, as is well known, a crucial role is played in Grice's account by the recognition of the speaker's intention. Examining this role will help clarify the specific "dependence on the freedom of the speaker" that I'm claiming is characteristic of the relation of testimony, and which distinguishes it from a relation of evidence.

Following Grice's progression, then: a handkerchief left at the scene of the crime may throw suspicion on someone and perhaps lead to genuine belief in his guilt. But as a piece of evidence it would induce that belief whether or not it were left there intentionally, and non-natural meaning (and "telling," surely) must at least be the upshot of something intentionally done. Further, it should be part of non-natural meaning that the intention to induce a particular belief is *manifest* to the person on the receiving end, and not like artfully planted evidence designed to steer him toward the desired conclusion while concealing any such intent. Further still, this belief-inducing intention must not simply be *known* to the audience, something he pieces together despite the speaker's best efforts at concealment; rather the speaker must fully expect and intend that her intention will be manifest to her audience. In this way, the audience can appreciate that another person is openly playing a role in directing him to learn something, by presenting a piece of evidence for them both to see and assess. This makes this knowledge, or at least this awareness of the evidence, "mutual"

---

12 Grice 1967, 44. Ross (1986) discusses natural vs. non-natural meaning at p. 74.

between them, and hence available as an object of cognitive and communicative cooperation between them. However, this is not yet non-natural
meaning, since these conditions are fulfilled when Herod presents the head
of St. John to Salome, or when the compromising photograph is flourished.
Here, although the audience has been directly and openly led to some belief, he or she has not been *told* anything. Rather, Salome has been shown
something and reliably left to draw her own conclusions. Herod manifests
a definite intention in bringing her this news, and he bears an obvious
responsibility for Salome's altered state of belief. But there is yet another
responsibility he does not assume here, which marks the difference between "'deliberately and openly letting someone know' and 'telling,'" and
this is shown in the fact that, while his intention regarding her belief is
indeed manifest, it is inert as far as Salome's belief is concerned, just as it is
when the person is shown a compromising photograph. It isn't doing any
epistemological work of its own. Both people would draw essentially the
same conclusions whether the evidence in question were deliberately and
openly displayed to them or not. So we might say that Herod's epistemic responsibility for Salome's belief is merely contingent, like that of the person
showing the photograph. In these cases they play a role in making a piece
of evidence available to another person, but they are not responsible for it
having the epistemic import it has.

For Grice, however, nothing can count as a case of non-natural meaning
if the relevant belief could be expected to be produced whether or not
the intention behind the action were recognized. The speaker must not
only intend that the audience recognize her intention, but this recognition
must itself *play a role* in inducing the belief in question, and that means that
the recognition of the speaker's intention must not just as a matter of fact
help to bring about the relevant belief, but must be *necessary* to its induce-
ment. In this way we arrive at Grice's original formulation of non-natural
meaning in his 1957 paper:

> A uttered x with the intention of inducing a belief by means of the recogni-
> tion of this intention. (1967, 45)

If the audience could not be expected to arrive at the intended belief *apart
from* the recognition of the speaker's intention regarding that belief, the
speaker must take upon herself the role of providing something with a
particular epistemic import that it otherwise would not have, and in this

way Grice sharply distinguishes non-natural meaning from the presentation of evidence. For any phenomenon with some independent evidential import will naturally be one which might well be expected to induce belief without the recognition of anyone's intention. That's just what it is for a phenomenon to be ordinary evidence for something else. To count as an instance of telling someone something, however, the speaker must present her action, her utterance, as being without epistemic significance apart from the explicit assumption of responsibility for that significance. In this way she announces that the reason for belief offered here is of a different kind from that stemming from externally obtaining evidential relations.

As Ross points out (75), from the point of view of the audience, considered as a reason for belief, the role of the recognition of intention is left somewhat mysterious here. The question is: just how does my recognizing that this speaker intends that I should believe P play a role in actually *getting* me to believe that P? If we compare this case with that of other things someone may want me to do, it's clear that the mere recognition that she wants me to do X does not, in general, provide me with much of any reason at all for complying. Why should we be so much more compliant when we recognize that someone wishes us to *believe* something? How can the mere recognition of someone's intention be expected to induce belief?

When looked at in this way, recognition of the speaker's intention may seem inadequate to induce belief. It may also seem pointless, adding nothing of epistemic value to what the audience already has. Again, compare this with the picture of radical interpretation, according to which the epistemic significance of speech is that of an indication of the speaker's beliefs. Once I employ this scheme of interpretation to learn what the speaker believes, I am then in possession of knowledge of a certain set of facts, viz., the speaker's state of belief, which *does* have straightforward evidential value for me, quite independently of how or whether the fact of this person's believing is explicitly presented to me. The speaker's state of mind is a phenomenon which has the same independent evidential import for me, regardless of how I may have learned of it, and regardless of whether it was manifested deliberately or inadvertently. And, as we saw, this same scheme of interpretation can provide a basis for me to infer to the likely *truth* of these beliefs, and so come to share them myself. I ascribe beliefs on the basis of someone's verbal behavior as I would from any other behavior, and in neither case do I rely on recognition of any *intention* to manifest some state of mind. And indeed, what could be the epistemic interest for me in learning of any such intention on the other person's part? By hypothesis, I already know what this person takes to be true, and I can now make of this knowledge what I will, deciding for myself whether this adds up to good reason for *me* to take this belief to be true. If the verbal behavior is evidence for the beliefs, then it doesn't *add* to my evidence as interpreter to learn that, in addition to believing P, the speaker also has the intention that *I* should believe P too (and come to this belief on the basis of recognition of that very intention, etc.). From my side, either learning of her belief is, on balance, sufficient for me to believe P too, or it is not. Nothing further about the intentions of the speaker, or just *how* she would like me to arrive at this belief, will be evidentially relevant for me at all. Or else, as before with the tainted evidence, learning that her belief was deliberately manifested now casts doubt on my ascription, because the evidence of her behavior is now contaminated by its aspect of performance.

What is needed is more direct focus on the speaker's *explicit presentation* of herself as providing a reason for belief. For it is *not*, in fact, the audience's mere *awareness* of the speaker's intention that is to provide a motivation for belief. If I simply *discovered* on my own that this person had the intention that I believe P, this need not count for me as a reason for belief at all. (Why cooperate with her designs on me, however benign?) The conditions given so far still have not accounted for any special importance to the overt act of *saying*, the explicit manifesting of one's intention, as opposed to simply doing something that allows one's intention to become known. If, unlike a piece of evidence, the speaker's words have no independent epistemic value as a phenomenon, then how do they *acquire* the status of a potential reason to believe something? It seems that this can only be by virtue of the speaker's there and then explicitly *presenting* her utterance as a reason to believe, with this presentation being accomplished in the act of assertion itself. The epistemic status of her words as a candidate for belief is something publicly conferred on them by the speaker, by presenting her utterance as an assertion. And indeed, it is *because* the speaker's words have no independent status as evidence that their contribution to the audience's belief must proceed through the recognition of the speaker's intention. Further, the intention seeking recognition must not simply be that the audience come to believe something, but must include the intention that the audience recognize the speaker's act of asserting as itself constituting a potential reason for belief. If it seems difficult to see how anything, even someone's words, could acquire some epistemic status through something like *conferral*, perhaps because this suggests something too arbitrary or ceremonial to constitute a genuine reason for belief, it should be remembered that for both parties this conferral is by its nature an overt assumption of specific responsibilities on the part of the speaker. This is no more (or less) mysterious than how an explicit agreement or contract alters one's responsibilities, actions which are also within the capacities of ordinary speakers. The speaker's intent, then, is that for the audience, the very fact that this speaker is freely and explicitly presenting P as worthy of belief constitutes her utterance as a potential reason to believe that P.

Of course, as with any public assumption of responsibility, the appropriate abilities and other background conditions must be assumed to be in place for it to amount to anything. For the speaker to be able to do this it must be assumed by both parties that the speaker does indeed satisfy the right conditions for such an act (e.g., that she possesses the relevant knowledge, trustworthiness, and reliability). These background conditions can themselves be construed as evidential, or at any rate not at the behest of the speaker to determine, but they are not themselves sufficient for giving any epistemic significance to the speaker's words, for the relevance of these conditions only comes into play once it is understood that a particular speech act is being performed with those words (i.e., an assertion or promise rather than something else). The speaker has to constitute her utterance as having this or that illocutionary force before the empirical background conditions can contribute anything to its epistemic significance. Hence the idea is not that the speaker's word's "all by themselves" should count as a reason for belief, or that the speaker's authority over the constitution of the particular speech act she is performing (e.g., as assertion rather than recitation) shoulders the epistemic burden all by itself. As with the explicit assumption of responsibility that goes with making a promise, its success will depend on the various conditions that go into the speaker's being in a position to take on any such responsibility, and which make for her public assumption's being anything for another person to count on. But in considering the speaker's words, the audience's belief in her knowledge and trustworthiness does not do him any epistemic good if it is still left open just *what* kind of action (if any) the speaker is presenting her utterance as. As far as relating to her words goes, the speaker's knowledge and trustworthiness are epistemically inert for the audience until the question of the particular speech act or illocution is settled. Determining her utterance as an assertion is what gets the speaker's words into the realm of epistemic assessment in the first place (or at least epistemic assessment of the sort that is relevant to testimony: we may indeed make evidential use of the words or inarticulate sounds made by someone while dreaming). And in this matter, the speaker and her audience are in essentially different relations to the epistemic import of the speaker's utterance. The speaker does not relate to the question whether her utterance is a committed assertion or not as something to be settled by evidence, because as a speaker of the language she plays an essential role in making it the case that her utterance is an assertion or not.

Hence Grice's original formulation needs some further refinement. The speaker intends not just that the recognition of her intention play a role in producing belief that P, but that the particular role this recognition should play is that of showing the speaker to be assuming responsibility for the status of her utterance as a reason to believe P. This addition is necessary since in principle there are all sorts of ways in which the recognition of intention could "play a role" in producing belief, ways that would not capture what is meant by "telling" or "non-natural meaning," or the correlative notion of believing the speaker. One such way would be manifested in the familiar situations of "double bluffing" where, e.g., I tell you I'm traveling to Minsk, knowing you'll take me to be lying and attempting to conceal my plans to travel to Pinsk, and hence meaning to deceive you about my genuine plans to go to Minsk after all. Knowing all this about me, however, you see through the ruse and conclude that I'm indeed going to Minsk, just as I told you. Here the recognition of intention does indeed play an essential role in the belief arrived at, and the audience comes to believe that what I say is true, but this is not a case of believing the speaker.[13] And there are other possible ways in which the recognition of intention might play a role, even a necessary one, but of the wrong sort.

Grice is sensitive to an incompleteness here, when he suggests toward the end that it should somehow be built into the definition that "the intended effect must be something which in some sense is within the control of the audience, or that in some sense of 'reason' the recognition of intention behind X is for the audience a reason and not merely a cause" (1967, 46). It is not the speaker's aim that the belief in question be

---

13 At the end of her paper, Anscombe (1979) points out that it is a requirement of any successful account of the phenomenon that it explain why we only speak of believing someone when we take her to be both right about the facts and truthful in intent.

produced by the audience's simply being so constituted that his awareness of the speaker's complex self-referential intention somehow produces the belief in him. That would fail in another way to describe the nature of the dependence on the person as such and the importance of mutual recognition. For the audience must not simply respond with belief, but must *understand* what the speaker is saying, and must understand what the speaker is *doing* in saying P, which is to say, purporting to present him with a reason for P. And the audience must believe P *because* he understands what the speaker is saying and what she is doing in saying it. In addition, and crucially, the audience must take this entire understanding to be *shared* by himself and the speaker. That is, he takes himself to be responding to just the kind of reason for belief that the speaker is presenting herself as offering (which is why cases of "double bluffing" are not cases of believing the speaker).

Any of the "proto-Gricean" ways of producing belief, the cases leading up to the full definition of non-natural meaning, provide us with something mediating between the audience and the speaker, something other than the person as such that is being depended on. Believing the speaker, on the other hand, involves accepting the offer to rely on *her*, and not something connected with her or as a consequence of what she has done. This direct dependence on the speaker's offer of responsibility is what is expressed in the "hereby" that is implied, and sometimes explicitly stated, in illocutions such as "telling," "warning" or "accepting," for it is in this very presentation of herself that the speaker assumes responsibility for the audience's belief (Austin 1962, 57). The implied "hereby" is thus also an expression of the self-referentiality of the Gricean formula, for it declares that it is dependence on the person as such, and not on something else she might point to, that is solicited in saying that she *hereby* tells her audience that P. In this way we can see the progressive refinements of Grice's definition of non-natural meaning as each aimed at laying bare the reliance of the audience on the other person as such. The belief is to be produced not simply by the speaker's action, or by her intention, or by the audience's awareness of her intention, or anything else outside their encounter. Just as the audience could treat the handkerchief or the photograph as evidence for P, and thus without trusting the speaker for the truth of P, so he could treat the speaker's action or intention as a similar kind of evidence without trusting the speaker, without his belief that P involving dependence on the person of the speaker as such.

When Grice says that the belief in question should be "something which in some sense is within the control of the audience," or that it should function as a reason for him and not a mere cause, this is not meant to suggest that the audience complies with the speaker's intention as a kind of favor, adopting the belief on request (as Ross notes [74]). But it does serve to clarify the kind of role that is to be played by the mutual recognition of the speaker's intention, how that can matter epistemically to the audience in the way suggested by Grice's progressive refinements of the account of non-natural meaning. The account of this role suggested by the assurance view is that the mutual recognition of intention can play the role for the audience of providing him with a reason for belief, because he sees the speaker as presenting herself as accountable for the truth of P, and asking, through the recognition of her intention, that this offer of assurance be accepted. And it is understood by both parties that this acceptance is something which the audience is free to give or refuse. The speaker is asking that a certain authority of hers be acknowledged, the authority to invest her utterance with a particular status as a candidate for belief, and this investment occurs by her explicit assumption of responsibility for her utterance's being such a reason for belief. This is the role for the recognition of intention that the speaker is asking for. And, I would argue, it is *only* such a role that could account for how, in the case of speech, the recognition of intention *enhances* rather than detracts from the epistemic status of the phenomenon (utterance), reveals it to be something other than doctored evidence.

The idea of assertion as providing reason for belief through the explicit assumption of responsibility for the truth of what is said accounts for a number of contrasts between belief through testimony and belief through confronting impersonal evidence. It points the way to understanding how the recognition of intention can play a positive role, rather than seeing it as something that is either epistemically irrelevant or undermining to the evidential value of the utterance. Further, a specific assumption of responsibilities is essentially an expression of a person's freedom, something that only makes sense as consciously assumed. It is for this reason that words spoken during sleep or under hypnosis do not have the value of testimony, because they do not count as *assertions*, whatever expressive psychological value they might still retain as evidence. Like a promise or an apology, something only counts as a person's assertion when consciously presented as such by him.[14]

---

14 Coady (1992, 45–46) distinguishes genuine testimony from the situation of someone who has

Promises and apologies, like acts of telling someone something, can be more or less reflective, more or less deliberate, done more or less voluntarily or under duress. Reference to the speaker's assumption of responsibility for the truth of what she says is not meant to deny that much of our speech is spontaneous and unreflective, or that much of what we acquire from the speech of others is more or less passively absorbed. "Telling" also includes telling something by mistake, to the wrong person, or just blurting something out when we meant to keep silent. We express our freedom not only in our considered actions, but also in the actions that go wrong, or are forced upon us, and the outbursts that we immediately regret. Blurting something out when you meant to keep silent is still a different matter from either talking in one's sleep, or having the utterance of those words be produced by electrical stimulation of the cerebral cortex. And the epistemic significance for the audience is entirely different in the two kinds of cases: in relating to the words produced by electrical stimulation we *may* learn something, but what we learn need not be dependent on such assumptions as, e.g., whether the person had any understanding of the words themselves, or any sense that she was providing anyone with a reason to believe something. These assumptions, however, are still indispensable to the understanding of the words that escape us or are forced from us, and they express the role of the person as such in providing a reason. This is confirmed by the fact that both speaker and audience relate to the blurting out differently than they would to the cases of talking in one's sleep or through electrical stimulation. In the latter case, the speaker would not *regret* what she said or try to make amends; in a sense what happened didn't involve *the person* at all.[15] And for that matter, a person may also *lie* spontaneously or out of panic as well as tell the truth. But surely the description of a

been hypnotized specifically to say something, perhaps even with the expectation of being believed. But his reason for excluding this case is different from mine. For Coady, this cannot count as "testifying" because it fails to satisfy the condition that the speaker "has the relevant competence, authority, or credentials to state truly that P" (42), since the words have more or less been "planted" in the subject. This focus on epistemic authority seems misplaced, however. For the speaker in this case *could* after all also happen to have the requisite competence and authority on the subject. Instead, the reason this doesn't count as testimony is that, in her present condition, she is not presenting herself as responsible for her statement's being true.

15 Holton (1994) provides an illuminating focus on the role of what Strawson refers to as the participant stance and the reactive attitudes, especially with regard to the distinction between belief through trust and belief through reliance. Holton says of the latter case, "Seen in this way, a person is like a measuring device: they respond to the environment in various ways, and we infer from their response to what the environment is like" (74).

person telling a lie makes reference to such things as the intention, whether conscious or not, to exploit the trust of one's audience and present oneself as providing them with a reason for belief. At the same time, it is consistent with the assurance view to think of assertions and tellings as something like the default assumption for the expression of indicative sentences in the declarative mood. It requires more, rather than less, sophisticated intentions to utter, "The rain in Spain falls mainly on the plain" and *not* mean it as an assertion. And so, barring any special reason to think otherwise, we may be entitled to treat an utterance of an indicative sentence as an assertion of its content.[16] But in a given case we may be wrong about this, and it remains true that what settles the question about the status of the utterance is whether or not the speaker is presenting it as true.

2.7 The Speaker's Conferral: Having Your Say, Giving Your Word

We are now in a position to clarify the problem Ross suggested with the idea of a speaker presenting her utterance *as* evidence for her audience. The problem is not that the speaker's words could not be *taken* as evidence by her audience. In principle, anything said or done by the speaker can be given a symptomatic reading. Nor is it true that the speaker could not privately *intend* that her utterance be taken as evidence. This would be the intention for many cases of deceit or more everyday manipulation, for instance. In a given case, my primary aim may be for my listener to draw the conclusion that I'm being scrupulously candid or self-revealing, and I accomplish this by confessing some minor fault of mine. Here, I am not *telling* anyone of my candor, giving my word on it (whatever good that would do), but rather doing something (in this case: saying something) that I hope will be taken as evidence for it. When it is a question of *non-natural* meaning, by contrast, the speaker is not relying on evidential relations alone to get her point across, but rather is counting on the explicit presentation of her intention to be the very thing which *makes* her words a potential reason for believing something in the first place. The recognition

---

16 This assumption is taken up further in the following chapter, in connection with Bernard Williams's idea of assertion as the "direct expression" of one's belief (Williams 2002, 74).

of her intention could only function this way if it was seen to be her assurance of the truth in question, her explicit assumption of responsibility for the truth of what she says. By contrast, the presentation of her utterance *as* evidence would be an implicit denial of this responsibility, breaking the link between the proposition she is giving her backing to and the belief she is hoping to induce, in which case there's no question of believing *her*. Thus for the speaker to present her utterance *as* evidence would be for her to present it as a reason to believe, while suspending the guarantee that gives it the epistemic significance of testimony in the first place. This is the problem Ross is pointing to.[17]

And as we have seen, to present something as evidence is to present it as having its epistemic value independent of one's own beliefs about it, or one's presentation of it, or the conferral of some status upon one's utterance. To offer some phenomenon as evidence is to present it as belief-worthy independent of the fact of one's presenting it as belief-worthy. When we present something as evidence for someone, we are inviting that person to "see for himself," to find it convincing as we do. And we may be prepared to offer reasons why it should be convincing, reasons independent of our simply *claiming*, once again, that it is belief-worthy. To present something as evidence is to be in a position to *report* that it is a reason for belief, and to be in this position one must be presenting that claim of belief-worthiness as having a basis in fact that is independent of one's reporting itself. A photograph has such an independent epistemic basis, independent of anyone's conferral. As a phenomenon, it counts as a reason for belief independently of anything concerning how the photographer may conceive it or present it. Because of this independence, its epistemic status is something the photographer himself may *discover* about it, or speculate about. His relation to this question is in principle no different from anyone else's. He may, of course, happen to know something about how it was produced that we don't know, and which may affect its epistemic status. But he may not know anything of the sort, and conversely we might know more about it than he does. He marshals the same kinds of reasons as any

---

17 "No abandonment of the agent's perspective, no abdication of responsibility for one's actions, is involved in seeing those actions as generating entitlements and obligations, either on the part of ourselves or on the part of others. (Compare the case of promising or issuing a command.) There is on the present account no difficulty in seeing the hearer as taking the speaker's words in the spirit in which they are honestly offered" (Ross 1986, 79). See also Robert Brandom's richly developed account of assertion in terms of the constellation of entitlements and obligations, in chapter 3 of *Making It Explicit* (1994).

other viewer in considering the question of what beliefs the photograph may provide a basis for.

But the speaker's relation to the epistemic status of her own assertion *is* different from anyone else's. For the speaker, it is not a matter of observation or speculation whether she is indeed presenting her utterance as something with the force of a committed assertion, and were she somehow unclear about this, then to that degree her utterance would be something less than a committed assertion. She may inquire into her own reliability, truthfulness, and command of the facts, but the status of her utterance as assertion rather than something else is a matter of what she is then and there prepared to invest it with. It has been noted by more than one philosopher that the relation of "believing someone" does not have a reflexive form; it is not a relation a person can bear to himself.[18] The problem with this, we can now say, is the problem with the idea of a person offering and accepting an epistemic guarantee from herself, which would require her to be simultaneously in command of and at the mercy of her own freedom. This is another basic feature of testimony not captured by an evidential perspective on it. Speaker and audience do not confront the utterance as a phenomenon with an independent or natural epistemic status which they could assess in the same spirit, for the speaker does not confront her own assertion as a *phenomenon* at all, but as an issue of her commitment. To speak of "conferral" of a candidate epistemic status is intended to register the fact that to count an utterance as, e.g., an assurance or a promise just is to count it as something presented with a particular epistemic status, the status of a potential reason for some belief (as contrasted with the status, say, of mere recitation of words, or ironic mimicry). To count as a competent speaker of a language is to be recognized as having definitive "say" over which illocution one's utterance counts as, whether as informative assertion, or as promise or apology, whether as a mere recitation or as a claim expressing one's commitment. An utterance counts as an assertion or an apology just in case the speaker presents it as such to her audience, in the appropriate context where this audience can be expected to recognize what it is being offered. The speaker cannot count as having promised or asserted something if she

---

18 After a "preamble," Anscombe *begins* her essay with the statement, "'Believe' with personal object cannot be reflexive" (1979, 144). See also Cavell: "A striking exception to the thought that I can stand in any relation to myself that I can stand to others is that of belief. Why apparently can I not, in grammar, believe myself?" (1979, 393).

had no such intention, or if she did not present her utterance to be seen as a promise or assertion, whereas the evidential import of what one says and does is independent of such conditions.

The speaker's authority to determine the illocutionary status of her utterance is the authority she has to present herself as accountable for the performance of some speech act. This is not a matter of discovery for the speaker, something she could investigate or report on, as she might with respect to the evidential status of something. When it is a question of the evidential status of something, even something the person herself has done, she and her interlocutors are on an equal footing with respect to establishing its standing as a reason for belief. A person does not speak with any special authority about the evidential significance of her actions, including her verbal ones. By contrast, the authority to present oneself as "hereby" assuming certain responsibilities in speech makes the speaker's epistemic position irreducibly different from that of the audience. For the speaker the import of her words is not an independently obtaining fact, something she has her own opinion about, but is directly dependent on the import she is then and there prepared to invest them with. And it is internal to the notion of the speaker's authority to confer illocutionary status on her utterance that she also has the exclusive authority to cancel or revoke such status. Words can be retracted, apologies or warnings taken back, but only by the speaker herself. At the same time, a person has no authority to determine, much less cancel, the evidential import of anything she has said or done, not even of her retraction itself.

When all goes well, in testimony a speaker gives her interlocutor a reason to believe something, but unlike other ways of influencing the beliefs of others, in this case the reason the audience is provided is seen by both parties as dependent on the speaker's making herself accountable, conferring a right of complaint on her audience should her claim be false. Whether this counts as a good or sufficient reason for belief is *not* a matter of the speaker's illocutionary authority, but will depend both on her sincerity and on her having discharged her epistemic responsibilities with respect to the belief in question.[19] But the presentation of her utterance as having this particular

---

19 Cf. Williamson: "To make an assertion is to confer a responsibility (on oneself) for the truth of its content; to satisfy the rule of assertion, by having the requisite knowledge, is to discharge that responsibility, by epistemically ensuring the truth of the content. Our possession of such speech acts is no more surprising than the fact that we have a use for relations of responsibility" (2000, 268–269).

illocutionary force *is* what makes it a candidate for epistemic assessment in the first place, and determines what kind of reason for just what proposition her audience is being presented with.

This way of looking at testimony makes much of the fact that in its central instances speech is an action addressed *to* another person, and that in testimony in particular the kind of reason for belief that is presented is one that functions in part by binding speaker and audience together, and altering the normative relationship between them. It doesn't follow from this, however, that someone outside that normative relationship can't avail himself of it and thereby acquire a reason to believe the same thing. If one person gives her word on something to another, whether as promise or assertion, someone overhearing this may derive a sufficient reason to believe, say, that the speaker will in fact do what she promised or that what she asserted is true. And the overhearer improves his epistemic situation in this way, without entering into the altered normative relationship of the two parties involved in giving and accepting of words. He has not himself been *told* anything, much less promised anything, and no right of complaint has been conferred upon him.[20] To say this much, however, does not provide a reason to assimilate his situation to that of someone confronting a piece of evidence, or suggest that the speaker's illocutionary and epistemic responsibilities aren't playing a genuinely epistemic role here. For even though the statement was not addressed *to him*, the overhearer is still in a different position from that of someone confronting a piece of evidence like a photograph or a footprint. It still makes a difference to his epistemic relation to the overheard report that what he is responding to is something whose epistemic significance is not independent in the way of a photograph or footprint, but is inherited from the speaker's assuming responsibility for the truth (and meaning) of what she says. This is so even if, as we might say, that responsibility was undertaken with respect to another person and not himself.

Naturally there is a certain vagueness as to just what situations will count as overhearing, and in a given case the addressee may be an indeterminate group of people. Nonetheless, while the overhearer may get a reason to believe without having the right of complaint that is conferred on the addressee, the fact that the overhearer of the assertion acquires any reason to

---

20 For further discussion of the assertions and promises, emphasizing their differences as well as similarities in their relations to the speaker's responsibilities, see Watson 2004.

believe from listening to these words is dependent on them being addressed to someone, with the force of assuming responsibility and thereby conferring a right of complaint. The overhearer of testimony is not in the same normative relation to the speaker as the addressee is, but his gaining any reason to believe is dependent on such a conferral having been given to some audience, even if indeterminate. Without that, the question of what speech act, if any, is being performed with these words would not be settled, whether anything has been asserted, and hence the overhearer could not get started on assessing their epistemic significance. (Imagine overhearing someone say, "The rain in Spain falls mainly on the plain." Until you know what speech act, if any, is being performed here, you don't know if considerations of reliability or trustworthiness are even relevant to the status of the words as a source of knowledge about the weather in Spain.) So, while in both cases (promising and telling), the overhearer can gain a reason to believe something without entering into the normative relation of promisor-promisee or teller-believer, in the overhearing of testimony he only gains a reason to believe something because such a relationship *has* been established by the original speaker and addressee.

This, then, is how I suggest we understand Ross's claim that the evidential view is inconsistent with the kind of reason for belief offered in everyday human testimony. In telling her audience something the speaker does not present her utterance as something with the force of evidence, because that would be to present her words as having their specific epistemic import apart from her assurance and the responsibility she thereby assumes. And in obscuring the speaker's responsibility, such a stance would also obscure the nature of the audience's dependence on her. For if it were a matter of evidence, then in principle both parties would be on an equal footing with respect to establishing its epistemic import. But this equity does not obtain with respect to someone's words, where it is up to the speaker alone to determine whether they are to count as an assertion or other committed speech act.

2.8 Evidence and Disharmony

The two broad views about testimony which I've been calling the evidential view and the assurance view are in no disagreement over the status of an assertion or a promise as essentially the action of a free agent. Both views are clear that speaking is a voluntary activity and that the speech of others has *that* kind of significance in our lives. Where they differ is in how that freedom is related to the status of the utterance as a reason to believe. For on the assurance view, it is not just that a particular free action is seen to have some epistemic import, but rather that the epistemic import of what the speaker does is dependent on her attitude toward her utterance and her presentation of it in a certain spirit, whereas by contrast, it is in the nature of genuinely evidential relations that they are not subject to anyone's conferral or retraction. It might still be asked, however, whether it doesn't still all come down to evidential relations in the end. The following reconstruction may be offered: Yes, the speaker freely assumes responsibility for the truth of what she asserts. But now this very act of assurance is a *fact*, which the audience confronts as evidence (of some degree of strength) for the truth of what has been asserted. Speech is acknowledged to be importantly different from other (indicatively) expressive behavior, but the audience's relation to it, as a reason to believe something, can only be evidential.

The claim of the assurance view, however, is not that an assertion could not be treated purely as evidence. It is always possible to treat anything a person says or does as constituting further evidence for one thing or another, and there is no level at which this somehow becomes impossible. The point instead is that refusing to acknowledge any epistemic stance toward the speaker's words other than as evidence means that speaker and audience must always be in disharmony with each other, for in the contexts of telling, promising, and apologizing the speaker is not *presenting* her utterance as evidence. And it is internal to the speech acts of, e.g., telling or thanking that they are not presented as evidence for one's belief or gratitude. To present one's utterance as evidence would be to do something other than to tell, promise, or apologize.

This claim may seem paradoxical. On the assurance view, the making of an assertion can be treated as evidence, can properly *be* evidence for various things, but the practice cannot coherently be described as the *offering* of evidence. But how could this be? If the speaker recognizes that her asserting can be, or even just *is*, evidence for the truth of the very proposition asserted, then how could there be anything amiss with her presenting it *as* something (viz., evidence) that she sees it legitimately *is*? But this general possibility for self-defeat should not be surprising. To allay the sense of paradox here, compare the assurance given in a *promise* with that of an assertion, and consider the incoherence or self-defeat in saying something like, "I promise; but of course I might change my mind, or forget, or cease caring." Here as well, the speaker is only saying something that both parties know to be true about herself and about promises in general. But to say so is, at the very least, contrary to the spirit in which a promise is made, contrary to the very point of making a promise. And what makes for this self-defeat is precisely the presentation of it in an evidential spirit. For notice: for someone to say, "I promise, but I might change my mind" is to refer to her promise as a fallible indication of future performance. That is, it is to present it as a kind of defeasible evidence for what she will do. And, of course, insofar as a promise is seen as evidence at all it can only be seen as *defeasible* evidence. Hence for the speaker to offer her promise as evidence means she must be offering it as, at best, defeasible evidence, with respect to which the promisee is on his own. And to do so is contrary to the point of making a promise, which is binding assurance.

The disharmony between speaker and audience entailed by the evidential view comes out in the consideration of two possible responses to receiving a promise. If someone promises to mail a letter for me, one thing I might do is accept her promise, placing myself in her hands and taking myself to now have sufficient reason for believing that she *will* mail the letter. If it turns out she *doesn't* mail the letter, either through carelessness or because she never really intended to, then I will feel aggrieved and let down. This is the ordinary expectation and liability to disappointment. I might, however, opt for another kind of response altogether. Here I don't *accept* the promise; I simply don't go in for that sort of thing, as I may not accept promises from a small child or (for different reasons) from someone I despise, but in another way I do take seriously the fact that she made one to me. In this spirit I may reason: "She is unlikely to make a promise she won't fulfill, since that would discredit her as a future promisor, and there are great and obvious advantages in remaining someone whose promises are accepted. Therefore, the fact that she made this promise to me makes it probable that she will in fact mail the letter. So I believe she will." If, on this second scenario, I later discover that she did not mail the letter after all, my reaction will be different. I will be disappointed, of course, and I will be surprised that she would discredit herself in this way. But I can't confront her with my complaint or my resentment because I never accepted the promise in the first place. My relation to this person's promise is similar to my relation to the person I suspect of "double bluffing" me. I don't believe her;

there's no question of that. But nonetheless her statement that she's traveling to Minsk functions as my reason for believing that this is what she will do. In both cases the speaker has made me a free declaration which I then make evidential use of to infer to the truth of what she says. On the evidential view, this second type of response to promises and assertions would have to be the only epistemically legitimate one, and yet such a reconstruction would yield an incoherent description of the practices of telling or promising. It would be incoherent because on such a view the speaker would have to be in the position of offering assurances that are never accepted, and which she knows are never accepted, and the audience would nonetheless be relying on the continued offering of such free assurances to serve as his evidential base.

The issue of harmony between speaker and audience goes deeper than this, however, and helps to delineate the relationship between the speaker's authority to determine the illocutionary status of her utterance and its actual epistemic import. In asserting that P, where the context is one of "telling," the speaker is not in a position simply to constitute her utterance as a good or sufficient reason for P, since that will depend on her credentials and success as a knower, as well as her honesty. But in the act of telling her audience that P, she does claim definitive "say" in determining that her utterance is being presented as a *reason for belief*, rather than, say, as a speculation or grammatical example, as well as determining just *what* it is that she is giving her word on. From the speaker's perspective both determinations matter to the alignment of speaker and audience that she sees herself as aiming at. From a purely evidential perspective, however, it shouldn't matter to the audience whether the route from the speaker's words to a true belief involves the loop in double bluffing or not. And just as clearly in such a case there would be failure of correspondence between the spirit in which the statement is made and that in which it is received. The speaker who asserts P is *not* indifferent to whether she induces belief in her audience through the loop of double bluffing. Her assertion is asking for belief in the *very* proposition stated and for the *very* sort of reason that she is then and there presenting to him. And *that* sort of reason is bound up with her presenting herself as accountable for this truth. In double bluffing, the reason for belief taken by the audience is different from the reason the speaker offers. What "telling" aims at, by contrast, is that there be a correspondence or identity between the reason the speaker takes herself to be offering and what the audience accepts as a reason, for the very content asserted. So we might say, in telling her audience that P, the speaker asks that her authority be acknowledged to determine what sort of candidate reason for what belief is up for consideration. This is her understanding of the speech act she is performing with respect to her audience, and it is this that is denied by treating the utterance in a wholly evidential spirit, in which the question of what is being considered a reason for what is anybody's business, and is not tethered to the speaker's awareness or intent. Conversation may of course move into and out of this "external" dimension of assessment, but for purposes of either agreement *or* disagreement it cannot begin there.

In the speech act of telling, the speaker commits herself to her audience with respect to a particular proposition and with respect to the kind of reason being presented. This follows from the difference between doing something that *has* a certain epistemic significance (as with taking or showing a photograph) and being responsible for something's *having* the epistemic significance that it has (as with a speaker and her words). In telling her audience something, the speaker aims at being believed, an aim which is manifest to both parties, and which binds the speaker and audience together with respect to a norm of correspondence between the reason offered and the reason accepted. When an act of telling completes itself, speaker and audience are aligned in this way through their mutual recognition of the speaker's role in determining the kind of reason for belief that is up for acceptance, so that when the speaker is believed, there is a nonaccidental relation between the reason presented and the reason accepted. The speaker says, in effect, "The kind of reason for belief you gain from my statement is precisely the kind of reason for belief I am hereby presenting myself as offering you. Insofar as there is a disparity between the two, I claim no special responsibility for whatever belief you may derive from my assertion." Presenting her utterance that way is a kind of declaration of transparency to her audience: the kind of reason overtly presented is precisely the reason that is meant to count for you. When the background of the speaker's knowledge and sincerity can be assumed, and the speaker is in fact believed by her audience (a common enough occurrence, after all), the two parties are in sync with each other in a way that they would not be if the audience were to take the utterance either as a reason for some other belief rather than the one stated, or a different kind of reason for that belief (as with double bluffing). Taking the utterance as evidence detaches the reason-giving significance of the utterance from the speaker's authority to determine what she is thereby committing herself to.[21] From an evidential perspective it may function as evidence for any number of things, for which the speaker's competence or responsibility may be irrelevant. This is manifestly not the speaker's perspective on the epistemic significance of her statement, which she sees in terms of the nexus of a specific responsibility assumed and a specific entitlement conferred.[22]

For the act of telling to complete itself there must be a correspondence between the reason being *presented* by the speaker and the reason *accepted* by her audience. This is the connection that is aimed at in the self-reflexive aspect of the Gricean formula, wherein the speaker asks that the very reason she is thereby presenting be the reason that the audience thereby accepts (i.e., through recognizing that very intention). Telling aims at being believed, which proceeds, via the speaker's overt assumption of responsibility, by joining together the particular belief proposed for acceptance, the kind of reason being presented for it, and the reason accepted by the audience. An evidential stance, by contrast, decouples all of these from each other, to be reassembled as the observer thinks best. But such a stance is contrary to the speaker's perspective on her act, insofar as it pictures her

---

21 That the directness of the audience's dependence on the person of the speaker as such is related to the directness of the speaker's own relation to the reasons on which she *bases* her belief is something I have been helped to see by Adam Leite's paper "On Justifying and Being Justified" (2004). Because the speaker's statement of her reasons is not a hypothesis she makes about the origin of her belief, her assertion makes *her* (and not, e.g., something inside her) directly accountable for the truth or believability of her claim. Leite puts it the following way: "Suppose that you consider reasons for and against a claim, find that certain reasons decisively support holding it, and sincerely declare that you believe the claim for those reasons. In the usual case, you thereby directly determine what the reasons are for which you hold the belief. Moreover, in declaring your reasons you both open yourself to epistemic evaluation or criticism on account of those reasons' inadequacy and incur certain obligations—in particular, an obligation either to give up the belief or to seek better reasons, should those reasons prove inadequate. A minimal adequacy condition for an account of the epistemic basing relation is thus that it allow (1) that the reasons for which a belief is held can be directly determined in this way, and (2) that one sometimes directly opens oneself to epistemic criticism and incurs further justificatory responsibilities by sincerely declaring that one holds one's belief for particular reasons" (227–28).

22 Putting it this way describes the relationship of speaker and audience in terms of an essentially correlative or "bipolar" normativity, of the sort that has recently been explored by a number of philosophers. By contrast, the non-personal nature of evidence, the independence of its epistemic force from its being presented as a reason *to* another person, expresses the "monadic" character of its normativity. In this connection see Ernest Weinrib 1995; Martin Stone 1996 and 2001; Michael Thompson 2004; and Stephen Darwall 2006. I explore some of these connections and their limitations in chapter 5.

presentation of herself as meaning, in effect, that as far as reason-giving force goes, the audience is on his own; as if the meaning of her utterance were, "Now I have spoken; make of it what you will," rather than, "Take it from me."

More is conveyed in our ordinary assertions than the specific proposition asserted, and more is often *intended* to be conveyed by the speaker, and much of this will be picked up in an evidential spirit. All of which is to say that not all, not nearly all, speech takes the form of one person telling something to another, testifying to its truth. Not everything we need to convey is best conveyed by being *told* to another, in part because not everything we need to communicate is something we could sensibly ask to be relied on for, present ourselves as accountable for, or ask to be accepted on our say-so (e.g., the occasional comedy or tragedy in someone asserting his own dignity or probity). Nonetheless, it is clear enough what Anscombe means when she speaks of the insult and injury in not being believed.[23] And the offense remains even when the speaker's audience takes the fact of her having made the statement to count as evidence for its truth, just as above he may take the speaker's having made the promise to make it more probable that she will do the thing in question. The offense lies in his refusing to accept what the speaker freely and explicitly offers him, in favor of privately attending to what the speaker's action passively reveals, just as someone might refuse an apology while still taking it in this case to be a reliable indication of remorse. What makes sense of such refusals is the fact that acceptance of an assertion or an apology doesn't just put one in a different epistemic position with respect to the facts, but brings with it certain vulnerabilities and responsibilities of its own. Accepting an apology, for instance, brings with it the responsibility to put away one's resentment, and makes one vulnerable to a particularly bruising possibility of deceit. These risks are avoided by simply taking the apology as more or less good evidence for remorse, and then making of it what one will.

The evidential picture puts speaker and audience into disharmony with each other in mislocating the connection between what the speaker does and the fact that it provides a reason for belief. From the speaker's point of view, it is not a matter of what her behavior passively indicates, but a matter

23 Anscombe 1979, 150. See also Austin 1979, 100.

of what she then and there presents herself as assuming responsibility for. Unlike an evidential relation, the connection between the speaker's words and what she asserts is entirely at her disposal to declare or to retract.[24] The possibility of such retraction is central to the meaning of the speech acts of assertion, order, and the like, and shows how different they are in meaning and consequence from other actions. Speaking, of course, *is* a kind of act; something with consequences in the world like other acts, and which leaves behind evidence of itself. But the exclusivity of the speaker's authority shows that retracting one's words is not to be confused with undoing the consequences of an action that went wrong. Often enough, another person could in principle clean up after the mess made by the speaker's careless remarks, but no one other than the speaker can take them back. Of course, the speaker's retraction is not the pretense that the original statement was never made. After the retraction it may still take a long time to undo the damage the hard or thoughtless words have caused, but the retraction itself will normally be a prior condition for the more practical (or consequential) work of starting to try to undo that damage. This is a different kind of task, for the speaker cannot "*hereby*" undo the damage or the hurt feelings caused; that takes consequential work, which may fail in unforeseen ways, like any other action. But again, that also doesn't mean that the sort of thing the speaker *can* accomplish "hereby" is something performed magically or effortlessly, or that it may not be something that can be managed only with great difficulty. It will, however, be a different kind of difficulty from that involved in repairing the further consequences of one's remarks. If the speaker tries and fails here, at the level of retraction or apology, it will not be for reasons of unforeseeable accidents, or the general resistance of the world to our wills.

---

24 Different speech acts will have different conditions of retraction, and for some, like promising, the speaker is *not* in a position to retract the promise unilaterally, once she has made it. The act of promising transfers a right to the promisee, who is then in a position to claim or waive that right. In a very useful paper which appeared after the article on which this chapter is based, John MacFarlane (2011) discusses the implications of taking the possibility of retraction as central to the meaning of assertion.

3

The Meaning of Sincerity and Self-Expression

3.1 Sincerity and the Telepathic Ideal

The difficulties of intimacy or the unobstructed meeting of minds are so various that it has occurred to more than one writer over the centuries that the fundamental problem here arises from our basic metaphysical condition as embodied human beings. In the *Enneads*, Plotinus describes the happy condition of souls when they have at last reached the heavenly region and are no longer encumbered by the physical bodies that once housed them, and makes a striking comparison between the soul's emancipation from physical embodiment and its freedom from the need for words or other signs to make itself known to others.

> We certainly cannot think of them [souls free of the body], it seems to me as employing words when, though they may occupy bodies in the heav- enly region, they are essentially in the Intellectual . . . [T]here can be no question of commanding or of taking counsel; they will know, each, what is to be communicated from another, by present consciousness. Even in our own case here, eyes often know what is not spoken; and There all is pure, every being is, as it were, an eye, nothing is concealed or sophisticated, there is no need of speech, everything is seen and known. (Plotinus 1956, IV. 3, 18)

So we might say: in a better world, there would be no need for speech, for the purpose of speech, and communication generally, can only be to make manifest the contents of one's mind, and there nothing would obstruct the view of one mind to another. A certain familiar picture of the meaning and value of sincerity gains expression in this passage. We value sincerity in speech, and in expression generally, because it is the closest we can come to unmediated access to the genuine state of mind of the person we are communicating with. In the context of putatively informative communication, we value speech because it is a reliable and fine-grained guide to the beliefs of the other person, and we value the person's beliefs themselves because they are often an indispensable and reliable guide to the facts in question. The smile, if sincere, takes us to the pleasure of the other person, and the statements she makes, if sincere, take us to her genuine beliefs about some matter we are interested in. And since the other person's words are only of interest to us insofar as they are a reliable guide to her beliefs, we would do just as well, and perhaps better, if we had more immediate access to those beliefs, dispensing with the need for verbal expression and all of its risks and inadequacies. Then we would be in a position to make up our own minds as to the epistemic value of her beliefs as a guide to the facts themselves, and we would be able to do this without the risks incurred by the additional inference from her possibly insincere speech to her beliefs and other states of mind. From the perspective of this ideal, sincerity belongs with the virtues that seek to make themselves unnecessary, but at the cost of treating speech itself as a lamentable expedient for purposes of ideal communication. The world of unimpeded communion of souls, as described by Plotinus, is for reason of that very purity an utterly silent world. There is nothing to say, simply because in that state of existence everything goes without saying.

This picture is a natural expression of the thought that sincerity matters to speech because its presence is our guarantee that what the speaker *says* is an accurate representation of what she actually *believes*. If what we hear from a speaker is to be believable by us, it is because the speech we hear provides us with access to what the speaker's own beliefs are, and her statements will be believable only to the extent that we are counting on her beliefs on this matter to be reliable. Hence since it is access to the beliefs of the other person that is doing all the real work here, it need not matter just how this access is achieved so long as it is understood that, other things being equal, we should prefer access that was free of the mediations of explicit speech and the risks inherent in the (often disappointed) assumption of sincerity.

This chapter argues against this picture, both as an understanding of what sincerity *is* and as an understanding of the importance of sincerity in speech. The epistemic status of another person's beliefs is importantly different from that of the words she speaks, and the importance of her speech is not simply that of an indicator of what her beliefs are. Further, the role of the assumption of sincerity in speech is not that of a guarantee that the speaker's words reflect her actual beliefs, but is in fact something both weaker than that in one way, and stronger in another way.

3.2 Williams on the Norm of Sincerity

We can begin with the following natural assumption about the role of sincerity in speech: since assertion aims at belief on the part of the hearer, this aim cannot be achieved unless the hearer assumes that the speaker believes what she says. This would provide a straightforward explanation of the norm of sincerity in assertion, and in recent years Timothy Williamson (2000) and others have argued that the considerations in favor of this norm in fact support the stronger norm that in assertion the speaker not only *believes* what she says, but knows it as well. I do not directly address the "knowledge requirement" here, except to the extent of arguing that even the belief requirement has a more restricted application than is usually assumed. In *Truth and Truthfulness*, Bernard Williams argues against the assimilation of the sense in which "belief aims at truth" to a norm of truth for assertion, for while falsity is a "fatal objection" to a belief (in that recognition of its falsity on the part of the believer amounts to abandoning it as a belief), there is no comparable fatality with respect to statements that are false. As he says, "We appropriately utter—that is, come out with—false sentences in all sorts of contexts" (2002, 70). This is so not only because not all statements present themselves as assertions, but also because not all assertions present themselves as candidates for belief, at least in the sense of being informative to the hearer (71). And yet, when it comes to assertions which do aim to change the beliefs of the audience, Williams suggests that the speaker must at least *present* herself as believing what she is saying. With respect to the idea that "we cannot typically make sense of someone who seems to be asserting something he does not believe to people who, as he well knows, know that he does not believe it," he says that "an explanation of it might be this: that an assertion is an utterance intended to bring it about that the hearer believes its content, and this is not an intention which, in these circumstances, the speaker can intelligibly have. This places assertion firmly in the context of one person's *telling* something to another" (70–71). I think it is indeed true that it is only the notion of *telling* and not the broader notion of assertion that can make sense of the requirement on the speaker's beliefs here, and the general importance of sincerity itself. As mentioned earlier, not all assertions aim at the beliefs of the hearer in the first place, and for these there may be no interest on the part of the hearer in whether what is said reflects the beliefs of the speaker. What Williams suggests above, however, is that when the aim of assertion *is* belief in the content of what is said, it will be clear to both speaker and audience that this aim cannot be achieved unless the speaker is assumed to believe what she says. This may seem obvious enough, especially if we are thinking of the audience asking itself the question, "Why should I believe this if *she* doesn't?" but in fact this question will often enough have a straightforward answer, with the reasons for believing what is said being quite independent of the speaker's own attitude toward it. For assertions are made, with the aim of being convincing, in the context of such activities as formal debate, ad hominem argument, or the following out of a proof, where the convincingness of what is said in these contexts need not depend at all on the assumption that the speaker herself believes what she is saying. In situations of this sort, assertions can function as reminders, challenges, probings, or orientations for the mind, and when successful they can be convincing on their own. Assertions are made and directions are given by the speaker helping someone follow a proof, but the aim here is that the reasons themselves will be found convincing, independent of any assumptions about the actual attitudes of the speaker.

The specificity of relating to the speaker as informant (1.3) has application here as well. In the context of Craig's discussion the notion of informant was defined by way of contrast with relating to the speaker (or agent) as mere source of information. In relating to the assertions made in the course of debate or following a proof we are not relating to the speaker as a mere source of information, but neither are we relating to the speaker as informant. The aim of the speaker may be to convey some truth, but she does not do so by *telling* the audience that truth, nor does the audience come to learn that truth by believing the speaker herself. The idea of a person speaking as an informant is tied to the speech act of telling, and the possibility of that person being believed by her interlocutor. In "What Is It to Believe Someone?" Anscombe understands this in terms of a certain form of reliance or dependence on the speaker: "believing x [the speaker]

that p involves relying on x for it that p" (1979, 145). In telling her audience
that p, the speaker does not only inform in the broad sense (as she may be
said to do when leading through a proof or in formal debate) but invites
that reliance on her as informant with respect to the content asserted. In
cases of "telling," the informant presents herself as in a position to inform
her audience of something which he is not presently in a position to know
by himself. This is different from either the way Socrates instructs through
questioning in the *Meno*, or someone pointing out the window and saying,
"Look, it's stopped raining," and cases like these are not described as cases
of testimony or where the interlocutor learns by believing the speaker. For
these reasons the question of what the speaker herself believes does not
have the same relevance for the hearer in the two cases, when he is considering whether to believe what has been said. There will be more to say
about the relevance of the speaker's beliefs later, as it pertains to the specific
form of informative assertion involved in telling; in particular there is more
to say about how the speaker's presentation of her own belief is supposed
to play a role in bringing the hearer to believe that very thing. But when
the context of assertion is not one where the speaker presents herself as informant in the first place, we might think that conveying beliefs about the
speaker's beliefs would only have *less* of a role to play. Williams, however,
disagrees and in so doing argues for a significant asymmetry between sincerity and insincerity.

> I have made the point that sincere assertions do not necessarily have the aim of
> informing the hearer; but insincere assertions do have the aim of misinforming
> the hearer. In the primary case, they aim to misinform the hearer about the
> state of things, the truth of what the speaker asserts. Derivatively, they may
> aim to misinform the hearer merely about the speaker's beliefs: the speaker
> may know that the hearer will not believe what he falsely asserts, but he wants
> her to believe that he himself believes it. We should say, then, that the standard
> conditions of A's asserting that P are that:
>   A utters a sentence "S," where "S" means that P, in doing which either he
> expresses his belief that P, or he intends the person addressed to take it that he
> believes that P. (2002, 74)

But the very asymmetry claimed here should give us pause. Why should the
general point of an assertion necessarily have anything to do with conveying
beliefs (true or false ones) about the speaker's own beliefs? If I open a book
and read the sentence, "The world is everything that is the case," surely an
assertion is being made here, and yet it does not matter to my relation to

this statement whether it expresses the actual beliefs of the author, nor does its functioning in my thought depend on my taking it that it does so. Most importantly for our purposes, it doesn't matter to the *believability* of that statement that I take it to reflect the beliefs of the speaker.

And if sincere assertion need not have any sort of informative intent (either about the facts or about the beliefs of the speaker), why cannot *insincere* assertion also take place in a context where informing or misinforming are simply not the issue? For instance, a teacher is examining a student and asks her to describe the chief causes of the American Civil War, and the student dutifully and intelligently outlines the causes as they were presented in lectures, which, let us assume, downplayed the role of slavery in the origins of the conflict. Perhaps the student herself is unconvinced by the line taken in the lectures, but is nonetheless quite good at outlining the approach presented there. So she speaks insincerely and does not go into her own thoughts on the matter. The context is one where both teacher and student assume that there is no reporting or exchange of information about the Civil War itself, so that is not the aim of the speaker. And in this situation I don't see why it should be the aim of the student to be misinforming the teacher about her *beliefs* on the matter either. In situations like these the beliefs of the speaker need not enter in as an object of concern at all. The teacher may simply want to know that the student has understood the lectures and can discourse on them competently. And if this is right, and situations like this are common enough, there seems no reason to deny that the student is engaged in making assertions when she says things like, "The issue of the scope and authority of the federal government divided North and South for reasons quite independent of the extension of slavery to the new territories." Similarly, when assertions are made in the context of formal debate and ad hominem argument, there need be no assumption that one is being informed either about the facts *or* about the beliefs of the speaker.[1]

What I think this shows so far is that not all assertions aim to be informative or misinformative at all, neither about the facts themselves nor about the beliefs of the speaker. And then within the class of assertions that *are* informative in the sense of aiming at the beliefs of the audience, some of these achieve their aim through something more like reminding or

---

1 And indeed, we can describe cases of outright *lying* (unlike the cases above) which involve no intention to deceive the audience. On this see Saul 2012, which draws on Carson 2006.

demonstrating and do not depend for their convincingness on assumptions about the belief or knowledge of the speaker. For these, sincerity need not play any role in achieving the aims of assertion. Finally, within the class of assertions whose aim *is* informative some of these have the aim that the speaker herself *be believed*, and these have the force or intent of *telling* the audience something. For these assertions the success aimed at does involve the hearer's assumption that the speaker believes what she says, for he is being invited or instructed to share that very belief.

But just what is the role of this assumption in the case of telling? In particular, if the hearer will not be convinced unless he assumes that what the speaker says reflects what she believes, does that mean that all the hearer is really concerned with is what the speaker's beliefs *are*, such that if he could arrive at this knowledge without being *told* anything, his epistemic position would be just as good or better? That would take us back to the conception of sincerity I derived from the picture of transparent communication in Plotinus, where the value of sincerity would be that of a fallible guarantee that the speaker's words reflect her actual beliefs. If we know her belief independently of the intention to make it manifest, it seems we can dispense with any reliance on the external signs of belief. But a person's beliefs, like her other attitudes, may gain expression in her behavior in various ways, and even her explicit statements can be revealing about much more than the particular belief being asserted. Not every belief that the hearer discerns in these ways will provide him with a reason to share that belief, so if sincerity contributes to the believability of what is said, it must do more than provide a glimpse into the mind of the speaker. The speaker herself, and not just the fact of her belief, must play a role in constituting a reason for her audience to believe something. We need to look more closely into just how beliefs gain expression in sincere assertion.

When Williams says that *in*sincere assertions must have the aim of *mis*informing the hearer, an important intuition guiding him here is that of the naturalness of sincerity over insincerity in speech. So, while saying what one genuinely believes about some matter may be the natural, default response to a question about it, and hence need not raise any specific question as to the *motives* of the speaker for speaking sincerely here, speaking *in*sincerely does seem to require something like an intent on the part of the speaker to deviate from the natural response, and hence does raise the question of the specific motives of the speaker for doing so. In this sense, then, there is a real difference between sincerity and insincerity.

Sincere speech does not immediately raise any question as to why the speaker chose on this occasion to express her actual beliefs. Expressing one's actual beliefs through assertion just is the immediate, natural response in speech situations, and as such it functions independently of the intent either to inform or to misinform. It is for reasons of this sort that Williams frequently characterizes sincere assertion as the spontaneous or "direct expression" of one's belief. By contrast, expressing something other than one's actual beliefs is something that calls for some explanation, specifically an explanation in terms of the motives of the speaker regarding her audience, and so it seems that these motives could only be deceitful, with respect to either the facts or her beliefs or both at once. Even so, I think examples such as the ones above show that such motives need not be deceitful at all. The person speaking in an examination or a debate may well have specific motives for departing from the spontaneous expression of her actual beliefs, but these motives need not have anything to do with misinforming her audience either about her beliefs themselves or about the facts in question.

3.3 Two Forms of the Expression of Belief

It is indeed significant that the natural, spontaneous response to any question calling for an assertion is to come out with one's actual beliefs, and Williams places illuminating emphasis on this throughout this chapter. ("Sincerity at the most basic level is simply openness, a lack of inhibition" [2002, 75].) It is also this emphasis on the naturalness of truthful expression over untruthful expression that accounts for his linking of sincere assertion with a special sense of *directness* in the expression of belief. This formulation is first introduced and emphasized on page 74, but is returned to throughout the chapter (78, 79, 80, 81).

> What better expression could there be of that belief than that sentence, and what belief could be better expressed by its utterance? There are, of course, other ways of expressing one's beliefs; we can say that someone who asserts that P and is sincere says something that is a *direct expression* of his belief that P. (74)

In this passage, there is a question about directness, and a question about what makes an expression of some belief "better" than some other one. If we restrict expressions to *verbal* expressions, then it may well go without saying that there is no better verbal expression of the belief that P than the utterance of "P" itself. But not all our beliefs, let alone other states of mind we report or give expression to, are so closely tied to words for it to be true that there can be no better expression of them than the utterance of some sentence. If we think of "expression" as covering a wider field than the verbal, and if a "better" expression is one that is more expressively adequate than some other one, then it won't be hard to imagine situations where there is indeed some more adequate expression (e.g., of my belief about the superiority of one performance to another, or about the quality of irritation in someone's voice) than the utterance of a roughly corresponding sentence. Or, alternatively, if what makes one expression better than another is that it is a more reliable guide to the truth about the state of mind in question, so that what is at issue is basic accuracy or reliability rather than expressive adequacy, then there are different reasons for doubting that the assertion of "P" will always be the better expression. For any assertion is an intentional act, and hence, as mentioned earlier, when considered as a reliable indication of a person's actual belief, explicit assertion is subject to the specific risks involved in relying on a deliberate expression that may be deliberately misleading. And even when the person's sincerity is not in question, the accuracy or reliability of her sincere assertion with respect to her beliefs will be affected by the quality of her own self-knowledge. As compared with other ways of reading off someone's beliefs from what she does (whether deliberately or not), relying on what she *says* involves the audience in further layers of mediation inseparable from the character of saying something as an intentional act. And this in turn raises questions about the idea of assertion as a "direct expression" of belief.[2]

The fact that beliefs and other attitudes gain expression in the absence of any intent to communicate, simply through our actions and how we perform them, might well suggest that these forms of expression are more *direct* than those involving the complexities of intention involved in *telling* someone something, however spontaneous truthful assertion may be. As Williams points out, "All sorts of inferences may be reasonably made from

2 As to "what belief could be better expressed by its utterance," there may be straightforward answers here too, according to which the belief expressed is not that of the truth of the proposition stated. In a given context, the belief being given expression by its utterance need not be belief in that proposition at all, but rather the belief that, for the present purposes of argument or demonstration or instruction, *this* is what my audience needs to hear.

what people say and the ways in which they say it. . . . [H]earers gather
more from a speaker's making a particular assertion than the content of
that assertion. As I put it earlier, the speaker expresses one belief, but they
acquire many. Speakers have countless beliefs and many different ways of
expressing them" (99–100). Some forms of the expression of belief involve
the speaker asserting or explicitly giving her word on something, whereas
other forms of expression may manifest beliefs or other attitudes which she
may not even be aware of, but which are evident to the right sort of audience. In Erving Goffman's formulation, there is the distinction between
"the expression that he *gives*, and the expression that he *gives off*."[3] In both
cases the hearer may gain access to the beliefs of the speaker, and from this
he may indeed learn about the facts themselves that these beliefs represent.
Corresponding to the difference between what the speaker "gives" and
what (s)he "gives off" is the difference between what I learn from *her* and
what I may learn from what she does and how she does it.[4] Only in the case
of what I learn from her, the person, does my relation to her beliefs involve
the speaker's assuming any responsibility for what I believe, and that makes
a difference to the kind of reason for belief that is obtained in the two cases.
The role played by the assumption of her sincerity here is thus something
more than a guarantee of access to what her beliefs are.

The central difference is that between expression in the impersonal sense
of the manifestation of some attitude or state of mind, and expression in
the personal or relational sense as the intentional act of one person directed
to another. To see this, let us leave the case of the expression of belief for
a moment and consider the case of an apology or an expression of gratitude. We do want these to be sincere, of course, and to reflect the actual
sentiments of the speaker. But it doesn't follow from this that the importance of sincerity in such cases lies entirely in providing a kind of guarantee that the verbal apology or thanks are indications of genuine remorse
or gratitude on the part of the speaker. For there are common-enough

---

3 "Many crucial facts lie beyond the time and place of interaction or lie concealed within it. For
   example, the 'true' or 'real' attitudes, beliefs, and emotions of the individual can be ascertained
   only indirectly, through his avowals or through what appears to be involuntary expressive behavior. . . .The expressiveness of the individual (and therefore his capacity to give impressions)
   appears to involve two radically different kinds of sign activity: the expression that he *gives*, and
   the expression that he *gives off*" (Goffman 1959, 2).
4 Cf. David Owens: "[M]y statements transmit knowledge only of that to which I testify. . . .You
   might learn that I am rich from my words but you didn't learn it *from me*, you didn't learn it by
   accepting what I said, and so it does not count as testimonial knowledge" (2000, 165).

situations where it is as clear as can be that someone is indeed sorry for what happened or grateful for the help, that the way she looks and acts is a more reliable and unequivocal indication of her state of mind than any words could be. Yet finding oneself in such a situation does not do away with the need for words. And this is because the words provide something more than an indication of the speaker's state of mind. For one thing, there is the difference between remorse or gratitude *expressing itself* in a person's face or action, and *the person* giving expression to her remorse or gratitude. When we need the person as such to get involved in the explicit expression of remorse or gratitude, this is not out of the assumption that this will always provide a more reliable guide to the state of mind we are interested in, more reliable than what may express itself in her face and gesture. In such a situation I may know everything I need to know about how this person is feeling, since this expresses itself in countless ways, in voluntary and involuntary behavior. When the person *expresses herself*, however, she doesn't simply provide a window onto her state of mind, but also "owns up" to the attitude in question, acknowledges it, and assumes a certain kind of responsibility for it, and for the hearer's knowledge of it. None of this is part of the story when her remorse or gratitude simply manifests itself, clear as day, in how she looks or what she does. Hence we need to attend to the difference between what the person does in expressing herself and what the gratitude or remorse within may do in making itself manifest. And the idea of an assumption of responsibility when the person expresses her remorse or gratitude is part of a further difference, which lies in the fact that only when the person as such is involved can we speak of the expression of remorse or gratitude being *directed or addressed* to some particular other person. When I can read the gratitude in her face, this may still leave me not knowing something, though by hypothesis it is not her gratitude itself which I fail to know. What I don't yet know is whether the person is willing to explicitly acknowledge it and address it to me; not only direct my attention to it, though that is of course important to the difference here, and not only make this knowledge explicitly shared between us, but also take up a role in constituting a reason for me to understand her as grateful or sorry. Putting all this into words highlights the fact that it is the person as such who is asking to be relied on, her choices rather than the natural generalizations linking states of mind with actions and appearances.

Sincerity is an issue where there is a question of believing the speaker as such, and this requires a notion of expression different from the "direct manifestation" of belief. The case of lying may help to clarify this distinction. In the case of explicit verbal expression of belief, considerably more of the speaker's attitudes may be given expression than the simple belief that P itself (e.g., the fact that she found this worth saying, that she is willing to help out, etc.). When the speaker is lying, of course, she expresses a belief that she does not have. At the same time, her action of telling a lie may express other beliefs and attitudes of hers, ones which the action of lying, and the way she carries it out, reveals her actually to have. Her choice of words or the creative elaboration of the lie may express her confidence in her powers, her contempt for her audience, or various other attitudes.[5] Hence in the lying assertion that P, the speaker expresses the belief that P, and while she is engaged in this lie various of her genuine attitudes also gain expression. And here we can see that the sense of "expression" cannot be the same in the two contexts, the context in which her attitudes are expressed in her behavior and the context in which she makes the explicit, though deceitful, expression of belief that P. One basic difference is simply that in her assertion that P she expresses the belief that P, whether or not she actually *has* any such belief; whereas when we speak of the beliefs and other attitudes which are given expression in someone's behavior, the very description itself implies that we are normally thinking of expression here in a "factive" sense, such that speaking of some attitude expressing itself implies the *presence* of that very attitude.[6] If I begin by characterizing someone's behavior as expressing her confidence in her powers, and then become convinced that she had no such confidence, then I withdraw the original claim that this is what her behavior expressed. Her behavior at the time *seemed* to express her confidence, but I now see this is

---

5 "Man lügt wohl mit dem Munde, aber mit dem Maule, das man dabei macht, sagt man doch noch die Wahrheit" (Nietzsche, *Beyond Good and Evil*, § 166). The Kaufmann translation, "Even when the mouth lies, the way it looks still tells the truth," doesn't capture the sense in the German that it is, nonetheless, the *person* ["man"] and not "the mouth" or the way it looks, which lies or tells the truth.

6 In "Testimony and Assertion" (2006) David Owens employs a very different notion of "expression." He restricts "expression" to the indicative sense such that "an expression of belief may be poor or inadequate but it can't be insincere: you can't express beliefs you don't have" (109). This naturally raises questions about how to characterize insincere assertion, which he takes up later in the paper. The restriction seems to have the implication that an insincere assertion of P can really only be the apparent expression of the belief that P. Even if we accept this reconfiguration of the idea of expression in speech, it seems that the insincere assertion that P should count as the actual, and not merely apparent, expression of *something*, and then it's hard to see what that could be if not the belief that P. The paper also employs a notion of sincerity such that an assertion may be either intentionally or unintentionally insincere (113), which I find hard to understand.

wrong. By contrast, were the person herself to have explicitly announced such confidence to someone, the claim that she expressed confidence in her powers survives any later revelation that in fact she felt no such thing. The main difference here is between expression as a quite general term for the various ways in which phenomena are made manifest, and "express" as verb of intentional action, something done by a person in a context of discourse, as addressed to another person. Hence we can refer to a "personal" or "relational" sense of expression as well as an "impersonal" one. A person's fear or belief may express itself in various ways that the person herself may not control or even be aware of. But the person herself can only express her fear or her belief if she is aware of it and means to make it manifest. Or rather, she can do this on the assumption that she *has* the fear or the belief in question. A person who makes a lying profession of belief that P is still said to have expressed the belief that P, in that this is what she intended to convey. But here too, the *in*sincere person will only be said to have expressed the belief that P insofar as she was aware that it was this belief (whether in fact hers or not) that she was seeking to convey. Thus in the case of either sincere or insincere expression, the *person* as such is said to have expressed the belief that P only insofar as she was aware of this belief, either as her actual belief or as the belief she was seeking to convey. "Expression" in this sense is a conscious act of the person, addressed to another.

The fact that speaking is itself a form of expressive behavior sometimes causes confusion on this point. The distinction drawn here between the personal and the impersonal senses of "expression" is sometimes assimilated to the distinction between linguistic and nonlinguistic expression, with the assumption that linguistic expression is personal expression, in being the conscious act of a person to make manifest a particular attitude. But since they *are* actions, speech and assertion will always involve consequences beyond the conscious intent of the person, and hence will always have the potential to be revealing of the person beyond what she intends to convey. Hence the example of lying not only shows the difference between the two dimensions of expression, but shows how both types of expression have application within the domain of speech and assertion itself. The liar expresses one belief with her assertion that P, while another belief (one that she actually has) gains expression through the act of lying itself.[7]

---

7 If someone can express some belief or some fear without having it, then the relation between the expression and the facts about my genuine attitudes cannot be a purely causal one,

3.4 Sincerity and the Speaker's Guarantee

The central question for the role of sincerity in assertion is the one Williams raises in chapter 5: "What is the relation between the speaker's beliefs and the beliefs with which the hearer ends up?" (2002, 96). What the foregoing discussion shows, I believe, is that the importance of the assumption of sincerity in speech cannot be reduced to providing the hearer with a kind of improved access to the speaker's state of mind, from which he draws his own conclusions. The speaker's state of mind is a state of affairs that has whatever epistemic import it may have for the hearer quite independently of any act of the speaker addressed to the hearer, or the speaker's presenting herself as an informant with respect to the truth in question. In this way the epistemic import of the *words* she addresses to the hearer is different from that of her *belief* itself, for her words will only have the import of an act of informative assertion on the assumption that the speaker is employing them to address the hearer in just that way. If the importance of sincerity were restricted to the idea of guaranteeing access to the speaker's beliefs, then in making the other person aware of her beliefs the speaker would have done her job as far as informing him is concerned. But if this were all that is involved in telling someone something, then the liar or the verbal misleader really would be able to say that she cannot be blamed because all she did was provide evidence for what her beliefs are and leave her audience to draw his own conclusions from this (Williams 2002, 107, 118). But telling someone something is much more directive than this, pointing the audience in a verbally specific direction, attesting to the truth of *what is being said*, and not just anything and everything that might be garnered from the person's speech and action. (The "directive" aspect of telling someone something shows up in the fact that the verb "to tell" has various imperative forms that are not shared by "to say" or even "to assert." I may not only tell someone the facts, but I may also tell him to back off, or tell him how to get back on the highway.) This directive aspect of the act of telling is only possible insofar as the person as such is

but opens up the possibility for such failings as error or misrepresentation. In short, there is a normative as well as a causal relation between expression in the personal sense and what is putatively being given expression. The applicability of such terms of criticism as error or misrepresentation for the personal sense of expression is only appropriate given that here the expression in question is the intentional action of a person, and persons and actions provide just the right sort of object for such criticism.

the agent of the act of expression. For the meaning of the act addressed to her audience depends on the speaker assuming responsibility for her utterance being a reason to believe something in the first place (as it would not be, for instance, if those same words are presented as some other speech act). This is not a relationship she stands in with respect to her beliefs or with respect to any other evidence, and in these ways the speaker is doing something quite other than allowing her beliefs to be known and leaving the audience to draw his own conclusions, as she would be when the epistemic import of some independent state of affairs does not depend on commitments of her own.

These considerations cast doubt on the idea that the value of words, the value of *sincere* words, can only be that of a reliable indication of the person's beliefs. The intentional act of the person in giving explicit expression to her belief and addressing this assertion to someone else provides her hearer with something more than he could have derived from the simple awareness of the speaker's beliefs themselves. In telling someone something, she does not simply lay her belief open to view (which can happen even with respect to an unconscious belief of hers), something for the hearer to make of what he will, but rather registers her consciousness not only of the belief itself but of the fact that she is engaged in providing her audience with a reason to believe that very thing. The "directive" aspect of telling, attesting to a specific proposition, is thus related to the speaker's presentation of herself as accountable for the hearer's believing what she says. Simply gaining awareness of what someone believes provides nothing of this relationship between speaker and hearer.

However, the role of the person as such in providing a reason to believe also means that in an important sense the hearer gets something *less* from sincere assertion than he would from direct access to the speaker's beliefs (and these two facts about the personal level of expression are related to each other, and characterize the nature of sincerity itself). This is because although sincere expression involves no intent to deceive, it also need not be terribly discerning about the self to which it gives expression. As Williams says, "It follows from the basic spontaneity of assertion that Sincerity does not typically involve a special exercise of Accuracy, namely, Accuracy in discovering what it is that I believe; rather, in the simplest case I am confronted with my belief as what I would spontaneously assert. There are, of course, other cases in which I do have to discover by inquiry what I believe" (76). Not only does sincerity not require any special exercise of accuracy, but it is a familiar fact about sincerity that it is compatible with error or simple shallowness about one's own attitudes, including one's beliefs. Matthew Arnold speaks of the "surface stream . . . of what we *think* we feel," and its stark contrast with the noiseless current below of "what we feel indeed," and he is clear that it is from this surface perspective that sincere expression takes place.[8] A person is credited with speaking sincerely when she presents herself as she takes herself to be, which may not involve reporting her own mind either deeply or accurately. In this way the demands of sincerity are weaker than the demands of accurate presentation of one's beliefs or other attitudes. If someone fails to know her actual belief about some matter, whether through self-deception or more innocently, she will still be speaking sincerely when she asserts the belief she takes herself to have.

In another sense, however, the requirement of sincerity is *more* demanding than the accurate presentation of one's state of mind. For again, if someone has the repressed belief, for example, that she is a coward, but takes herself to believe no such thing, she will have failed to speak sincerely if, for her own reasons, she nonetheless says that she *is* a coward, even though by hypothesis what she asserts here expresses what she actually thinks about herself. As D. H. Mellor and others have pointed out, a person speaks sincerely when she says what she *takes* herself to believe, and not simply when she says what she in fact believes.[9] Just as it is possible to lie while inadvertently reporting the actual facts, it is possible to speak insincerely while asserting what is in fact one's actual belief. Saying what I actually believe is not *sufficient* for sincerity, if my intent was deceptive but my apprehension of my own belief was distorted. And saying what I actually believe is not *necessary* for sincerity either, since I still speak sincerely if I am somehow wrong about my actual belief but nonetheless assert what I take myself to believe. Despite Mellor's own formulation, the truth in this idea does not require appeal to "second-order states," which would appear to have the consequence that children and others without

---

8 "Below the surface-stream, shallow and light, / Of what we *say* we feel—below the stream, / As light, of what we *think* we feel—there flows / With noiseless current strong, obscure and deep, / The central stream of what we feel indeed." Quoted in Trilling 1971, 6.

9 Mellor uses the term "assent" for second-order belief, believing that one believes, and says, "Sincere assertion is saying what one assents to, that is what one believes one believes, not just what one believes" (1977–78, 97). The account Mellor gives of assent in that paper has been superseded by the richer account he gives in "Consciousness and Degrees of Belief" (1991).

the concepts of such states cannot be said to be sincere or insincere. The underlying thought is consistent with Williams's basic idea of sincerity as naturalness or spontaneity, for it would be a bad picture of spontaneity itself that would suggest that a spontaneous declaration cannot be the expression of a person's self-deception, confusion, or simple shallowness with respect to her own mental life.[10] There is indeed such a myth of natural or spontaneous expression as guaranteeing its source in the truth of the person, without any distorting admixture of reflection or interpretation. In the context of verbal expression, however, the basic meaning of spontaneity or naturalness is the absence of either inhibition or the intent to mislead. If we are assuming that the truth about a person's attitudes can indeed be distorted or masked from the person herself in various ways, then there is no reason to think that spontaneous or natural expression is somehow guaranteed to penetrate through such interferences to the undistorted truth itself. For example, a person's sincere declaration of confidence in some outcome may be made in the absence of any acknowledgment of her own doubts and fears about it, and thus fail to accurately display her real state of mind, even to be at variance with her deeper convictions about the uncertainty of the outcome. This sort of situation does not require the postulation of second-order attitudes, and may describe the situation of someone without the capacity for such attitudes.

In these ways, sincerity fails to be a guarantee of access to the speaker's actual beliefs, and hence from the point of view of the picture of sincerity that we began with, all this should make it quite mysterious why sincerity should have any central importance at all to the epistemology of testimony. What it suggests is that we cannot make sense of the importance of sincerity for testimony unless we separate this from the assumption that the importance of sincere assertion is that of providing access to the speaker's beliefs. As we saw, the believability of some assertions doesn't rely on assumptions about the speaker's beliefs in the first place (when she is not speaking as an informant), and what the current considerations aim to bring out is that with respect to the class of assertions where the beliefs of the speaker *are* crucial, whereby the speaker *tells* her audience something, sincerity does not function as a guarantee of access to

---

10 "This is not to say that M. Legrandin was anything but sincere when he inveighed against snobs. He could not (from his own knowledge at least) be aware that he himself was one, since it is only with the passions of others that we are ever really familiar, and what we come to discover about our own can only be learned from them" (Proust 1998, 181).

the speaker's beliefs, but provides something both stronger and weaker than that. Sincere assertion is a weaker guarantee than that, since it only provides us with the speaker's own apprehension of herself, which may be limited in various ways. But this same fact leads to an understanding of how sincere assertion provides the hearer with a kind of epistemic relation to the facts that he could not get merely through knowing what the speaker actually believes.

It is only with respect to the sense of "expression" involving the person as such, the intentional action of expressing one's belief, that the person is in a position to speak for the meaning or epistemic import of what she is attesting to. With respect to whatever may express itself unconsciously or inadvertently in someone's speech or other expressive behavior, while this may indeed be a source of knowledge for the audience, he is on his own as far as assessing its epistemic significance goes. Since beliefs which are revealed in these ways need not even be known by the speaker herself, the hearer (or observer) cannot assume that the speaker is in a position to offer support or justification for what may be garnered in this way, nor that she speaks with any authority about the meaning or general significance of the belief which manifests itself in her speech or other behavior. Ultimately the speaker's relation to what expresses itself in her behavior is no different from her relation to what her act of lying may reveal about her. And indeed, this is true for beliefs which someone may learn of in ways that have no basis in overt expression at all. In such a situation, the audience cannot look to the person as such to say anything helpful about the belief's meaning, its justification, or how it would alter in response to counterevidence of various kinds.[11] Mere access to the other person's beliefs provides nothing like what is taken for granted in the continuation of a conversation. By contrast, in the ordinary speech exchanges associated with testimony, it is taken for granted that if someone asserts that P, the hearer is *not* on his own in the task of assessing its meaning or its epistemic significance. In making the assertion, the speaker has taken on the burden of responding to a request for clarification, interpretation, or justification. This is one way in which it distorts the philosophical discussions of testimony when the topic is taken

---

11 In connection with the distinction between an informant and a "mere source," Craig mentions a related point that an informant "can often empathize with the inquirer, and react not just to the question but to the presumed point of asking it, so giving the inquirer useful information that he did not know he had need of" (1990, 36).

up atomistically, outside the conversational context of anything longer than a single utterance or two.

If something I say or do provides *evidence* for some fact, it is irrelevant to this evidential force whether or not I *know* that what I said or did provides such a reason for belief. Nor, in such a case, do I need to understand *how* it constitutes such a reason for belief. But when a person makes a committed assertion, she must recognize the sort of reason she is offering, and her role in constituting it as a reason for belief. Hence sincerity matters to testimony because it is from this position that the speaker assumes responsibility for the meaning and justification of what she says. This is a genuine epistemological difference for the hearer, providing something different from what he would get simply from access to the other person's beliefs. And in this way the linguistic nature of testimony is related to the role of self-understanding and awareness in presenting someone with a reason for belief. It is only from a position of understanding what she is doing that a speaker can make a promise or give her word on something. A speaker performs specific illocutions (of asserting, promising, refusing) in self-consciously assuming or declining to assume specific responsibilities. A mature speaker of a language does not only have command of the formal resources of that language (grammar, vocabulary, etc.) but is credited by others with the ability to invest her words with the force of, say, an assertion rather than a question or a recitation (not to mention such further stages of development as the age of consent). And from the hearer's point of view, he cannot have any idea of the epistemic import of what he has heard until he knows which illocution the speaker is presenting herself as enacting. Hence for the hearer to know what to make of this utterance, whether as evidence or anything else, he must assume that the speaker is speaking from within the authority to constitute her utterance as, say, an assertion rather than a paraphrase of someone else's statement. If the person is not assumed to speak for herself here, then the hearer cannot take himself to be receiving any kind of testimony from her at all, whatever epistemic stance the hearer may ultimately want to adopt toward the utterance.

We do want and expect what people tell us both to be true and to express their actual beliefs, and often enough we are not disappointed in these expectations. But the importance of sincerity is not simply that of learning the speaker's beliefs, because that would suggest that just any way we might come to know these beliefs would have the same epistemic import as the speaker's assertion. And that would fail to account

for the person's own role in constituting her utterance as a potential reason to believe something, her addressing her assertion to another
person, and her attestation to a specific candidate proposition; none of
which is part of the person's relation to her expressive behavior or indeed to her beliefs themselves. In addition, the understanding of the
role of sincerity in terms of access to the speaker's beliefs leaves unexplained the importance of the limited way in which sincerity does relate
to such access, since it is neither necessary nor sufficient that sincere
speech reflect the actual beliefs of the speaker. One can fail to speak sincerely while nonetheless giving expression to one's actual belief, just as
one can speak sincerely in a way that reflects a very imperfect grasp of
one's actual attitudes. Sincerity matters epistemically to the hearer not
because it provides him with a window onto the speaker's beliefs but
because it tells him what the person as such is assuming responsibility
for, as this relates to the hearer's own belief. The difference made by the
speaker's accountability doesn't simply lie in the fact that the audience
now has someone to blame should he turn out to be misled, but lies also
in the more epistemically relevant fact that, rather than having simply
come upon someone's belief to make of what he will, the hearer can
assume that the belief in question has survived the speaker's reflection
on it and is being presented to him with the speaker's epistemic backing
and answerability for its justification and general (including contextual)
significance. As with any assumption of responsibility, this can be something shallow, confused, or deluded, but the speaker's explicit presentation of what she says as belief-worthy, and the joint responsibility for
belief expressed by this, nonetheless provides the hearer with something
of an epistemic import different from the private or telepathic discovery
of someone's beliefs.

4

The Claim and the Encounter

4.1 Grice: The Production of Belief (in Others) through the Revelation of (One's Own) Belief

A "telepathic ideal" of communication is a fantasy of unmediated contact between two minds, one which itself rests on a particular conception of minds themselves and how they relate to one another in the sublunary, nonideal case. On this picture, a person's words, like her gestures and other reactions, are to be seen as the visible or audible indication of the person's belief, the state of mind itself being something which is neither visible nor audible. The person's state of mind is the direct object of interest, but it needs some intervening medium of expression to become known by another person. The available forms of such manifestation come with their own risks, however, since they can be misleading in various ways. And in the case of communicative speech, that is, a speaker's deliberate manifestation of her state of mind, these risks are amplified by the addition of the possibility of deliberate deception, or imperfect self-apprehension. In light of this, the ideal, it might seem, would be if we could dispense with such mediation altogether and proceed directly to the other person's state of mind. As opposed to this, we have seen that in at least a broad class of speech acts (thanks, apologies, contracts, retractions, and other "social acts of mind" in Reid's sense) this fantasy does not in fact even represent an unrealized ideal, since the overt act of self-expression is in fact not one that the partners in the exchange would wish to dispense with even if that were possible. The explicit manifestation to someone of one's intent or one's remorse goes beyond what could be gained by that other person through any act of mind reading. And in that case, the value of sincerity in such acts would have to be understood differently than as the next best approximation we could get to unmediated access to the speaker's state of mind.

On one way of seeing Grice's story, it fails to take a decisive step away from the Indicative picture of the speaker's words as signs of her belief, precisely in virtue of the roles given to the beliefs of the two parties to the communicative exchange, and the character of the act that the speaker is described as engaged in. For on this picture the speaker is described as doing something (i.e., saying something out loud) with the intent of bringing another person within earshot to believe something. It is thus the state of mind of her audience that is the *object* of the speaker's action, something she wishes to affect in a particular way. And the description of the effect that she wishes to produce in the mind of the audience is itself described in terms of the speaker's *own* state of mind: that is, (in Grice's post-1957 formulations) the speaker aims to produce the belief in the audience that she, the utterer, believes that P. She wishes to produce this effect in a particular way, of course, one that necessarily proceeds through the hearer's recognition of that very intention of hers, but nonetheless the description of the speaker's general aim is made in terms of producing a certain result in the mind of another, viz., a belief about her own belief. That result concerns the *beliefs* of the audience, and the content of the beliefs to be produced in the audience concern the beliefs of the speaker. Of course, Grice presented his account as an account of communicative *meaning* and not testimony, but we can understand this last condition in terms of a familiar demand of testimony: if the ultimate aim is for the audience to gain the belief that P from the speaker (which is how the transmission of knowledge is being understood here),[1] then this result cannot be hoped for unless the audience first comes to believe that the *speaker* herself believes that P. Hence we can see this as a way of generating the requirement that the speaker making an assertion present herself as sincere.

Various philosophers have objected both to the characterization of the *act* of the speaker in terms of affecting the beliefs of the audience, and to the description of the desired *effect* as the audience's coming to believe that the *speaker* believes something. In "Meaning, Communication, and

---

1 A problematic assumption, about which see Welbourne 1986 on the "commonability of knowledge," as contrasted with beliefs.

Knowledge," John McDowell criticizes the description of the desired effect, by reference to the relation between asking a question and receiving an informative response.

> The primary point of asking questions is not to acquire beliefs about one's interlocutor's beliefs, but to find out how things are. Correspondingly, the primary point of making assertions is not to instill into others beliefs about one's own beliefs but to inform others—to let them know—about the subject matter of one's assertions (which need not be, though of course it may be, the asserter's beliefs). Strawson's proposal represents a communicator as engaged in the manipulation of his audience's beliefs.[2]

Grice, of course, has his own story to tell about just how this conveyance of beliefs about the speaker's beliefs is to be accomplished, but even if we accept the importance Grice gives to the explicitness of the speaker's expression of intention, and the role that is to be played by the audience's recognition of this intention in coming to believe that P, it may still seem that this picture places the emphases in the wrong parts of both sides of the exchange. Surely the point of the speaker's telling his audience that P is to put that person in touch with the *fact* of P itself, and not with merely another representation of P, the belief-state of the speaker. The general description of the speaker's aim must be that she seeks to directly *inform* her audience that P, and not provide him with the next best thing to that, by way of indicating something about herself. The primary object of attention for both parties is some feature of the world, not the psychology of either of them, and that focus is part of what constitutes their understanding of what kind of act they are engaged in. In asserting "P," the speaker may not care that the audience come to any conclusions about her own state of belief, nor is she presuming an interest in her belief-state on the part of the audience. There will certainly be a role for the speaker's beliefs in this exchange, and this role is part of the speaker's own understanding of what she is doing. But it would be contrary to her understanding of this role to think that, although bringing her audience to learn of her beliefs through the Gricean mechanism may be the most efficient way of achieving that aim,

---

2   McDowell 1998, 38. The last thought about manipulation McDowell credits to Tom Ricketts. McDowell's primary target here in this article is Strawson's "Intention and Convention in Speech Acts," but Strawson's own context is a progressive refinement of the Gricean picture. See also Ian Rumfitt's very helpful discussion in "Meaning and Understanding" (2005, in particular 430–32).

her primary aim of providing such access would be accomplished were her audience to learn of her belief in some other way, and then reason his way to the facts from this. By the same token, it would be a mischaracterization of the character of the act of telling or informing to define it as that of a speaker seeking to produce an effect on the beliefs of the audience, for that suggests a purely instrumental understanding of the act, with the audience as the purely receptive object of the influences of the speaker.

The Gricean agent is described as both too passive and absent from her own act of informing and also as too active, or active in the wrong way, in aiming to produce a result on the state of the other person in a unilateral way. That is, we seem to have a picture according to which access to the speaker's beliefs is doing all the epistemic work, and hence in which the speaker herself is curiously passive or absent from the scene of instruction once she has made such access to her own mind possible. She has opened the window on her beliefs as she might open the window to reveal the rain outside and may now go about her other business. The reasons that should count for her audience are no longer her affair, but are given by the evidential value of her belief-state as it is currently constituted, which the audience may assess on his own. And at the same time, in describing the speaker's aim in speaking as that of producing an effect on the beliefs of her audience, the speaker is pictured as having too instrumentally active a relation to the state of mind of the other person. The speaker seeks to produce a change in a certain direction, and availing herself of this special way of bringing her audience to believe something about her own beliefs seems the best way to do this. It is of course true that Grice's account goes to great lengths to specify the particular way in which this is to be achieved (i.e., through the recognition of the speaker's intention), but this specification of the way in which the audience's beliefs are to be affected can still be understood as an *instrumental* specification, a description of the most efficient way for this independently described end to be achieved. And as for the reason for belief that is provided by the speaker's utterance, it still looks as though this is derived entirely from learning what her beliefs are, and hence depends on a particular understanding of the meaning of the assumption of sincerity. The characterization of the kind of act in question and the characterization of the way in which the influence of the speaker's act is supposed to play a positive epistemic role for the audience are split off from each other in a way that seems to occlude the understanding of how the speaker's act and the reasons provided by it are aspects of one phenomenon when two people are in active communication with each other. Here the speaker is not so much addressing her audience as she is seeking to produce a result on his belief state, and she is not so much presenting her reasons to her audience as she is purporting to provide access to something else, namely her own belief-state.

4.2 Verbal Communication and Perception

Several philosophers have made criticisms of what seems overly inferentialist or psychologistic in Grice's basic approach, but in retreating from this McDowell and others have stressed an analogy between testimony and ordinary perception which obscures what Grice was rightly seeking to capture in his account. The comparison of testimony with ordinary perception can seem attractive both epistemologically, in assimilating testimony to a familiar paradigm source of knowledge, and phenomenologically, in affirming what is spontaneous and unreflective in the ways we learn from what we see around us and from what other people tell us. Toward the end of "Meaning, Communication, and Knowledge" McDowell sums up one of the important strands of the positive picture he arrives at through the criticism of Strawson and Grice in the following way.

> When the communicative process functions properly, sensory confrontation with a piece of communicative behaviour has the same impact on the cognitive state of a perceiver as sensory confrontation with the state of affairs that the behaviour, as we may say, represents; elements of the communicative repertoire serve as epistemic surrogates for represented states of affairs. (1998, 45)

The comparison of verbal communication with perception is made by philosophers from a variety of philosophical commitments, and collectively represent what Mitchell Green has called the "extended senses model of communication."[3] McDowell and others are drawn to the analogy with perception out of the desire to avoid the implication, stemming from Gricean-styled accounts, that informing someone that P proceeds most immediately by providing an indication of the speaker's *beliefs* (and by means

---

3 Green 2007, 9. In her book *Varieties of Meaning*, Ruth Garrett Millikan gives an especially forthright expression of this view: "I will argue that understanding language is simply another form
of sensory perception of the world" (2004, 113).

of this indication, to influence the beliefs of the audience). Rather, it is said, the correct picture should be one in which the speaker directly informs her audience of the fact itself, and does not do so only indirectly by means of providing an indication of her belief concerning that fact.

However, the complaint about the indirectness of the Gricean story, and its suggestion that the primary aim of communication is to instill beliefs about one's beliefs, should not be thought to lend support to the comparison with perception. Any account of directly informing someone of some fact by telling him so must have something to say about how learning this fact from someone in this way depends on the hearer's recognition that a particular *speech act* has been performed by the speaker (an informative assertion, normally), one in which she declares the truth of some proposition. The words of the speaker do not count as a reason to believe their content if they are spoken without any understanding of what they mean, or that they are being presented as a reason to believe something. By contrast, the reasons for belief provided by "sensory confrontation with [a] state of affairs" do not depend on a person's presentation of that state of affairs as a reason to believe something or her understanding the epistemic significance of her act when she does so. There is nothing analogous to this dependence of epistemic reasons on the self-understanding of an act that presents something for belief in the perceptual case of being shown something or seeing it for oneself. As with other comparisons, there are innocuous ways of understanding the comparison with perception as well as more substantive ones, and some of these will not be in any conflict with either a Gricean account or one invoking practices, institutions, and "social acts of mind." For instance, often what people mean to defend in stressing the perceptual analogy is just the idea that learning about the world from what people say is "direct" and "noninferential," and that the giving and receiving of testimony is normally something spontaneous and unreflective. But we may say much the same about many explicitly institutionally grounded social interactions, like accepting cash for goods and services, or stopping at a red light. If the comparison with perception means only that we respond to the assertions of others spontaneously and without any labored inferences, the specific comparison with sensory contact is not doing any real work. Everyone will want to agree that ordinary speakers are normally spontaneous and unreflective in their daily talking and unaware of performing any complex inferences, while at the same time acknowledging that speaking and understanding a language is an enormously complex and sophisticated social and cognitive ability. As with other complex skills and institutional practices, we can surely say both things in the same breath. Similarly, sometimes all the comparison with perception comes down to is that, just as we normally and justifiably take the deliverances of the senses at face value as revealing the world to us (which is what "trusting the testimony of the senses" comes to), so in responding to what people tell us we normally and justifiably operate with a default assumption of trust in the word of others.[4] Here again this is a similarity at such a level of generality that the specific comparison with perception is not contributing anything to the understanding of verbal communication. And apart from that, the fact that we operate with a default assumption of trust does nothing to suggest that the recognition of the intentions of others and the aim to be understood as a speaker play no role in the constitution of something as an assertion, and thus a candidate reason to believe what is asserted.

McDowell's comparison of verbal communication with "sensory confrontation with the state of affairs" suggests something more specific and substantial than either of these thoughts. He is motivated here by some of the same concerns that ground the views he has defended elsewhere about the directness of perception itself. So he is primarily concerned to preserve the sense that in ordinary informative communication the focus of both parties is on "the subject matter of one's assertions," the facts themselves and the world around them, and not on the beliefs and intentions of either of them. In asking a question we wish to be informed about nothing less than the subject matter of our question, we wish to be put in touch with the facts themselves. But even so, the idea of testimony as "the extension of the senses" or the claim that receiving an answer to one's question has the same impact as "sensory confrontation with the state of affairs" itself is not a claim that can be taken literally, and is a misleading comparison even in the limited range of cases where we might speak of actual perceptual contact with a state of affairs. That is, for one thing, the topics of ordinary informative communication go well beyond anything for which it would make sense to speak of sensory contact or

---

4 Reid's own earlier comparison of our trust in testimony with our trust in the reliability of the senses is basically of this sort. This is a theme in his 1764 *Inquiry* (chap. VI, "Of Seeing," sec. 24, "Of the analogy between perception, and the credit we give to human testimony") before his conception of "social acts of mind" in the *Essays on the Active Powers of Mind* in 1788.

perception. When I ask someone the time, or whether he could do me a favor, or why he couldn't turn his paper in on time, I wish to learn the facts all right, but the state of affairs I am concerned with is not one for which it makes sense to speak of being in "sensory contact." This applies as well to what we may be told about the past and future, the chances of getting caught, or what couldn't possibly happen unless the banks fail. The extension of the senses model could only seem to have application to the limited ranges of cases where there really is the possibility of being in sensory contact with the state of affairs, and then we would need an account of all the remainder of verbal communication, and an explanation for why we must somehow be content with a bifurcated account of testimony to accommodate discourse about both sensory and nonsensory contents.

However, even in those cases where there is the possibility of being in sensory contact with the topic of the speaker's assertion (the cat on the mat, the milk in the fridge) the comparison of testimony with perception suggests the irrelevance of the fact that when I am *told* about the milk in the fridge, as opposed to seeing it myself, I am peculiarly dependent on someone's self-conscious act for this information, and that I couldn't get this information from the speaker unless she understood what she was saying and that she was making an informative assertion. Testimony involves the presentation of a reason to believe something by someone who means to be presenting such a reason. There is nothing analogous to this in the extension of the senses. Grice's account took the form it did because he was seeking to capture what is self-conscious in an act of verbal communication and how its success depends on one person aiming to be understood in a particular way by her interlocutor, and for that aim itself to be recognized and understood by her interlocutor. A person who fails to understand what she is saying, or who is speaking in a trance, is not in a position to inform anyone of anything, whereas someone's making some state of affairs evident or obvious to another person need not involve her having any understanding of the epistemic significance of her gesture, or that she is providing a reason to believe something at all. The comparison of testimony with perception leaves unexplained how it matters to the status of the speaker's utterance as a reason to believe its content that the speaker means for her utterance to have precisely that significance as a reason to believe its content, and that if she didn't mean it that way, or didn't mean it at all, her utterance would lose that epistemic significance. In this respect, the comparison with perception is not an improvement on the picture it rightly rejects, according to which access to the speaker's beliefs is what primarily matters, access that may be obtained either by communicative speech or in other ways, and where the epistemic significance for the audience of the speaker's beliefs, unlike that of her utterance, does not depend on the speaker's meaning for them to count for her audience as a reason to believe something. On either picture, the meaning of the speaker's act is that of producing an observable phenomenon whose epistemic significance for the audience is independent of either the speaker's particular understanding of her own act or the audience's understanding of the speaker. The speaker does something that provides her audience with something to interpret and respond to (thereby making some portion of the world noticeable, or making her own beliefs evident), but the epistemic significance of the result to which her audience responds has nothing itself to do with the speaker's own understanding of that result or how she means for it to count for her audience.

It may be a just criticism of the Gricean picture that it presents the speaker as engaged in a kind of unilateral effort to produce a particular effect on the beliefs of her audience, and in this way it fails as an account of interpersonal communication as a social act. Insofar as the Gricean picture describes a particular set of conditions for providing another person with access to her own belief, it seems that this aim could always be fulfilled without there being any actual encounter between the two people, and with the audience on the receiving end being more a private interpreter of the psychological evidence than a genuine interlocutor or partner in the exchange. However, the comparison with perception, or bringing another person to "sensory contact with the state of affairs," is also unilateral in its own way, and does no better in this regard since it provides no place for the social act that two people in verbal communication with each other are engaged in. In retreating from a picture of informative communication as a complex interpretive process of providing and gaining access to each other's beliefs, the comparison with perception still pictures verbal communication in terms of producing a result on another person, and fails to give proper place to the interrelation between the speaker's understanding of her own act and its epistemic significance, and her seeking for it to be understood by her audience, which is the basis for his gaining a reason to believe something.

4.3 Sincerity, Self-Understanding, and Self-Manifestation

We have seen that not all assertions convey knowledge in virtue of assumptions about the beliefs of the speaker (e.g., the examples given of the use of assertions in following proofs or other forms of instruction), but these contexts are also not ones in which the communication of knowledge involves the speaker presenting herself as informant or her being believed by the audience. In the central class of cases in which one person *tells* another person something, by contrast, it seems unavoidable that, considered as a reason to believe something, the speaker's statement will count for nothing if it isn't taken to reflect what she herself believes, or if her beliefs themselves are not seen as likely to be true. What we've seen so far is that the Indicative picture fits uneasily with several of the central features of what makes testimony a distinct source of knowledge, but there is more to be said in explaining how those features which are not captured by the Indicative picture can themselves be understood as contributing to the hearer's gaining a reason to believe something. In thinking about the role of knowledge of the speaker's beliefs, we have drawn attention to a number of features that distinguish the way they are *made known* in testimony, the type of act of presentation in question, from the various other ways that a speaker's beliefs may manifest themselves. The immediate task is to see how these features of verbal expression can be understood as mutually reinforcing in a way that makes sense of testimony as a reason for belief, and explains the normative assumption of sincerity in speech in a way that does not reduce to the question of gaining access to the beliefs of the speaker. The Sincerity condition itself tells us that a speaker's telling another person that P will count for her audience as a reason to believe P, only insofar as the speaker presents herself as believing what she says. The remainder of this chapter raises a set of questions about the meaning of this requirement, insofar as it combines with two other commonplaces about verbal communication (the Sincerity condition being the first one), as instanced in the central cases of telling, promising, warning, etc.

The second of these commonplaces has already entered the discussion, and that is the fact that the accomplishment of such acts presumes that the speaker is not only acting with awareness, but that she knows what she is doing, that she understands the meaning and import of the kind of verbal act she is engaged in. We may call this the Understanding condition on verbal testimony, and it has several dimensions that will be explored later. For now, we can think of it as beginning with the simple condition on the success of speech acts that the person will be acting intentionally and thus aware of what she is doing, and not, e.g., talking in her sleep. Words and cries are produced in all sorts of circumstances, consciously and unconsciously, and another person may learn much from them, but a testimonial reason for belief is only on offer if in the speaking itself the person is acting with awareness and understands what she is doing. More than simple awareness of what one is doing, however, the understanding in question must include both semantic understanding of the language she is speaking, and pragmatic understanding of the kind of speech act that she is engaged in and its broader significance and consequences. Just as promising, for instance, requires an understanding of such things as what it is to commit oneself to another person, to be held to one's word, and to fulfill one's promise, so telling another person something requires an understanding of such things as what it is to provide someone with a reason to believe what one has said, what it is to believe what one is told by someone else. Awareness and understanding of what one is saying is necessary for the accomplishment of acts like telling or promising, but not just in the way that awareness and understanding of what one is doing will normally be a practical requirement of a moderately complex task like unlocking a door or going to the refrigerator and making a sandwich. Actions like these will normally go better under conditions of awareness and understanding, but can also be done unintentionally and even unconsciously. By contrast, understanding what one is saying is not just an enabling condition for an act that might in unusual circumstances be performed without such understanding; rather, for "social acts of mind" like telling or promising, such understanding is a constituent feature of such actions themselves. Actions like asking a question or making an assertion or a promise are essentially and not contingently expressions of awareness and understanding.

The third commonplace requires a word of clarification about the Sincerity condition itself, implicit in what has been said so far. There is an ambiguity in many presentations of the Sincerity condition, between the condition that a speaker *be* sincere, or believe what she asserts, and the condition that the accomplishment of the speech act of assertion (or apology, thanks, etc.) requires the *presentation* of oneself to one's audience as sincere.

In his original presentation of the Sincerity condition for assertions, Searle himself wavers a bit between these two formulations.

> For assertions, the preparatory conditions include the fact that the Hearer must have some basis for supposing the asserted proposition is true, the sincerity condition is that he [the Speaker] *must believe it to be true*, and the essential condition has to do with the fact that the proposition is presented as representing an actual state of affairs. (1969, 64; emphasis added)

But a few pages earlier, when he is discussing sincerity in connection with promising, he is clear that the relevant requirement for the speech act itself concerns the explicit presentation of oneself to one's audience as sincere, rather than what we may think of as one's actual state of mind.

> A promise involves an expression of intention, whether sincere or insincere. So to allow for insincere promises, we need only to revise our conditions to state that the speaker takes responsibility for having the intention rather than stating that he actually has it. A clue that the speaker does take such responsibility is the fact that he could not say without absurdity, e.g., "I promise to do A but I do not intend to do A." To say, "I promise to do A" is to take responsibility for intending to do A, and this condition holds whether the utterance was sincere or insincere. (62)

When Searle speaks here of the "expression of intention, whether sincere or insincere," he is clearly referring to a sense of "expression" defined by a social practice, and not the factive sense of "expression" as indication.[5] The expression of intention is here a social act, and the sense of "expression" is a relational one, the expression *to* some audience of a particular intent. The assumption of responsibility Searle refers to is likewise responsibility to another person. Hence if we are thinking of the Sincerity condition as a condition for the making of assertions or promises, which may themselves be sincere or insincere, then the requirement is for the *presentation* of oneself as sincere.

The distinction made in the previous chapter between an "impersonal" and a "personal" or active sense of expression can now be better put in terms

---

5 It is clear one page later that Searle does not mean to restrict this "social" sense of expression to promising, but extends it to the illocutionary in general: "Wherever there is a psychological state specified in the sincerity condition, the performance of the act counts as an expression of that psychological state. This law holds whether the act is sincere or insincere, that is whether the speaker actually has the specified psychological state or not. Thus to assert, affirm, state (that p) counts as an expression of belief (that p)" (1969, 65).

of a distinction between the sense of expression as indication, or what reveals itself in someone's speech or other behavior, and the sense of expression as a social-relational act addressed to another person. Lying and other forms of insincerity are familiar facts of life, and are only describable as such because a person counts as nonetheless having asserted that P, and thus having expressed the belief that P, even when she had no such belief to give (indicative, factive) expression to in the first place. In the very accusation of insincerity we describe the speaker as having expressed the belief, the desire, or the hope that P when in fact she had no such belief, desire, or hope. In a sense, the social notion of expression of belief through explicit assertion is all on the surface of the encounter: the person counts as having asserted that P, and thus expressed the belief that P, simply in virtue of having deliberately and explicitly *presented herself* in this mode to someone who recognized her as doing so. So the third commonplace, which follows from the social-relational notion of expression, may be called the "Manifest condition" to capture the idea that this form of expression is what it is because the speaker presents herself that way, and this presentation is recognized by her audience. From the side of the audience, the primary meaning of the Manifest condition is that the speaker counts as having asserted or promised, and incurred the responsibilities that go with having done so, even if insincere, simply in virtue of the audience's correctly recognizing her as presenting herself as doing so. As with illocutionary speech acts generally, given the appropriate circumstances, to present oneself to one's audience as telling or promising, where that presentation is recognized by one's audience, is to do the thing itself. The speaker cannot say that she never actually promised or told him anything simply because she didn't in fact have the intention or belief that she expressed, and the illocutionary practices of telling, warning, and promising could not play the roles in our lives they do if this were otherwise.[6]

In his discussion of promising, Hume gives succinct expression to how these three conditions hang together.

> It is evident, that the will or consent alone never transfers property, nor causes the obligation of a promise (for the same reasoning extends to both), but

---

6 Austin marks this early on in *How to Do Things with Words*: "Do we not actually, when such intention is absent, speak of a 'false' promise? Yet so to speak is *not* to say that the utterance 'I promise that . . .' is false, in the sense that though he states that he does, he doesn't. . . . For he *does* promise: the promise is not even *void*, even though it is given *in bad faith*" (1962, 11).

the will must be expressed by words or signs, in order to impose a tie upon any man. The expression being once brought in as subservient to the will, soon becomes the principal part of the promise; *nor will a man be less bound by his word, though he secretly give a different direction to his intention*, and withhold the assent of his mind. But though the expression makes, on most occasions, the whole of the promise, yet it does not always so; and *one who should make use of any expression, of which he knows not the meaning*, and which he uses without any sense of the consequences, *would not certainly be bound by it.* . . . Nay, even this we must not carry so far as to imagine, that one, whom, by our quickness of understanding, *we conjecture, from certain signs, to have an intention of deceiving us*, is not bound by his expression or verbal promise, if we accept of it; but must limit this conclusion to those cases where the signs are of a different kind from those of deceit. (*Inquiry Concerning the Principles of Morals*, sec. III, "Of Justice," n. 13; emphases added)

First, Hume says that "expression" is essential to these forms of binding one-self to another; the mere facts about the person's will, even when known, are not sufficient for such binding. Second, although he speaks of "signs" in this regard, they cannot be natural or indicative signs if, as he goes on to say, the man is "no less bound by his word, though he secretly give a different direction to his intention," for in that case the presence of a contrary in-tention would mean that the interlocutor had simply misinterpreted the actual meaning of the natural sign. The sign seemed to indicate the presence of a certain intention, but the interpreter of the sign was mistaken about this. Rather, the person is bound by her promise in virtue of presenting herself as intending to fulfill it and having that presentation recognized by her interlocutor, despite any secret contrary intention on her part, which gives us a version of the Manifest condition. Third, Hume says that the person is not bound by her words if she does not know the meaning or understand the significance of what she is saying, which is to endorse the Understanding condition. And finally, Hume notes that a person is none-theless bound by her word, even if "by our quickness of understanding, we conjecture, from certain signs, . . . [that she has] an intention of deceiving us." The promise or the assertion is still made, even when we may know "from certain signs" that the person is insincere. Hume's point here only makes sense on the assumption that the sense of "signs" which may reveal to us a deceiving intention, while still preserving the obligations of the promise made, is different from the sense of "sign" in which the person's will must be "expressed by words or signs in order to impose a tie upon any man."[7] If the words of a promise or an assertion were mere indicative signs in the same sense that the furtive glance or the hesitant tone of voice may be signs of the speaker's deceiving intent, then the presence of the latter would undermine our reason for thinking that the speaker's words had in fact expressed any commitment in the first place, and with that would go the obligations of a promise or the assurance of an assertion. We would be in the position of someone who misinterpreted a person's sudden grimace as an expression of pain when it was really an expression of relief, in which case we correct our original impression of what the sign was an indication of. The preservation of the obligation in the face of evidence of insincerity requires tacit recognition of the distinction between what we have called the Indicative sense of "expression," in the manner of a natural sign, and "expression" *to* someone in the sense of a social act. In the same way that mere knowledge of the other person's will or consent is not sufficient for the transfer of property or the obligations created by a promise, so mere knowledge of the promisor's private contrary intention of deceiving us does not obviate the obligations of the promise. In promising or assertion, the person presents herself as sincere, but the accomplishment of the speech act takes place on the level of self-conscious explicit expression and its recognition, and the actual existence of the state of mind that is overtly expressed is neither sufficient nor necessary for this transaction.

4.4 Two Forms of Knowing What One Is Doing

The Understanding condition as applied to illocutionary acts like assertion involves practical understanding of a particular kind, and is accordingly tied to a notion of agency of a particular kind. Knowledge and understanding of what one is doing are important to successful action generally, of course, but not always in a way such that their absence annuls its character as an act of a certain type. Knocking a bottle off a table may be done utterly unconsciously or inadvertently, or it may be done with full deliberate intent. It is the kind of thing that can be "done" by someone who has no idea what he

---

7   And indeed, in the last clause of this sentence Hume may be read as noting the need for a distinct notion of "sign" to cover the overt promise: "but must limit this conclusion to those cases where the signs are of a different kind from those of deceit." I am grateful to Jed Lewinsohn for pointing this out to me.

is doing. More complex actions, such as driving a car, require skill, attention, and a knowledge both of the kind of thing one is doing and of what one is doing *right now*. Such knowledge is employed in the successful execution of the action and, accordingly, will be something that can come in degrees, with the less knowledgeable or less attentive person normally performing the action less well. Someone driving to an unfamiliar address may be a poor driver generally, and may operate under various false assumptions and make particular mistakes along the way, and yet still manage to make it to his destination. In a general sense, of course, such a driver "knows what he is doing" (he is not, e.g., operating the car while in a trance), but in other ways, ones which are indeed relevant to the successful completion of the act, his understanding of what he is doing may be very imperfect. In such a case his execution of the action will be imperfect, but not so much so that it fails to count as intentionally driving to such and such an address. Here his knowledge and understanding of what he is doing play an enabling role toward the end of arriving safely at a certain address, but that end could conceivably have been reached with little or no understanding of what he is doing.

On the other hand, someone uttering the sounds associated with the English sentence, "The rain has finally stopped," but who has no idea what the words mean, or perhaps even that they are words, has not asserted anything, not even poorly. And the utterance of the words, "I promise to meet you tomorrow at three" fails to be a promise at all, if produced under hypnosis, or by someone asleep, or without understanding of what she is saying. The failure of these conditions for the act of asserting or promising do not simply impair it as a good instance of its kind, but destroy its character as an act of that kind altogether. Zeno Vendler puts the point the following way.

> An illocutionary act is not a mere mouthing of a sentence in a certain situation. The circumstances may be right and the sentence well-formed, the 'I' prefixed and the performative verb in its due place—nevertheless, no illocutionary act will be performed if, for one thing, the speaker does not understand what he is saying, or, for another, he does not intend to perform such an act, that is, does not intend his audience to take him to be performing one.[8]

The person must understand what she is doing for her verbal act to be the kind of thing that a promise or an assertion is. A speaker who, in Hume's

---

8 Vendler 1972, 25–26. See also Reid (1788), Book V, sec. 6: "It is obvious that the prestation promised must be understood by both parties. One party engages to do such a thing, another accepts of this engagement. An engagement to do, one does not know what, can neither be made nor accepted. It is no less obvious, that a contract is a voluntary transaction."

words, "knows not the meaning" of the verbal expression or uses it "without any sense of the consequences" has not just done the thing of promising or asserting *poorly*; she has not done it at all. The knowledge and understanding that are necessary conditions for performing such acts as these will naturally include semantic understanding of the language in question, practical knowledge of what one is doing with these words on this particular occasion, and the understanding of the social practices of asking, answering, promising, etc. What matters for the understanding of speech acts like assertion is the general distinction between knowledge the absence of which may impair the execution of an action (as with the driver), and knowledge or understanding the absence of which annuls its character as an action of a certain type at all. The speaker's understanding of her action is not relevant simply to the production of a result that could have been described and achieved without such understanding but is rather constitutive of the kind of action it is. A "social act of mind" like promising or asserting is not just made possible by certain forms of self-understanding but is essentially an expression of a form of self-understanding that aims at a kind of shared understanding with another. In this way, as we will see further, the constitutive role of knowledge and understanding is related to the characterization of the type of act in question, as a form of mutual understanding rather than a unilateral act of producing a result on the beliefs of another, something which might well be enabled by self-understanding of the significance of one's action but is not constitutively dependent on it. The relevance to the epistemology of testimony lies in the fact that, in acts of assertion or telling, if the speaker does not understand what she is doing and the meaning of what she says, then *no* epistemic reason relevant to the content of what she says is provided by her action. Here the provision of a reason for belief in what is said is dependent on the speaker's understanding of what she is doing and the hearer's understanding of the speaker, a form of epistemic dependence that does not obtain, for instance, when the speaker's regional accent reveals where she is from.

4.5 Moore's Paradox and the Meaning of Overtness in Assertion

Taken individually, the three conditions under discussion (Sincerity, Manifest, and Understanding) seem like commonplaces of the ordinary practice of speaking and telling, but together they raise a set of questions about how to understand the actual role of the speaker's beliefs or other states of mind in the exchange. The Sincerity condition tells us that the speaker's utterance must be presumed to be sincere, as reflecting her actual beliefs (or intentions, etc.), if it is to fulfill the function of an act of telling, which is to provide a reason to believe what is said. The Understanding condition tells us that an utterance will not count as an act of assertion or promising if the speaker does not understand what she is doing, either acting without awareness altogether or without the relevant understanding of the kind of act in question (the social practice of the particular speech act and its significance). And the Manifest condition tells us that, when the speaker *is* acting with knowledge and understanding of the relevant kinds, the utterance may still count as an act of telling or promising even when insincere, purely in virtue of the speaker's presenting herself as doing so to an audience who understands and recognizes her act.

Of course no one *wants* an insincere promise or assertion, and even an *insincere* promise or assertion must nonetheless *present itself* as sincere to accomplish anything. The Manifest condition tells us that an utterance may in fact fail to be sincere and yet still be the performance of the act in question: an act of telling or promising. The fact of the speaker's insincerity does *not* annul its character as an act of that type, and, as Hume notes, even if the hearer *knows* that the speaker is insincere, the hearer will nonetheless understand the speaker to have told him that P or promised him to X. Indeed, that is precisely her interlocutor's complaint when he discovers the insincerity: "But you promised, you *told* me . . ." And yet, for the speaker to *announce* her insincerity in the course of her utterance *would be* to annul its character as an act of the type in question. The words, "It's raining out, and I don't believe it" fail to constitute an assertion about the rain, or an assertion of any kind, just as saying, "I promise to pay you back, but I have no intention to do so" fails to constitute any sort of promise.

We can thus see another way in which the *presentation* of sincerity is decisive for the accomplishment of the act in a way that the question of the speaker's actual beliefs or intent is not. It is understood by both speaker and hearer that an act of promising or telling has been performed even when insincere, and it is even acknowledged to have been performed when the interlocutor *knows* the speaker to be insincere. And since, when the speaker's insincerity is known to the hearer, it will surely also be known to the speaker herself, it will thus be true that this insincerity will be known to both of them. If each of them may know this, without this knowledge destroying the character of the act of telling or promising, why then *will* it destroy the character of the speech act for the speaker to *announce* this insincerity in the course of making her statement? To say, "It is raining out, and I don't believe that it is" is familiar as a form of incoherence associated with Moore's Paradox. Coupling "I don't believe it" with the utterance "It's raining out" does destroy its character as an assertion about the rain. Whatever sense may be made of the utterance, it will not be treated by either party as even a faulty assertion about the weather. Here we see that the meaning of the Sincerity condition, as a condition for the performance of certain speech acts, concerns what is overtly presented in the encounter, in the social act itself, and not what may be privately known by each party. If we learn that the speaker does not understand what she is saying, then we don't count her utterance as a promise or an assertion; she cannot count as having assumed the responsibilities that go with promising or asserting. If, however, we discover that she does not believe what she says or intend to fulfill what she promises, this discovery does not annul the character of the speech act. As Hume says, we must not suppose that a speaker about whom "by our quickness of understanding, we conjecture, from certain signs, to have an intention of deceiving us, is not bound by his expression or verbal promise," and nor should we assume that a speaker is not responsible for telling a lie even when we can conjecture from certain signs that she does not believe what she tells us. And what this points to is the difference between the significance of what we may be able to conjecture from certain indicative signs (positively or negatively, as it were) and what a speaker commits herself to in her overt declaration. For the situation is such that even when the speaker and hearer both know that the speaker does not have the relevant belief P when she makes her assertion "P," she will still be understood by both of them to have asserted "P"; and yet if the speaker herself announces this to her hearer, she will *not* have asserted anything.

Clearly, for the conditions on making an assertion or promise there is a decisive difference between what each person in the encounter may *know* (about the other's beliefs or intentions) and what is made genuinely *explicit* between them, what they share as common ground in their discourse. We could imagine a situation of what is called "mutual knowledge" in which the hearer knows "from certain signs" that the speaker addressing him does not in fact believe what she is saying, and where the speaker in turn, by the quickness of her own understanding, discerns that her interlocutor mistrusts her sincerity, and where the speaker's awareness of the hearer's mistrust is picked up on by the hearer himself, up through whatever levels we may like, without this producing the cancellation of the speech act that would result from the speaker's saying outright to her interlocutor that she does not believe what she is saying. The Moore-utterance would not simply make evident what both parties already know, and in the absence of any such overt announcement, no iteration of levels of knowledge they may each have about the other's beliefs concerning one other would have the consequence that the speaker had failed to make a lying assertion (transparent and unsuccessful perhaps, as lies often are). Beyond the fact that the truth about the speaker's beliefs has *revealed* itself, become known mutually, is the fact that in the Moore's Paradox statement the speaker is *presenting herself* to her interlocutor as disbelieving what she said in the first part of her utterance. It is thus not either the *fact* of insincerity or the *knowledge* of the speaker's insincerity ("mutual" or not) that is incompatible with the performance of the act of telling someone something, but rather the overt presentation of oneself to one's audience as not believing what one says.

Thus, what matters for the accomplishment of an act like assertion, and thus for the provision of a reason for believing someone's assertion, lies on the level of the explicit presentation of oneself in speech, as opposed to everything that may reveal itself in one's speaking and other behavior. We are now in a position to see how these three conditions (Understanding, Sincerity, and Manifest) work together to form the conditions for a speaker's capacity to make assertions in the first place. If a person can *say* anything with words at all and not simply pronounce them, if she can affirm some proposition in speech, then she clearly must be able to *present it as true* as a public act, and have that presentation be recognized and taken up. It is the accomplishment of this act that makes for the specific possibility of believing what is said, and hence the communication of knowledge through testimony. Only when it is determined which particular speech act is being performed by someone's utterance is there a possibility of believing what the speaker says or believing the speaker. The performance of some other illocution, such as asking a question, does not provide the possibility of believing what is said, though of course, like the revelation of a person's regional accent, it may provide the occasion for believing something about the speaker or her beliefs. But it is paradigmatically an assertion that provides a candidate object of belief, and to assert that P is to present P as true and hence as belief-worthy. The positive meaning of the Sincerity condition follows from this since to present P as true to one's hearer means to present P as belief-worthy as such, for both speaker and hearer, and not just the hearer alone. For the speaker to affirm some proposition as true to her audience is to thereby present herself as in possession of the same truth, and its believability cannot be thought to apply to the hearer alone and not to the speaker as well. The reliance on the idea of truth in assertion means that the speaker must present her statement as expressing a truth they now hold in common, rather than as a way of producing a result in the mind of the hearer. Rather than aiming at an effect on the hearer's beliefs, the speaker making an assertion must present herself as *sharing* the truth of P with her interlocutor. The role of truth in assertion means that the parties to the exchange must understand the nature of the act of telling or informing not as a unilateral one but instead as part of a common activity.

This puts the Sincerity condition in a different light from that suggested by the Indicative picture of the expression of belief. The assumption of sincerity matters not because this will often provide our best (but fallible) guarantee of access to the speaker's beliefs, which is all that really matters in the exchange, but rather because the presentation of oneself as believing what one says follows from the understanding of the speech act in question as presenting the proposition as true to one's interlocutor, and hence as a truth they share. We can see this by considering the "positive" version of Moore's Paradox, that is, an utterance of the form "It's raining out, and indeed I *do believe* that it is," which is as fully paradoxical as the more familiar "negative" forms. The peculiarity of this version consists in the fact that, in the course of an apparent declaration about the rain, the speaker presents her own belief in that fact as *additional information* for the audience. But if the audience is to take the first part ("It's raining out") as an informative assertion about the *weather*, he must take himself to already know, or be entitled to believe, that the second part is true ("and I believe it"—that is, that the speaker believes it). If it were truly an open question for the audience whether the speaker is even presenting herself as believing what she is saying, then it would be an open question whether the speaker is presenting the first part ("It's raining out") as something *true*, which would leave it open whether the audience is presented with something as a candidate for agreement or disagreement, that is, as an assertion rather than some other speech act or none at all. So, for the audience to see the utterance "P" as a reason to believe that P, he must see himself as already entitled to believe that the speaker herself believes that P. Suspending that assumption would mean suspending the question of what illocution, if any, is being performed by the speaker with her words, and apart from the question of the utterance being part of an illocution such as assertion, there is no question of either believing or disbelieving what is said. Further, we can see that the assertion that "P" will be canceled by the overt presentation of oneself as not believing it, even if that very statement of disbelief is *itself* insincere. That is, the person who says, "It's raining out, and I don't believe it" may nonetheless actually believe that it *is* indeed raining out (she was lying in the second part, about not believing that it's raining). However, the private presence of *that* positive belief of hers doesn't matter, for it is her explicit presentation of herself as *not* believing it which cancels the utterance as an assertion about the rain, and not her actual state of belief.

It is natural enough to think of the kind of self-presentation in question as a public performance which necessarily leaves open the question of the speaker's sincerity. In one way this is right, but in an important way it is not right. It is right in that the audience may hear the speaker tell him that P, and not yet know whether she is speaking sincerely. That question is open. But the question of the speaker's sincerity is not open in the following sense: If the audience is to understand the speaker as making some kind of statement at all, even if responding to it with doubt and suspicion, he must understand her to be presenting herself to him as sincere. That question is not an open one for him, for it is a condition of understanding or knowing how to respond to the speaker's act as an informative assertion *at all* that he understand it in those terms. In that sense, as a condition for the comprehensibility of the social act they are engaged in together, the question of the speaker's presentation of sincerity is not for him an open question. This is not to say that he must assume the speaker really is sincere, but that if he is to make sense of her act as one of telling or asserting at all, and thus know how he is to respond to it, he must relate to it as something that gives itself out as sincere. If the speaker announces that she does not believe what she says, this means that the audience cannot understand what the speaker could mean to be *doing* in addressing these words to him, and hence cannot understand what *he* is to do in response. The audience cannot understand his own *role* in this exchange ("Is something being presented for belief or agreement or not?"). By contrast, when the speaker is insincere but does *not* announce this to her audience, the meaning of the encounter will yet remain clear to the audience. If the audience *knows* that the speaker does not believe what she is saying (where the speaker has not announced this), then he *does* understand what the speaker is doing perfectly well. For in that case he understands the speaker to be engaged in the familiar practice of making a lying assertion (or to be just kidding, etc.), and the audience will understand what modes of response and reply will make sense for him here.

The Moore-utterance cancels the speech act of assertion by undermining the assumption that something is being presented as true and thus as a candidate for belief. The act misfires because it fails to provide a place for the possible responses of agreement or disagreement with what is said on the part of the addressee. Contrary to the appearance suggested by much philosophical discussion of the topic, assertions are rarely made in "one-off" situations by a speaker who utters some words within the hearing of another person, with the intent of influencing his beliefs in a certain direction, and who then disappears from the scene. Verbal interactions between people can approximate to this, of course, but acts of telling and the like are normally part of an ongoing conversation within which each party alternates between the roles of speaker and hearer. The particular illocutions that speakers express to each other within a conversation make for different possibilities of response within the conversation. For instance, being asked a question makes for the possibility of replying to it with an answer or replying that one doesn't know the answer, or asking another question. One can ask a question without wanting to know the answer, or even without wanting any reply at all, but it still belongs to the kind of speech act that a question is that understanding it means understanding the specific forms of reply that it calls for. Similarly, it belongs to the nature of being *told* something by someone that it opens up the possibility of replying in the form of agreement with what is said, disagreement, or replying with a question. Aside from the possibility of an overt verbal response, being told something also provides for the possibility of believing or disbelieving what is said, which again are different forms of response from those provided for by the asking of a question. (Someone's question may be suspicious or insincere, but as a question it does not provide for the possibility of believing or disbelieving what is said.) The comprehensibility of the original speech act of assertion depends on the comprehensibility of such responses of agreement, denial, belief, or doubt. There is only the kind of reason for belief on offer that an assertion provides if the making of it provides a place for a set of possible replies by the person being addressed. In undermining the assumption that the speaker is presenting the proposition as true, the Moore-utterance undermines itself as an assertion in that it fails to define a set of possible replies from the person it is addressed to. While understanding that people can indeed disbelieve what they say, the interlocutor is nonetheless at a loss to understand how the utterance could be seen as presenting a proposition as true if the speaker does not present herself as sharing that same truth with him. There is no place for the interlocutor to make a reply, on the assumption that both parts of the Moore-utterance are indeed addressed to him as part of a single illocutionary act. For the assertion would not be canceled, and the interlocutor would still occupy a space of possible replies to it, if the second part of the Moore-utterance ("and I don't believe it") were said to someone else, turning away from him as the original addressee. Even if they were all within earshot of each other, the first interlocutor, to whom only the first part had been addressed, could reply to it as an assertion which he now had excellent reason to believe was untruthful and could bring this up against the speaker. That is, he could still respond to the first half as presenting to him a proposition for belief, and with this he would understand the possibilities of reply open to him in the conversation. But with both parts addressed to him in a single conversational act, he would be at a loss to understand his own role in the conversation. Open hypocrisy can make for delicate conversational maneuvering, but it is still different from conversational breakdown. Assertion and testimony do not always in fact involve the actual continuation of the conversation, but a speech act proposing itself as an object of belief must nonetheless make sense of the role of the interlocutor in the exchange and the set of possible responses his interlocutor's act opens up for him. The possibility of believing what is said requires that the potential object of belief be expressed in a particular illocutionary form (e.g., as an assertion rather than a question), one which creates the reciprocal possibility of certain forms of reply (e.g., agreement or disagreement, "yes" or "no"). From here we will see further reason to reject the unilateral model of linguistic communication in terms of the production of a result on the mind of another, whether as associated with the original Gricean formulation or with the comparison with perception.

Various philosophers have remarked on what John McDowell calls the "special overtness which is characteristic of verbal communication."[9] We are now in a position to see that this overtness is not a matter of making

---

9 McDowell 1980, 40. This is emphasized in the Strawson article that McDowell is responding to (Strawson 1964; McDowell 1980, 32), as well as in the writings of Grice and Austin that Strawson is responding to, and more recently in Robert Brandom's *Making It Explicit* (1994).

something obvious or hard to miss but rather of how the interlocutors
address each other in the context of conversation. For we have seen that a
speaker's disbelief in what she says may be known to her hearer, and this
realization may itself be known to the speaker, etc., without this knowledge
they each have annulling the character of the assertion. What is incompatible with the assertion P is not either the fact or the revelation of the
speaker's non-belief in P, but rather her declaration of her non-belief in P to
the same person to whom she presents that assertion. Hence the difference
is made not by what is "mutually known" by the two parties (in the sense of
a set of higher-order beliefs they may each entertain about each other), but
rather by their being in a position to address each other, with the interplay
between first-person and second-person pronouns, as in "I'm telling you
that it's raining out and I don't believe it." It is only when both parts of the
utterance are spoken to the same person addressed as "you" that the speech
act of assertion undermines itself, and not when the speaker makes it known
in some other way that she does not believe what is asserted. The difference
made by "overtness" thus cannot be made out without appeal to the idea
of one person addressing another, in a context where it would make sense
for each party to use the second-person pronoun in referring to and in
addressing the other. And *that* difference, the difference made by a genuine
encounter between the two people, cannot be made out by any elaboration of further levels of beliefs and intentions they may have with respect
to each other ("mutual knowledge"). The significance of sincerity in verbal
communication is thus not that of a best approximation to the telepathic
ideal of one mind's immediate access to another, for that would still leave
out the actual encounter that goes with addressing and being addressed by
another person, where each party has distinctive and alternating roles to
play. The souls described by Plotinus, whose mental lives are utterly transparent to each other, merely know everything that is to be known about
each other, and are not yet in communication with each other. For in
overcoming the need or the possibility of externalizing themselves in overt
forms of expression, they are by the same stroke removed from the forms of
encounter between minds made possible by what Reid calls "social acts of
mind," and thus the knowledge they have of each other remains essentially
unshared (perhaps "mutual" in the "higher order" sense but still private
and unshared). The assumption of sincerity in speech is not a substitute for
such undifferentiated transparency, but rather follows from a practice that
defines the possibility for a speaker to share what she knows with another

speaker by overtly assuming responsibility for its truth, by presenting her utterance with the specific illocutionary force of an assertion and having that recognized by her interlocutor. It is only when *that* question has been settled, and it is understood that an assertion has indeed been made, that the hearer takes a reason to believe something to be so much as on offer. Prior to the fulfillment of the conditions for the performance of that speech act, the epistemic reasons relevant to believing what one has been told have not yet come into play.

5

Illocution and Interlocution

5.1 Addressing, Claiming, and the Second Person

Recent discussions of what is called "correlative" or "bipolar" normativity have emphasized the dimension of moral and legal obligations that relates specific individuals to each other in pairs such as promisor and promisee or debtor and creditor, as contrasted with generalized norms that relate a person either to the moral law as such, or to the promotion of some good. In such a relationship, one member of the pair is obliged to recognize the demand of a specific other person upon her (whether to pay back the debt, fulfill her promise, respond to a complaint, etc.). There is more than one notion at play in these discussions, but several of them center around the correlativity of person-directed rights and duties (i.e., a duty *to that person*), and the idea of *claiming* a right or demanding recognition. In chapter 1 we saw how natural it is for the notion of rights to express itself in terms of claims and assertions (e.g., Feinberg 1970), and in his recent development of the idea of "second-personal normativity" Stephen Darwall refers to Feinberg's formulation, and lays equal stress on the notions of claiming and affirming in characterizing the normative realm in question (Darwall 2006, 18, 121, and 138). The situation of one person addressing another is treated as paradigmatic of the type of relation he has in mind, whether it be making a promise, or a contract, or telling someone to get off your foot. The act of addressing another person in speech is presented as in some way emblematic of this type of normative relation between people. If this is so, it raises the question of how the fact that claiming, demanding, and promising, etc., are all specifically verbal acts reveals something of the structure of "relational normativity" in general, as well as how the most basic acts of speech, such as simply saying something or claiming something to be true, rely on a dimension of something like relational normativity.[1]

One broad tradition of thinking about assertion sees it as a kind of social act in which a speaker makes herself responsible for the truth of her assertion that P (Peirce 1934), entitles her interlocutor to the belief that P, licenses the reassertion that P (Brandom 1983), or overtly commits herself to the truth of P (Searle 1969), where the force of "overtly" here is that of a public commitment to some possible audience (and not simply the sense of being "committed to the truth of P" just in virtue of *believing* P itself).[2] Theories of assertion in this tradition place it as a speech act squarely in the context of interpersonal communication, the transfer of truths from one person to another, and the acts of entitlement and commitment underlying such transfer would thus seem to belong somewhere in the normative realm of correlative or relational normativity. This appearance is strengthened by the fact that, as we have seen, the very acts of addressing, claiming, and asserting themselves are so often presented as exemplars of the form of second-personal relations, by Darwall as well as others. In this light, however, Darwall's discussion is of special interest, not only because he has given one of the most well-worked out versions of this idea, but more specifically because it is important to his story that the realm of "second-personal reasons" is restricted to *practical* reason, and has no analogue in theoretical reason. The notion of second-personal reasons themselves, he says, marks "a fundamental difference between theoretical and practical reason" (22). Even while still just getting into view the idea of "second-person reasons," one can see the point of such insistence. In promising someone to do something, for example, a speaker may be said to create a reason for doing something in incurring a (second-personal) *obligation* to do it, an obligation that does not precede the promise itself. By contrast, in the act of *telling* someone that P, it is the understanding of both speaker and audience that the truth of P *does* precede any act of telling, and does not itself depend on the interpersonal act relating of speaker and audience itself. The truths in question in ordinary testimony are matters

1 There are by now several different developments of related notions in Weinrib 1995;Thompson 2004; Stone 1996 and 2001; Darwall 2006; and others, and I will not be concerned here to keep their specific differences straight, hoping that the general notion I develop here will be clear enough.
2 This is not an uncontested tradition of thinking about assertion. See MacFarlane 2011 for a very helpful discussion of this tradition in comparison with some of its contemporary rivals.

of theoretical and not practical reason. At the same time, it is surely not accidental to the idea of communication through testimony that what the speaker presents and what the audience responds to is a speech act of a particular kind. Speakers do communicate truths to each other, by means of the particular speech acts of asserting, claiming, and telling. That much should not be a matter of controversy. It is in responding to illocutions of *this* form that a recipient of testimony believes, doubts, or disbelieves what was said, and may believe or disbelieve the speaker herself. If, as suggested by the broad tradition of thinking about assertion in terms of relations of entitlement and overt commitment, this aspect as social act is what makes an utterance so much as a candidate for belief, we need to understand better how this social aspect of assertion can be the vehicle for the communication of ordinary theoretical truths, which are not themselves "bipolar" or relational in nature.

5.2 Theoretical Reasons and Their Transmission

A central theme in the development of the contemporary idea of the "second-personal" is that of reasons which by their very nature depend on the authority of a person to address them to another.[3] Darwall illustrates this with the case of someone standing on another person's foot, and the demand that he remove it.

> Unlike reasons for belief and practical reasons one might give in advice, reasons of this kind are second-personal in their nature. Their very existence depends on being able to be addressed person-to-person. Unlike the reason having to do with the simple badness of your being in pain, the fact that you can and do reasonably demand that he move his foot simply would not obtain

---

3 My focus here will be exclusively on reasons or norms which are second-personal in a sense which depends on an explicit act of address, made by one person to another. Darwall, for one, is equally interested in a broader notion of the "second-personal" which encompasses one's relation to the "moral community" as such, apart from any explicit acts of address or recognition (e.g., "Moral obligations involve implicit demands that are 'in force' . . . even when actual individuals have not explicitly made them" [2006, 290 n. 22]), and he remarks that reactive attitudes themselves "implicitly address second-personal reasons to the violator" (60). For questions concerning this extended sense of the second-personal, see Lavin 2008 and Wallace 2007.

but for the common competence and authority to enter into second-personal relations of reciprocal address. (Darwall 2006, 59)

Thus, there are reasons which refer to the simple badness of someone's being in pain, which are independent of that person (or creature) having any standing to complain, let alone having made an actual complaint. For now, we may call these "monadic" reasons (Thompson 2004), in that their status as reasons does not in its very nature relate two people to each other, aligning them in a two-place relation of complainant and complainee. Rather, both parties may be said to relate themselves individually, and in the same way, to an independently obtaining normative fact, the badness of this pain. To this is contrasted the reasons which obtain only in virtue of the fact that one person, with the authority to address complaints and demands to another, makes such a demand that the other person get off her foot. In doing so, the person making the demand does not "simply point to a reason holding in normative space" (Darwall 2006, 259), as might any independent observer of the situation, but rather purports to direct a claim upon a particular person and hold him responsible. Reasons such as this by their very nature express a relationship between the two people, like that of debtor and creditor, which grounds the force of the reasons in question in the nature of their relationship to each other, rather than in how each of them is related to an independent order of value.

It is this contrast between reasons which depend on the authority of one person to address another person, and reasons which obtain independently of any such relationship binding them, that suggests that the idea of the second-personal marks a divide between practical reason and theoretical reason. Immediately after the passage just quoted Darwall says,

> I argue therefore that the authority to address practical reasons can take forms that are quite different from the epistemic authority that is presupposed by theoretical reason-giving or by other forms of practical reason-giving, like advice, where the reasons are not second-personal. (2006, 59)

This contrast is thematic in Darwall's account, but it is ambiguous between a claim about the monadic nature of epistemic reasons themselves and a picture of how epistemic reasons are given by one person to another in ordinary testimony.[4] And it is here that the role of speech and addressing in testimony and in the notion of the second-personal itself matter to each other.

---

4 Kukla and Lance (2009) argue that, in either the practical or the theoretical domain, Darwall fails to clearly distinguish the "second-personality" of the pragmatics of speech acts from a

For while the confrontation with evidence is an unmediated relation, for
example, between a person and a photograph, the speech act of asserting or
telling is second-personal in its very nature, something establishing different
and complementary relations between speaker and hearer. In describing the
relation to evidence as unmediated, I mean that a person's epistemic relation to the photograph does not depend on any other person's relation to
the photograph or attitudes toward it (as discussed in 2.5). But with respect
to an *utterance*, the speaker and hearer stand in essentially different relations
to it, and this difference in roles is essential to how the utterance comes to
be a reason for belief in the first place. The status of the utterance as a reason
to believe something depends on how the speaker makes herself accountable in speech, and that determination is a matter of the speaker's authority
to declare herself to her audience. The audience, for his part, cannot occupy
or usurp that role but must instead defer to the authority of the speaker to
determine what sort of reason is or is not on offer here. Unlike the monadic
relation which they may each separately bear to the photograph as evidence,
the constitution of the utterance as an illocution of telling requires the two
parties to be playing distinct but reciprocally related roles in the exchange.
So while we may agree that epistemic authority itself is a monadic notion, it
wouldn't follow from this that the verbal transmission of epistemic reasons
was a monadic affair like the confrontation with evidence.[5]

"second-personality" of reasons themselves, and express skepticism about the latter idea. See
Jeremy Wanderer's "Alethic Holdings" (2014) for a particularly insightful discussion of some of
the issues raised by Kukla and Lance's book.

5 For a discussion of Darwall, testimony, and the second-personal that understands the reasons
for belief in testimony to be themselves "second-personal" in nature, see McMyler 2011. In a
related discussion (critically sympathetic to McMyler), Berislav Marušić (2015, chap. 7) argues
for the possibility of a kind of "rational doxastic partiality" in the context of certain forms of
testimony. I believe that both thoughts rely on an understanding of what is "relational" in the
act of testimony that is different from the account developed here. Neither doxastic partiality
nor the second-personality of reasons for belief follow from the thought that the transmission
of knowledge in testimony proceeds by believing the speaker that P, where that is understood
as something different from either simply believing the proposition expressed, or inferring to
the truth of that proposition from the speaker's behavior (i.e., relating to the speaker as what
Craig [1990] calls a "mere source" rather than as an informant). Through testimony we learn by
believing speakers who are self-consciously presenting themselves as informants, and if we have
truly learned and come to know something in this exchange, we are then ourselves in a position to occupy that same informing role with respect to an indefinite number of interlocutors,
who may in turn come to know what we tell them. This is a primary way knowledge circulates
in the world, beyond the original speaker and interlocutor. I think the way the idea of a "relationship" between speaker and hearer is understood by McMyler and Marušić makes this
feature of ordinary testimonial transmission difficult to understand. The sense of the interpersonal developed here is not "affective" but rather concerns the reciprocal roles of speaker and

If these features of ordinary speech acts of telling and informing point to a genuine contrast with the confrontation with evidence and suggest that the interpersonal act of telling must be relevant to its character as a reason to believe something, any such account will still want to accommodate the genuine differences between the role of the second-personal in the communication of practical and theoretical reasons. A speaker's epistemic authority is a matter of her relation to the independent facts, not her relation to her interlocutor. The speaker reporting some fact does not constitute something as a reason for belief the way the complainant makes her very complaint a reason to get off her foot, for instance. If the speaker giving testimony has reasons to offer in favor of believing something, they have that status as reasons independently of her, or the fact that she is presenting them to another person. Further, theoretical reasons are not agent-relative in the sense described by Darwall (9). The complaint directed to the person standing on one's foot directs a reason to *that person*, a reason of a different kind from an impersonal reason to anyone who might be in a position to improve the situation. By contrast, a theoretical reason, a reason to believe something, cannot be agent-relative in this way. If one speaker addresses another and swears to the truth of some assertion, her interlocutor will indeed have a special claim against her should she turn out to be wrong or deceitful, but in making this declaration the speaker does not take her assertion to count as a reason for belief that applies exclusively to the person she is addressing, having no application to someone outside their particular relationship. In swearing to the truth she commits herself to her interlocutor, but what she swears to is an ordinary public truth.

5.3 Perlocution, Illocution, and the Idea of a Normative Power

The second-personal aspect of testimony, and the authority that is relevant to it, is tied to the verbal nature of testimony, specifically the illocutionary dimension of speech acts like telling and asserting. Hence, in bringing it into view we need to distinguish epistemic authority from another kind

interlocutor in a "social act of mind." (See Wanderer 2013 for a discussion of McMyler which deploys a helpful distinction between what he calls "philial" and "transactional" senses of interpersonal relationship in the context of thinking about testimony.)

of authority, the authority of the speaker to constitute her utterance as an illocution of some kind, and hence to make it count as, e.g., a statement rather than a question, and thus as a possible object of belief. This is a capacity of any mature speaker of a language that is as fundamental to communication as the command of the syntax and vocabulary of one's language. For a speaker to be in a position to *say* something, state some truth by some form of words, it is not enough for the utterance to be correctly formed. The speaker must be recognized to be in a position to determine that her utterance counts as either the statement that this is so, or the *question* whether it is so, or the representation of someone *else's* belief that it is so, etc. It is here that the difference between the audience's relation to the speaker's *utterance* and his relation to the speaker's *beliefs* becomes important. For when Darwall speaks of "epistemic authority" as outside the realm of the second-personal (123), he is thinking of one's relation to another person's presumed knowledge or beliefs. But the second-personal aspect of testimony relevant here is in the first instance a matter of one's relation to the speaker's *utterance*, where what counts is the speaker's authority to determine its particular illocutionary status, a status it has as part of a social-relational act in that the illocution is essentially something made *toward*, or with respect to, another person. When confronted with someone's utterance, the assumption that the speaker is both knowledgeable and sincere is of no use to an interlocutor wishing to be informed unless he knows how to understand what speech act the speaker is performing with those words. Without that knowledge, the interlocutor will have no idea what relation the speaker's words might bear to her belief regarding its content, let alone what her belief itself may be. Hence, the speaker's illocutionary authority must first be recognized before her epistemic credentials can be so much as an issue for her audience. The illocution of asserting or telling is what makes the utterance so much as a *candidate* for belief. It is what makes it possible for there to be a question for the addressee of believing *what the speaker tells him*, that very thing.

As described in previous chapters, the notion of "expression" relevant to assertion and other illocutions is not in the first instance a psychological notion or a notion of behavioral manifestation (3.3). The relevant notion of expression is rather that of an intentional act of self-representation, an act of the person as such, directed to some other person. In claiming P as true, a speaker expresses *to* some possible audience the belief that P, by way of affirming the truth of P itself. For the verbal acts of telling, claiming, or warning, the way that the utterance comes to be a reason for belief (or, indeed, a reason for *dis*belief) is dependent in a familiar way on *how* the speaker presents her utterance. In presenting her utterance as a promise, for instance, rather than as an exercise in diction, the speaker exercises the authority to constitute her utterance as having the illocutionary significance of a promise. The relevance of the notion of authority here lies in the fact that, not only is the speaker free to present her utterance one way or another, but also this ability to make her utterance count as one illocution rather than another (or none at all) rests with the speaker alone. This is not to say that the speaker's role in determining which illocution she is performing guarantees her against the various forms of misfiring, but rather that no other person makes it count as a particular illocution of claiming or promising (successful or not).[6] This distinguishes the place of authority in the *illocutionary* dimension of a speech act from that of its *perlocutionary* dimension. For while the speaker plays an authoritative role in determining the illocutionary status of her utterance (e.g., as promise or assertion), the speaker does not play a similar role in determining what Austin calls the perlocutionary effects of her speech (e.g., as persuading, alarming, or annoying).[7] The question of the perlocutionary status of one's speech, e.g., whether one has succeeded in persuading or annoying one's audience, is something that the speaker does not pronounce upon with any authority. Another person (her audience, for example) may well know better than she does about the actual perlocutionary effects of her speech.

Since Austin (1962) first developed the notions of the illocutionary and the perlocutionary, it has been clear enough that the former notion is to

---

6 As Austin emphasizes in his original presentation of these ideas (1962), various background conditions must be in place for an ordinary illocutionary act to come off, including the recognition or "uptake" on the part of the audience, and the speaker's authority only obtains under the assumption of these background conditions. Hence, for example, some illocutions such as passing a sentence or adjourning a meeting depend on the speaker occupying a particular institutional role and being in a particular institutional setting. Absent these conditions the speaker has no authority to determine which illocution is being performed. The following discussion concentrates on the more basic illocutions that any mature speaker of a language can be recognized to perform, such as telling, promising, or apologizing.

7 This distinction will come in for more discussion soon, but for now we may settle with Austin's characterization of the illocutionary as what is done *in* uttering some words, as in promising or requesting, as opposed to what is done *by* uttering them, as in surprising or annoying. Speaking of the perlocutionary, Austin says, "Saying something will often, or even normally, produce certain consequential effects upon the feelings, thoughts, or actions of the audience, or of the speaker, or of other persons: and it may be done with the design, intention, or purpose of producing them" (1962, 101).

be understood in terms of the enactment of the speaker's commitments, as shown in the central cases of promising and asserting. In his analysis of speech acts, William Alston (2000) is explicit about the relation of the illocutionary quite generally both to the speaker's authority and to the adoption of a specific normative stance toward another person. As Alston puts it,

> Take some P that I am capable of asserting and a sentence, S, that is usable to assert it. Then in uttering S it is wholly up to me whether I am thereby asserting that P rather than, for example, practicing pronunciation or giving an example. Whatever it takes to make my utterance of S the former rather than the latter is something I can institute at will. (2000, 36)

In speaking of something which is "up to me" or which "I can institute at will," it must be a specific notion of agency that Alston has in mind. For the bare invocation of freedom does not distinguish the freedom that is relevant to the basic act of saying the words involved, as with any action of the speaker, from a notion of agency which is relevant to gaining a specific illocutionary status for one's utterance. Hence the need to distinguish the agency that is specifically relevant to the illocutionary as the normative power involved in delimiting one's claims and responsibilities: "An utterance is most basically made into an illocutionary act of a certain type by virtue of a normative stance on the part of the speaker" (71). For the central case of assertion, the nature of the illocutionary is understood in terms of the speaker making herself responsible to her audience for the truth of the proposition asserted.[8] In making an assertion rather than practicing pronunciation, the speaker makes it the case, among other things, that she is now subject to a range of criticism or forms of assessment to which she would not otherwise be subject. This is an aspect of the difference made by the "normative stance" expressed in her presenting her utterance in the guise of one illocution rather than another (or as no illocution at all). Hence the specific freedom in question is not to be understood simply as the freedom involved in making something happen, not even in making some normative

---

8 There is a progress of formulations of the illocutionary in Alston's book, all of which employ the notion he abbreviates as the act of "R'ing" on the part of the speaker, which is defined as follows: "In uttering S, U took responsibility for its being the case that P" (2000, 55). Thus, in filling out the formula we have: "In uttering S, U R'd that P—In uttering S, U knowingly took on a liability to (laid herself open to) blame . . . in case of not-P. . . . [T]aking responsibility for P is something that U *does*. It involves U's *instituting* a state of affairs, rather than just being a matter of U's *recognizing* an already existing state of affairs (55).

difference, but more specifically in the second-personal terms of making oneself responsible toward another person in specific ways. Thus the normative stance that defines the category of the illocutionary, as well as its more specific instantiations (e.g., as the particular act of warning rather than promising, etc.) is itself a matter of relational, or second-personal, normativity. That is, it is not only that the speaker assumes a certain responsibility for her action (e.g., takes responsibility for its consequences), but more specifically that in illocutions generally the speaker makes herself responsible in particular ways *to* another person. It is in the nature of an illocutionary act to be undertaken toward another person, to be an act performed with regard to, or to, another person, as in "I told *him* the news," "I asked *him* to leave," "I warned *her* about the car."

The notion of a normative power, as developed by Joseph Raz and others, is itself often illustrated by reference to the speaker's relations to the speech acts she performs, and specifically with respect to the contrast between the instituting of a different normative relation between people (illocutionary) and the effects, both normative and non-normative, which the speaker's words may produce (perlocutionary). And this is only natural given the close relationship between the very idea of the illocutionary and that of the exercise of a normative power. We can see several of the elements of this idea in the following example from Raz:

> Imagine that John wants to know whether he can rely on Harry giving him a lift to town tomorrow. Harry tells him: "I am almost certain to offer you a lift to town tomorrow. In the circumstances it would be far wiser for you to rely on me rather than make alternative arrangements, but remember, I do not promise anything, I am merely advising you." Harry is intentionally inducing John to rely on him but he does not promise anything. Promising is surely more than inducing reliance, by promising I bind myself and confer a right on the promisee. (1972, 99)[9]

The speaker here says that he is not promising but merely advising. In this example, the speaker (Harry) means to fix or restrict the normative relation with respect to his audience (John). While displaying a kind of perverse fastidiousness about the precise commitments he is prepared to make, Harry is nonetheless exercising a familiar capacity in his speech. He *is* advising, but

---

9 For more on normative powers, see Raz 1999. Early in his book, Darwall cites Raz's 1972 paper in the context of describing "a distinctively second-personal kind of *practical authority*: the authority to make a demand or claim" (2006, 11).

he is *not* promising, and he *may* offer a lift tomorrow, but has not done any offering yet. In saying, "Remember, I do not promise anything, I am merely advising you," he announces that the normative power to promise is his to exercise here, but he is choosing not to exercise it in this speech act. It is understood by both parties that in saying "I do not promise . . ." he has in fact *not* promised. That is, he assumes, and is credited with, a particular authority over the question of how his words are to *count* with respect to John. And in this, he speaks with a different authority than he does with respect to the question of inducing reliance by his words or other actions. Harry fully expects and intends that his words will have the effect of influencing John to rely on the fact that he will give him a lift tomorrow. We may speak here of Harry's words having the perlocutionary effect, the intentional effect, of encouraging John to rely on him for a lift. In doing so, he undoubtedly incurs a certain responsibility for inducing this reliance, especially should he change his mind and leave John high and dry. But while incurring this responsibility, Harry presents himself to John as declining to assume another responsibility, one associated not only with creating reliance in John, but with binding himself and conferring a right on John, a specific right of complaint should he fail to come through with the ride. It is assuming or declining *this* responsibility that is specifically an exercise of his normative powers as a speaker and moral agent.[10] The conferral of a specific right of complaint on John is an alteration of the normative relation between them, and it is an alteration which he is acknowledged to be free to make or to refrain from making. It is an alteration in a different sense from that produced by his statement that he will almost certainly offer John a lift tomorrow. That verbal action of his would change things certainly, and may make Harry liable to blame should he change his mind and fail to alert John. But the alteration in the case of actually promising or offering is of a different sort, and is the exercise of a different capacity on Harry's part, specifically the capacity to make something he does *count* in a certain way, rather than

10 Compare Reid: "As the contract is binding without any regard to the purpose, so there may be a purpose without any contract. A purpose is no contract, even when it is declared to the person for whose benefit it is intended. I may say to a man, I intend to do such a thing for your benefit, but I come under no engagement. Every man understands the meaning of this speech, and sees no contradiction in it: Whereas, if a purpose declared were the same thing with a contract, such a speech would be a contradiction, and would be the same as if one should say, I promise to do such a thing, but I do not promise" (1788, Essay V, chap. VI, "Of the Nature and Obligation of a Contract," 336).

the capacity knowingly to produce certain effects.[11] In this case, he exercises the speaker's authority over whether his words are to count as a promise or another kind of statement of intent. And the difference this makes is not in the first instance a difference in the effects produced. Promise or no promise, John *could* always complain should Harry not show up in the morning with his car, and the fact of a promise might make no difference to the likelihood of his complaining.

While the exercise of such a normative power is an expression of the person's autonomy, and belongs to the authority of the speaker to determine what illocution his words perform, it is at the same time a normative power that is undertaken with respect to another person, and hence involves two distinct freedoms. In conferring a certain illocutionary status on his words, the speaker in the example deliberately and explicitly alters the status of his action so as to expand or restrict the scope of his accountability to the other person. Hence this is one way in which the normative power described above is at once an expression of the speaker's autonomy and of his ceding a certain authority to others. Within bounds, it may be up to him to determine whether in his speech he has promised or merely advised, but once having done so, it is *not* up to him to decide whether, for instance, he has faithfully kept his promise, or whether his advice was helpful or well timed. The power exercised in this act is a power governing one's relations to others, and while the speaker's freedom is expressed in making his utterance count as a promise or a piece of advice, what the speaker thereby accomplishes is that he is now subject to a range of assessment (e.g., as to whether he has *kept* his promise, or given *relevant* advice) the authority over which is given over to the freedom of others, or at any rate shared with them. The freedom invoked in Alston's account of the illocutionary is thus not simply the power to produce effects, nor simply the self-assertion of autonomy, but must be seen as the freedom to make oneself *subject* to the freedom of another, in specific ways.

So a certain dependence on the freedom of another person is already contained in the normative power described in the account of illocutions thus far, given that the normative status that is conferred on the utterance is a relational normative status. The illocution is addressed to another person, and in making it count as a promise or a piece of advice the speaker at

---

11 On this distinction, see Tamar Schapiro: "Whereas empirical power is the power to make things *happen*, authorial power is the power to make things *count*" (2001, 111).

the same time grants a related authority to her audience, in that now her words are subject to a range of assessments from the other person to which they would not otherwise be subject (e.g., the responsibilities that go with having *told* someone something about the rain in Spain, rather than having only uttered the words). However, there is a prior involvement of others in the speaker's ability to confer a particular status on her words, one that adds a further dimension to the authority that is specifically illocutionary and its second-personal dimension. For naturally the speaker can only appeal to the freedom of another person, and bind herself to it in specific ways, if this appeal is *recognized* by the other person. The names "illocution" and "perlocution" describe different aspects of the assessment of speech as an action. A given utterance may have the illocutionary status of an assertion and the perlocutionary status of being, e.g., an insult or an incitement. Both dimensions involve recognition on the part of the speaker's audience, but they do so in quite different ways, and the speaker's authority is correspondingly different with respect to these dimensions of the speech act. A well-known marker for the illocutionary is the possibility of naming the action in the very performance of it, with the inclusion of the demonstrative "hereby" before the performative verb; as in "I hereby warn you, promise you, congratulate you . . ." Assuming the conditions of what Austin calls the "uptake" of the performative (e.g., that the speaker is heard and is recognized to have the authority to perform the kind of act in question), the speaker explicitly assumes the power to declare that she has indeed, then and there, performed that very action. Normally, for someone to declare to another person that she warns or congratulates him, is for her to have done that thing, and done so in the very saying itself. But a familiar difference of the *perlocutionary* is that the speaker is *not* in a position to make it the case in her declaration itself that she has indeed insulted, persuaded, or surprised her audience. Unlike the performance of an illocution such as "telling," the perlocutionary does not admit of announcements of the form "I hereby persuade (or insult) you."[12] And yet both aspects of the speech act obviously aim at and depend on the recognition of the audience, so both the authority and the recognition involved in the illocutionary must be of a particular kind.

---

12 On this and much else relevant to the topic, see Cavell 2006. See also the discussion in Anthony Laden's *Reasoning: A Social Picture* (2012) within a broad and illuminating account of reasoning within an ongoing conversation.

5.4 Recognition and Reciprocity

It is in seeking to make out the specific difference between the illocutionary and the perlocutionary that Jennifer Hornsby (1994) identifies what she calls the "Reciprocity condition" for illocutions. What she notes under this heading is that, for there to be an illocutionary dimension of speech at all (and hence for speakers to be able do things like tell or invite), there needs to be a reliance on recognition between speakers that is *sufficient* for the speaker to have done what she presents herself as doing. She first motivates this idea by reference to John Searle's account in *Speech Acts* (1969).

> Searle was quite explicit about the crucial element of what is going on here, which he illustrated for the speech act of *telling A that P*. "If I am trying to tell someone something . . . as soon as he recognizes [that I am trying to tell him], I have succeeded. . . . Unless he recognizes that I am trying to tell him [it], I do not fully succeed in telling it to him" (Searle, 1969: 47). . . . What reciprocity provides for on this account is the success of attempts to do certain speech acts. It allows there to be things that speakers can do simply by being heard as (attempting to and thus) doing them. (Hornsby 1994, 193)

In the passage she quotes, Searle shifts between a claim of necessity ("unless he recognizes") and a claim of sufficiency ("as soon as he recognizes"), but since Hornsby's target is specifically the different roles of recognition in the perlocutionary and the illocutionary, her concern is with the apparent *sufficiency* of recognition for the success of the *ill*ocutionary dimension of speech. This is the ordinary ability of a speaker to perform a verbal act of claiming (or warning, or refusing . . .) sheerly by being recognized as meaning to do so.

> Illocutionary acts (such as stating or warning) are those things for which reciprocity suffices—things which, even if they can be done without anyone's taking them to be done, are such as to be done when an audience takes them to be. (Hornsby 1994, 198)

And Hornsby's general thesis is this:

> The line between illocutionary and perlocutionary comes between those acts on the one hand which need invoke only reciprocity to have their proper consequences, and those acts on the other hand which invoke either more than reciprocity or something quite else. (1994, 195)

For a speaker to succeed in telling someone something, it is normally sufficient for her to be recognized by her interlocutor as meaning to tell him,
where that means both seeing that this is her intent and recognizing that, as
a speaker, it is indeed up to her whether her utterance is to count as telling,
denying, or conceding.[13] The success of the illocutionary is in this way "especially immediate," in that there is no further thing the speaker needs to
do or hope for once the recognition expressed in the Reciprocity condition has been secured. Under these circumstances of mutual recognition the
speaker can say, e.g., "I *hereby* tell you, warn you," and thus declare what she
is in fact accomplishing in speech with an authority that she cannot claim
when it is a question of perlocutionary acts like comforting or persuading.
The speaker can do this because she is announcing this to the very audience whose recognition of her intent is sufficient for the success of acts of
this type.[14]

In this way, while authority and recognition are conditions of the success
of both the perlocutionary and the illocutionary they play different roles.
When we say that the act of illocution *aims at* being recognized by its audience, this is something that it has in common with perlocutions like comforting or insulting. But in the case of perlocutionary acts, the recognition
by the audience of the intent to comfort or persuade is at best necessary and
never sufficient for the accomplishment of the aim.[15] Or perhaps it would
be better to say that for perlocutionary acts the recognition of the intent
can only contingently be sufficient for success. For in a given situation a
person might well be comforted, or insulted, simply by the recognition that
in this person's act she overtly *means* to comfort or insult him. By contrast,
the illocutionary force of an utterance, which is the prior condition for its
having the status of an assertion or an act of telling, has an internal relation

---

13 Illocutions such as telling or claiming are basic to being a speaker at all, while others, such
    as commanding or sentencing, are dependent on occupying some institutional office. For
    illocutions which are dependent on the holding of some office, the recognition of what the
    speaker means to be doing in her utterance will not be sufficient if it is assumed that she does
    not, in fact, have the authority to perform such a speech act.

14 Is recognition always *necessary* for the performance of an illocution? Hornsby notes the am-
    bivalence we sometimes have over describing someone as "trying in vain to warn" and having
    warned all right, but without succeeding in alerting to the danger (1994, 197). Whatever we
    decide about particular cases, however, it cannot be denied that the act of warning, like other
    illocutions, *aims* at being recognized and fails to complete itself without it.

15 See Bach and Harnish 1979: "In general, hearer recognition of perlocutionary intentions is
    incidental to the production of perlocutionary effects. . . . What distinguishes illocutionary
    intentions, we suggest, is that their fulfillment consists in their recognition" (12–13).

to the recognition of its audience, for it is made possible by that very recognition. Insofar as the speaker's audience sees that in this verbal act she is intending to warn, promise, or tell him something, then the speaker has in virtue of that fact succeeded in warning, promising, or telling him. And this sufficiency is not something which contingently obtains in this or that instance, but is a defining feature of the illocutionary as such, the kind of act one means to be performing.

The sufficiency of recognition for illocutions is also part of what is essentially overt or manifest in "social acts of mind," as expressed in the fact that, for instance, a "false promise" is still a promise, as false testimony is still testimony (Austin 1962, 11). The sense of "false" in speaking of a false promise is thus not like the sense of "false" in "false pearls," for the responsibilities that are incurred with a promise or an assertion are not dispelled by the fact of one's insincerity.[16] In the realm of the second-personal and the illocutionary, the manifest appearance counts as the deed itself, whatever mental reservations the speaker may harbor. As discussed in the previous chapter, if a speaker is recognized as having presented herself as freely assuming the responsibilities of a promise or an assertion toward another person, then she has done so, whether or not she has the intention of following through. It is the sufficiency of recognition that distinguishes the illocutionary from the perlocutionary dimension of an ordinary speech act, because it is the illocutionary dimension that expresses the ways in which speakers render themselves accountable to each other (as well as restrict those forms of accountability in specific ways), as opposed to the other ways in which they may hope in their speaking to have some kind of influence on each other.

5.5 The Observer's Perspective and the Perspective of the Interlocutors

Here we are in a position to see how the possibility of acts for which the recognition of meaning to perform them is sufficient for their success belongs to the understanding of both speech acts like "telling" and the structures of relational normativity generally, as well as how implicated with

---

16 As Bernard Williams puts it, "in the phrase 'insincere promise,' the word 'insincere' is not what the scholastics called an *alienans* term, that is to say a qualification which weakens or removes the force of the term that it qualifies (as 'bogus,' 'imitation,' 'pretend,' etc.)" (1973, 215).

each other are the speaker's illocutionary authority, on the one hand, and her making herself subject to the freedom of another. At various points the comparison with other illocutions like promising has been useful for bringing out the dimensions of the speaker's authority to constitute her utterance as a particular illocution that binds her to her audience in a particular way and gives that audience some new set of reasons. Prior to the act of promising her interlocutor to mail his letter, the speaker was free to do or not do that thing, but now having made the promise the speaker has a reason (an obligation) to mail the letter, and the promisee has a reason to believe that this is what the speaker will indeed do. Both sets of reasons are grounded in the completion of the act of promising itself. But the sense of the illocution of "telling" as a social act does not mean that the speaker presents herself as reporting to her audience a truth which consists in the meaning of the speech act itself, something that would not be true but for her statement. To the contrary, it is part of her understanding of what she is doing, and the understanding she wishes to communicate to her audience, that she is communicating some fact whose truth precedes and is independent of her statement itself. It might be thought to follow from this that the illocutionary aspect of the act of telling, the sense in which the speaker binds herself to her audience in "making herself responsible for its truth" (Peirce), cannot be relevant to the reasons for belief gained by the audience. Here again one could appeal to the situation of one person overhearing a conversation between two other people. When the speaker promises her friend to mail a letter for him, she commits herself to her friend, and in doing so she not only incurs an obligation but also provides him with an epistemic reason to believe that his letter will be safely delivered. The friend's reason to believe this about his letter is grounded in the speaker's overt commitment to him. Another person who overhears this exchange between the speaker and her friend and who has no reason to doubt the sincerity and fidelity of the speaker will now *also* be in a position to conclude that the friend's letter will get mailed.[17] And yet, it will be pointed out, the overhearer has not received any commitment of any kind from the speaker, so therefore the reasons for belief that a speaker provides in acts of telling

17 This point is emphasized in my original 2005 paper (22), now incorporated into chapter 2 of this book, where I also stress the disanalogies as well as analogies between telling and promising. This seems to have been missed by Lackey (2008, 224), Schmitt (2010, 232), and Owens (2006, 117–18).

cannot depend on forms of "making oneself responsible" that characterize illocutions like telling. The conclusion does not follow, however, for while the overhearer's epistemic reason for believing that the speaker will mail the letter is not dependent on any commitment the speaker made to *him*, this reason is dependent on the speech act in question being a committed one and not, e.g., part of the recitation from a phrase book or the rehearsal of some scene. Were the utterance overheard not part of any committed illocution, the overhearer would not gain any reason to believe something relevant to its content.[18] The differences between assertions and promises remain, of course. In promising, the speaker commits herself to some performance, to making something true, where the performance and the truth are "up to her," something she can fulfill, whereas in ordinary assertion the truth that is claimed is not up to the speaker and is not presented as such. This is perfectly true, but *making* some proposition true is not what Peirce or others have in mind in connecting the act of assertion with "making oneself responsible for its truth." Rather the claim concerns making oneself *accountable* for the truth of what is claimed, so that the speaker shall be held to account both for the meaning of the claim and for its truth should it turn out to be false. For the speaker, making herself accountable in this way *is* something that is fully "up to her" in the relevant sense. She might have remained non-committal, but now that she has made her assertion, the eventual truth or falsity of the claim has consequences for *her*, for she will now turn out to have spoken truly or falsely, with justification or without, etc. If the speaker had not explicitly staked herself on this proposition in her speech, thereby making herself accountable for its truth, then neither her audience nor anyone overhearing her would have any reason to believe what she said, since she would not have "said" anything in the sense of claiming something as true.

We have seen that, unlike other ways in which someone's behavior may provide another person with a reason to believe something, a speaker's utterance only has the status of a claim or assertion insofar as the speaker is acting with the understanding and awareness of what she is doing. In the absence of such awareness and understanding, no claim or assertion is made, and there is therefore no possibility of believing or disbelieving what

---

18 Elizabeth Fricker makes a similar point: while one may well learn something by overhearing a conversation, "that there is such an entitlement available depends on the fact that the utterance is an audience-directed speech act" (2006, 598).

is claimed or asserted, and no reason for believing something connected with the meaning of the words. This condition on the accomplishment of illocutions like assertion has no parallel for other acts by means of which we may inform or draw someone's attention to some fact. What is done when a person shows her friend something by pointing across the room may indeed be more effectively accomplished when she knows and understands what she is doing and what she is showing to her companion. And her success in bringing him to see something may in various circumstances be made more likely if this person takes her to be doing so knowingly and intentionally. But the role of acting intentionally and with understanding (and the audience's recognition of such intention and understanding) is a contingent factor in such success, an enabling condition for success in some circumstances and not others. The reason for belief gained by the audience (or observer) on such an occasion does not depend on the agent's acting intentionally or understanding the epistemic import of her own behavior. The connection between the first person's behavior and the reason for belief gained by her audience or observer would be the same if the observer's attention was drawn to the other side of the room by her involuntary and unconscious glance. From the perspective of what I've called the Indicative picture it doesn't matter to the epistemic position of the audience or observer that he is confronting an intentional act, an involuntary response, or any kind of action at all.

This point has been expressed in terms of the condition that an act with the epistemic significance of a claim or assertion depends on the act being performed intentionally and with awareness and understanding of its import. And according to the Manifest condition for illocutions (4.3) a speaker will count as asserting that P in virtue of presenting herself as doing so to an audience who recognizes her as so presenting herself (an act of self-presentation that, from the first condition, is understood to be self-conscious and intentional). As a social act, then, the speaker counts as expressing the belief that P in virtue of this interplay between overt self-presentation and recognition, even if she in fact believes otherwise. From the perspective of the classical epistemological situation of the observation of objects and events and the interpretation of the evidence they provide, these conditions can seem hard to understand. For the evidence of a person's belief (or other attitude) in her behavior does not depend on her awareness or understanding of that evidence, and on this model it will be difficult to see how someone's behavior could *become* evidence for her belief just in virtue of being presented that way. But if we are looking at the act in question as a social act involving the explicit assumption of responsibilities by one person toward another, these two conditions will seem perfectly appropriate. For the explicit assumption of a particular form of accountability is precisely an expression of the person's freedom whose enactment requires the person's awareness and understanding of what she is assuming, and making oneself accountable to another person in specific ways is accomplished in presenting oneself to that person as doing just that, and having that self-presentation recognized and taken up. The Manifest condition governs the practice of voluntarily assuming relational responsibilities with respect to each other: the person is bound insofar as she *presents herself* as binding herself to another person who "acts a part" (Reid) in a reciprocal act of recognition or uptake. The responsibilities are assumed in the overt social act itself and remain in force whatever private thoughts and feelings one may have to the contrary. The way that an assertion provides the audience with a reason to believe what is asserted is not by way of providing evidence for the speaker's belief (for such evidence may be provided with or without the speaker's understanding and awareness) but rather by way of the speaker's overt commitment to her audience concerning the truth expressed, with the speaker's expression of belief as a byproduct of that overt presentation of a proposition as true.

Unlike the reasons that are constituted by an act of promising, the facts which make someone's assertion true or false are independent of any "normative powers" exercised by the speaker or the act of address itself. But it doesn't follow from the fact that theoretical reasons may be said to be "there anyway" that when a speaker presents her statement as true to her audience, she is doing something other than *informing* her audience of that very fact and can instead only be said to gesture at the evidence for its truth. In making her statement, the speaker *declares* the truth in question, and does not simply do something that makes its truth noticeable, as she might in showing a photograph or the broken china lying on the floor.

A story about speech and testimony that places a notion of human communication at the center of its account will insist that, in addition to other ways in which one person may acquire knowledge of something from another person's behavior, there is the phenomenon of acquiring the knowledge of P *from another person* (and not simply from "what she does," or the "state of affairs" of her belief-state) because that person overtly communicated that very knowledge to him. The truth in question, and the reasons in favor of it, may be said to be "there anyway," but at the same time we must describe the way in which this truth, these reasons, are directly and openly communicated from speaker to audience by means of the speaker's intent to do just that, contingent on the audience's recognition and under-standing of her act. There is no way to understand ordinary speech on the assumption that the only way genuine theoretical reasons can be conveyed from one person to another is through a medium whereby one person's understanding of what she is doing, and another person's understanding of her, are irrelevant or incidental to the conveyance of reasons (as they are in the case of the photograph). The communication of reasons between people through overt commitment and entitlement is not a supplementary way that reasons get around in the world, but is internal to the notion of reasons themselves. Human communication (informing, reporting, telling, etc.) is the transfer of knowledge (or misinformation) between people, and it accomplishes this as the direct aim of an intentional activity, conducted by people who understand themselves to be doing just that. The transfer of knowledge is not something that happens *in spite of* what they do or as the byproduct of what they do (as with what may be revealed by the speaker's regional accent), but rather as the very meaning of what they do. And the participants in this practice take the *fact* that they *mean* to be communicating knowledge to each other to be central to the preservation and transfer of epistemic reasons from one to another. It is not seen as accidental to the preservation and transfer of epistemic reasons that the speakers understand themselves to be conveying a particular truth to an audience who needs to understand them if they are to learn the truth they are seeking to convey.

We have stressed the first-personal aspect of the speaker's knowledge of what she is doing in her illocution, and we are now in a better posi-tion to see why it matters that this is the form such knowledge takes, and how this differs from the speaker's knowledge of the perlocutionary effects of her utterance. If we are conceiving the illocutionary act in terms of the self-conscious exercise of a normative power with respect to another person, then we can see the speaker's awareness of which illocution she is performing as a matter of how she is staking herself in the utterance, and thus as a form of practical knowledge. This is not something she learns from observation of herself, nor is it a question to be answered by another person.

At the same time, however, the speaker's "illocutionary authority" is other-dependent in that, as mentioned above, the content of *what* she knows (which illocution she is performing) must include the perspective of the other person on her performance. This dependence is connected with the general notion of authority, for the speaker's illocutionary authority obtains insofar as it is recognized by others to obtain. This is perhaps most clearly seen when we consider that ordinary illocutions exist along a spectrum from the minimally institutional to the fully bureaucratic and judicial. While any mature speaker can expect to be recognized as being in a position to ask a question or declare an intention with a form of words, only certain people holding certain offices can do things like adjourn meetings or commute sentences by means of their authority to constitute their utterances as the illocutions in question. The institutional context is present throughout the spectrum of illocutions; it is just that it embraces a more or less universal class of speakers and a more basic set of speech acts at the minimally institutional end.[19] In speaking of the "illocutionary authority" of the speaker, and the normative power to constitute her utterance as having some illocutionary status, there should be no suggestion that this is somehow a kind of unilateral authority, or that the various illocutionary statuses in question are not, like other statuses generally, dependent for their very substance on being recognized by others. The speaker may be said to "confer" a certain illocutionary status on her utterance, but only against an institutional background that is not hers alone, and with the cooperation of the others in her speaking community.

And even prior to the illocutionary dimension of speech, there are several dimensions to the dependence on, and incorporation of, the other person's perspective on one's act for its own self-understanding that are basic to the idea of ordinary discourse. The speaker incorporates the perspective of her interlocutor in the unfolding of her action itself, in facing her addressee, and speaking at a volume that she imagines will be loud enough for him to hear and understand her. In so doing, she adopts an imaginative perspective on her own performance of how it may appear to her audience. Doing so is not merely the entertaining of a kind of outside perspective on her own action, not merely the incorporation of that perspective in thought but also in her action itself. In the progress of her speech act she seeks to conform her performance to this imagined point of view so as to be perceptible and comprehensible to that other person, since the very point of what she is

---

19 This spectrum of the institutional context of what I've been calling "illocutionary authority" relates to the broader political context of Hornsby's essay, as well as the issues raised by Miranda Fricker (2007) and others.

doing is to make herself understood. In both the first-person understanding of her act and in its actual guidance the speaker must incorporate the perspective of her addressee.[20] At the same time, it is also part of the speaker's perspective on her act as a communicative one that her interlocutor is to incorporate *her* perspective on what she is doing, that the success of communication here depends on her addressee understanding her act as she herself understands it. The success of her act depends on her own reflective practical understanding of its meaning (illocutionary and otherwise) being adopted and shared by her addressee, and on his doing so because they see themselves as participants in the same practice. The relevant incorporation of another perspective on one's act and including that in one's own reflective understanding of it is not the same thing as taking an "outside" perspective on what one is doing, something that each of the parties could do separately. The speaker does not imagine a third-person perspective on her act but rather a second-person one, that of her addressee; in adjusting her performance to this perspective she is not speaking so as to be overheard by an observer, but rather inhabiting the perspective of a shared participant in a practice, the shared consciousness of what they are doing together.

20 This mutual incorporation of perspectives is, of course, not restricted to linguistic communication, and there is by now a great literature in developmental psychology and elsewhere about the emergence in play and other activities of what Tomasello calls "conceptual perspective-taking." See Tomasello 1999, 128 and 170–73.

6

The Social Act and Its
Self-Consciousness

6.1 The Bearing of the Agent's
Understanding on the Description of What
She Does

Toward the end of her book *Intention*, Elizabeth Anscombe says that many of our descriptions of happenings are "directly dependent on our possessing the *form* of description of intentional actions" (1976, sec. 47). She notes that while "offending someone" is something that can be done unintentionally (and indeed unknowingly), there would be no such thing as offending someone if this were not something normally done intentionally. This distinguishes "offending" from descriptions of happenings and activities like "sliding on the ice," which while it describes something that *may* be done intentionally refers to something whose concept does not depend on the form of description of intentional action. But the range of descriptions that do so depend is vast and encompasses most of the descriptions we give of human activities and happenings. Within this class of descriptions she makes a further division, between "descriptions in which a happening may be intentional or unintentional" and "those which can only be voluntary or intentional." The first list includes "offending," "abandoning," and "kicking" and other descriptions relating to the vital movements of animals. These descriptions are linked to forms of activity that are normally directed and under the creature's control, but whose conditions of accomplishment do not depend on their being intentional in a particular instance. For our purposes, it is the second list that is interesting, those descriptions under which an action can *only* be intentional, for it includes "telephoning, calling, greeting, signing, signaling, paying, selling, buying, hiring, dismissing, sending for, marrying and contracting." In the context of the present discussion what is striking about this list is that it both encompasses Reid's initial list of "social acts of mind" and could easily be seen as a continuation of it.[1] Anscombe does not return to this point in the remainder of *Intention* (the ensuing discussion is restricted to the first list and the dependence on "vital descriptions"), nor does she in that book mark any particular "social" character in the descriptions in the second list. It is in her later essays on promising and related topics that she picks up the thread of this principle of division and its significance for understanding the form of self-understanding that characterizes social acts of mind.

First, however, what would it mean to say that a certain class of action descriptions can *only* apply to actions insofar as they are "voluntary or intentional"? From within the perspective of Anscombe's understanding of intentional action generally it will mean, among other things, that these descriptions apply to someone's action only insofar as the agent is aware of what she is doing under that description and where this awareness is not based on observation of herself. Hence, as we have been arguing with respect to illocution in particular, to describe an action as one of "signing," "selling," or "hiring" will be to do so on the assumption that the agent in question is aware that this is what she is doing and understands its significance. This distinguishes acts of these kinds (or under these forms of description) from other human acts which are normally perfectly voluntary and intentional, like "offending," "abandoning," or "kicking," but whose character as acts of *those* kinds does not depend on their being done intentionally or with awareness and understanding of what one is doing. What is the nature of this dependence of the applicability of a certain action description on the assumption that the agent in question was aware of what she was doing and that this awareness was of a certain type, i.e., the nonobservational knowledge associated with "practical knowledge"? And what could this condition (which we can see as a version of what we've been calling the Understanding condition for illocutions) have to do with the social character of the acts on Anscombe's second list? She begins her paper "On Promising and Its Justice" with the following question and challenge:

---

1 I have omitted "groping" and "crouching," the latter of which Anscombe admits may be a doubtful example.

> What bearing can what the agent thinks have on the description of the action? If an action is a physical happening, someone may want to say that a physical happening is what takes place, whatever the agent thinks. Such things as marrying, making a gift, swearing an oath seem to be counter-examples. It is essential to getting married, as it is to the other things, that someone who is doing it should think he is doing it. ([1969] 1981, 10)[2]

Here the concern is more focused on the dependence of the action description on "what the agent thinks" rather than on its character as "voluntary or intentional" (as in the passage from *Intention*) but the point is the same. The phrase "what the agent thinks" is less than ideal in this context, since it suggests something more like a mere set of thoughts the agent might be entertaining about what she is up to, and obscures the connection with Anscombe's own earlier idea of "practical knowledge" which she is clearly drawing on here.[3] Drawing out this connection helps in understanding the nature of the dependence she has in mind between the applicability of a certain action description and the agent's own understanding of the act. The section of *Intention* containing the two lists is immediately followed by the section in which she makes her famous invocation of the dictum from Aquinas that "practical knowledge is the cause of what it understands" (1976, 87). It is only briefly indicated in that context that this point concerns the *formal* dependence of an action description on the agent's practical (i.e., nonobservational) knowledge of what she is doing.[4] The thought is that the description of something done, such as "breaking an egg," will apply to it as an intentional action only insofar as that description is known to the agent, and where that knowledge is not had by observation of herself. It may be that another description such as "breaking the only egg left" also applies to what was done, but if this description is not known to the agent, then, for Anscombe, the action does not count as intentional as so described. The agent's "thought" or her "practical knowledge" of what she is doing is the "formal cause" of the (intentionally described) action itself, in that the

---

2 The same question in nearly the very same phrasing and with the same examples occurs near the beginning of "Two Kinds of Error in Action" ([1963] 1981), which opens with a discussion of the legal maxim "Fraud vitiates consent."

3 In any case, in the parallel formulation in her paper "Two Kinds of Error in Action" ([1963] 1981) Anscombe is happy enough to invoke the idea of knowledge, as when she says, "There are some descriptions X of things done that cannot hold unless the subject knows that he is doing X; for example making a contract" (4).

4 I discuss the idea of the "formal dependence" of intentional action on practical knowledge of what one is doing in "Anscombe on Practical Knowledge" ([2004] 2017).

applicability of a certain description to the action (intentionally "breaking an egg") is formally dependent on the agent's nonobservational awareness of what she is doing, as so described.

However, the idea of formal dependence comes into sharper relief when taken up in connection with the action descriptions in Anscombe's subdivision, that is, those she says can *only* be done intentionally, such as marrying and contracting. It is with respect to *these* that she says, "there are events such that their occurrence is formally dependent on the thought that they occur."[5] For the description itself ("breaking an egg"), while it may often enough be the description of an intentional action, is not as such a description of something done which is formally dependent on the thought of its occurrence. The description "breaking an egg" applies just as fully to what someone is doing whether or not it is part of an intentional action or done with practical self-knowledge. But for the explicitly social acts in her subdivision, such as marrying or contracting, the applicability of these action descriptions at all is said to be formally dependent on the agent's awareness and understanding that she is doing that very thing. What is the difference in the role of such self-awareness here, and what does it have to do with the social character of the action types in the second list of Anscombe's subdivision? Many action descriptions, such as those in Anscombe's first list, identify an action in terms of the result aimed at and achieved (e.g., offending someone, switching something on or off), and hence we can describe *what* the agent is doing or has done in terms of the production of a result. The result can be identified extensionally and is not itself formally dependent on it being the content of self-aware intentional action. We can describe the desired result independently and we can thus describe circumstances in which the result was produced inadvertently or unconsciously.

Among things done through speaking, "offending" will belong with the perlocutionary rather than the illocutionary. It can be done wholly unconsciously, even though, as with ordinary actions, success here may well be aided by care and attention to what one is doing (Wilde: "A gentleman is someone who never gives offense unintentionally"). But even when it is something done intentionally and with full awareness, the applicability of the description ("offending") is not dependent on that fact. In one sense, of

---

5 Anscombe [1969] 1981, 2; or more briefly: "facts which are formally dependent on human thought of them."

course, "offending" is a social act in that it takes place against a social background of cultural expectations and meanings, as when one causes offense by failing to observe the rules of some custom or the local formulas of politeness. Offending essentially involves more than one person, at least one of whom is responding to the other (difficult to imagine the conditions for "offending oneself"), but it is not a social act in the full-blown sense that necessarily involves both people in mutual awareness, and with both parties understanding the part each plays in the act in question. Insofar as "giving offense" is the description of the result of one's remarks, that result is specifiable independently of any reference to the speaker's intent or awareness of that result. The role played by the speaker's knowledge and understanding of that result is contingent. That is, there need be no such agent-awareness for the result, so described, to be produced, and when such awareness *is* present, it either plays an inhibiting role (as when the offense is unintentional and unwanted) or it plays an enabling role in ensuring and perfecting the production of just that result.

What is contained in the idea of a set of action descriptions which *only* apply insofar as the act is performed intentionally, and what is the significance of the fact that the actions Anscombe lists under this heading seem overwhelmingly to be social acts of mind, and indeed to be the names for various illocutions? It is striking that Anscombe herself does not pursue this question explicitly in the later essays on promising which raise the question of the bearing of "what the agent thinks" on the nature of the actions of that sort, but we can draw out a few implications. Something already suggested is that action descriptions in this category will not be descriptions of actions in terms of results which could in principle be produced in some other way. Both "breaking an egg" and "contracting with someone" are descriptions of getting something done, but "contracting" does not refer to a result which could be described independently of a social practice and the self-understanding of its practitioners. Unlike "breaking an egg," the description of the thing done in the case of illocutions and other social acts of mind is the description of something for which there is no purely extensional way of picking it out. It is a perfectly contingent matter that some broken egg is the result of a human action, whereas the reality of a contract or an act of apology is essentially and not contingently an enactment of the understanding of the action as being precisely a contract or an apology. And indeed we describe acts like selling, buying, hiring, and contracting in terms of "coming to an understanding," the idea being that the act itself, the thing done, just is arriving at a certain shared understanding among the parties and hence not some independent result that could be picked out or aimed at apart from such understanding. Something else suggested by the idea of an action description whose application is formally dependent on the agent acting knowingly and intentionally is that the agent's knowledge (or awareness or understanding) is seen as a constitutive element of the action-type itself, rather than as an antecedent causal condition for successful production. The question of the bearing of "what an agent thinks" on the description of an action is the same as the question of the role played by the agent's awareness and understanding of what she is doing on the reality of the action itself. The relation of the agent's knowledge to what it is that she knows (her act, her illocution) is not like the knowledge-relation someone may have to an object or result external to her because, for this category of things known, their being consists in, is formally dependent on, the agent's knowledge embodied in them. It is not knowledge that can be explained by appeal to any contingent relation between a knower and some object of knowledge (e.g., as with perceptual knowledge), for here the object of the agent's knowledge, the illocution, is itself a form of self-understanding.[6]

Earlier, in chapter 4 (4.4), we distinguished two different roles that an agent's knowledge can play in the success of an action. Knowledge can play an efficacious or "enabling" role with respect to achieving a result independently conceived, such that ordinary practical and theoretical knowledge, as well as ordinary care and attention to what one is doing, will be contingently but reliably related to success. The person who knows what she is doing will do a better job and be more likely to produce the result aimed at. By contrast, for certain action descriptions, knowing and understanding what one is doing will be a constitutive condition of doing the thing at all, and not just an enabling condition for doing it well. If the speaker does not understand the language she is speaking or if she is speaking in her sleep she cannot be said to assert or promise anything at all. We can now say: her awareness and understanding of what she is doing is the formal condition for the applicability of action descriptions such as "asserting" or "promising" to what she does.

6 For a related discussion, see Anton Ford, "Action and Generality": "It bears emphasis that getting married depends on knowledge, not merely as an efficient cause but also for its own internal constitution. It is not as though the agent's thought were instrumental in bringing about something whose existence we could perfectly well understand on its own. . . . This means that a person's knowledge that he is getting married is related to its object quite differently than his vision is related to its object" (2011, 101).

We might ask at this point how it could be, or what it means to say, that there is a class of action descriptions which only apply insofar as the action is performed intentionally and with awareness, and what that has to do with the apparently social character of the actions listed in Anscombe's subdivision. Even for actions which are "social" in the sense that their accomplishment involves the coordination of more than one person it may be contingent to the result that it was achieved intentionally and consciously. From this point of view it may seem unmotivated to carve out a subclass of such actions which are such as to *only* be done intentionally and with awareness, where such awareness is the formal condition for the applicability of that description of the thing done. However, one natural way to motivate the category of actions satisfying those conditions would be to describe the class of actions which aim at being recognized as such, and indeed whose success *consists* in such recognition (as in Hornsby's Reciprocity condition). An act of this kind could *only* be one the description of which was formally dependent on the parties' practical self-consciousness of what they are doing, for it is the very aim of such an act that this self-consciousness (the self-understanding of the act) be mutually recognized. This would not be to claim that *only* a social act can make sense of Anscombe's subdivision, but we would be claiming that social acts (acts which aim at and are completed by the recognition of another) can only be understood within Anscombe's subdivision, as acts which can *only* be intentional, and which are formally dependent on the agent's understanding of them as such.

Anscombe herself does not point up the social character of the action descriptions whose intentional and self-aware character are constitutive rather than contingent, and when in the later essays she does relate this condition to the *formal* dependence of the action description (e.g., "promising," "contracting") on "what an agent thinks," the emphasis still seems to be on the constitutive role played by the thoughts of an individual agent. What we can see now, I believe, is that clarity about the very idea of a class of action descriptions for which a form of self-awareness plays a constitutive role is helped by bringing the social character of the actions in question into more explicit focus. For there is something misleading, or at least incomplete, in the phrasing of her initial question about the bearing of "what an agent thinks" on the description of the action, since it is of the essence for actions of this type that there is more than one person involved and that they *share* an awareness and understanding of what they are doing together that is constitutive of and not merely an enabling condition for the completion of the act in question. These acts are not only forms of intelligibility

the way any intentional action is, but actions which consist in *making* themselves intelligible to another intelligence "who plays his part" (Reid). The
speaker and her interlocutor must both be aware of and understand the
speaker's utterance, and they must understand together what illocution is
being performed by these words. Hornsby's Reciprocity condition tells us
that such shared understanding is not only necessary but sufficient for the
accomplishment of an illocutionary act. The shared understanding and recognition of the illocution in question is the formal cause of that which is
understood by the two parties, the social act of mind enacted by them.

6.2 The Illocutionary, the First Person, and "Hereby"

The social act of accepting . . . admits only of the present tense. To the
"I have inwardly assented" and "I shall inwardly assent," there is on the
other side only the "I hereby accept." *One should not overlook the distinctive function of the "hereby."* It refers to an event which is happening
along with the performance of the act, that is, to the "accepting,"
which here as it were designates itself. By contrast, there is no least
sense in saying, "I hereby experience an inner assent." Here it is precisely not the case that the experience is performed in and with the
expression.[7]

Earlier we referred to the "illocutionary authority" of the speaker to determine which illocution she presents herself as enacting, which form of
committing or declining to commit herself she is engaged in. It is not by
self-observation that the speaker knows this, and no other person is in
a position to constitute or practically determine what particular illocutionary force the speaker's utterance is meant to count as (the incoherence or bad faith in, "I don't know. You tell *me* whether I'm promising or
just giving advice"). This was the upshot of the discussion of "normative
powers" and Joseph Raz's nonpromisor of a ride to work tomorrow. It is
part of the authority recognized in a mature speaker to determine that she

---

7 Reinach [1913] 1983, 30, sec. 3, "The Social Acts"; emphasis added. I am grateful to Bruno
  Ambroise for drawing my attention to Reinach's remarkable work and its place in the prehis-
  tory of thinking about speech acts.

is, e.g., *not* promising but merely advising, or that she is indeed asserting the proposition uttered rather than reciting it. The illocutionary authority of the speaker determines the *identity* of the particular illocution, but not its realization, for that does not depend on her alone. We are now in a better position to see how, far from being an individual capacity of the speaker, this illocutionary authority depends not only on her participation in a social practice that precedes her, including her recognition as a mature speaker with the institutionally recognized power to perform certain illocutions and not others, but also on the participation of an interlocutor whose uptake is the constituting condition for the accomplishment of the illocution.

Since Austin it has been recognized that the first-personal aspect of illocutions is not accidental to them. The grammatical form of a performative utterance is first person because the reality of the act, the act of promising, for example, depends on its first-person expression. To say of someone *else* that she promises or that she thanks is not to accomplish any promising or thanking, but rather to describe (truthfully or not) what someone else is doing. Further, we now see how a further dimension of the first-personal form of the illocution is expressed both in the idea of the exercise of a normative power and in the first-personal (practical, nonobservational) understanding the speaker must have of what she is doing in order to be doing it at all. That is, we have to understand the speaker who says, "I promise you, I warn you . . ." as presenting herself as both *doing* the promising or warning in question, and doing so *self-knowingly*, not only because there is no such thing as doing these things unknowingly, but because the explicit form of the words spoken, "I promise you, I warn you," is not only the accomplishment of an act but the *announcement* of that very accomplishment to the interlocutor. The act is named in the declaration that one is performing that very act, and this self-consciousness on the part of the speaker is expressed in the "hereby" that is, as has been noted since Austin, the touchstone of the illocutionary in contrast to the perlocutionary.[8] Perlocutionary acts or consequences like "alarming" or "comforting" are not for the speaker to

---

8 Anscombe also discusses the meaning of "hereby" in "Rules, Rights and Promises" ([1978] 1981, 319–20), and makes the important point that the sense of something accomplished "hereby" is not either that of a mechanism or that of the self-fulfilling demonstration in writing on the blackboard, "I am hereby writing on the blackboard," but that rather it is *"by its significance"* that the promise creates a new obligation. Here again, however, the social context and the constituting roles of the speaker's understanding and the interlocutor's recognition are far in the background of her discussion.

pronounce upon, these action descriptions not being formally dependent on their being intentional and self-aware. Nor are perlocutionary acts accomplished in the uptake and recognition by the interlocutor, such that "nothing further need happen" for the act to be done,[9] as the Reciprocity condition does not apply to acts like "alarming" or "comforting." For these reasons it would make no sense (or only as a joke) to say something like, "I hereby comfort you, alarm you . . . ," for the accomplishment of the actual comforting or alarming is outside the speech situation, not something the speaker can present herself as making true then and there.[10]

However, in relating this understanding of the meaning of "hereby" as a touchstone of the illocutionary to the speaker's practical self-consciousness, understood as playing a constituting and not merely enabling role for the act, it should not be thought that this source of the speaker's ability to declare that she is indeed (and "hereby") doing the thing named in her illocution lies in the fact that what the speaker is pronouncing upon is something utterly self-referring and independent of any contingencies outside herself. That would obviously be the wrong way to interpret the difference between how a perlocution like "alarming" depends on how things turn out and thus cannot be pronounced upon in a first-person manner, and how an illocution like promising or telling is accomplished in the speech situation itself. For in fact the speech situation includes the interlocutor *more* integrally in the case of the illocutionary than the perlocutionary, for the illocutionary acts can *only* be accomplished by the interlocutor's playing a corresponding role in the illocution. That is, the first-person authority that distinguishes the illocutionary from the perlocutionary and which is expressed by the speaker in the "hereby" has to be understood in relation to the speaker's *dependence* on her audience, a dependence that is given by the role of reciprocity for the accomplishment of the act she announces herself as doing. We can look at the question of the speaker's knowledge and authority in the following way.

An utterance such as, "I (hereby) renounce all claim to possession" has the outward form of an assertion of some fact, and it is natural to see the speaker of an illocution as presenting herself as speaking from *knowledge*, knowledge of the truth of what is stated in her utterance. Within a conversation, this self-presentation of the speaker is normally accepted, the

---

9 "Recognition by an audience that such an intention has been made public in this way leaves nothing further needing to happen for the intention to be fulfilled" (McDowell 1980, 41).
10 Here again, see Cavell (2006).

performative is normally a "happy" one, and the speaker can be said to have done the thing in question while saying that she is doing it. However, for the speaker to be able to present herself as speaking from knowledge of what she is doing, she has to incorporate the other person's point of view in that very expression of knowledge, for if her interlocutor does not hear or understand her, then she is simply not doing the thing she announces herself as "hereby" doing. The speaker's first-person declaration of what she is doing depends for its truth (and hence for any knowledge of its truth) not only on the speaker but on the interlocutor's knowing and understanding the same thing that is known and understood by the speaker. The form of an illocutionary utterance is the speaker's first-person announcement to her interlocutor of what she is doing, but this is something that must be known and understood by both speaker and interlocutor in order for "warning" or "promising" to be the thing that she is in fact doing. This is a matter of what the speaker and interlocutor must know *together*, such that, if the interlocutor doesn't know it, the speaker can't know it either. This is the sense in which, as Reid puts it, social acts of mind like promising or "testifying a fact" depend on "another intelligent being, who acts a part in them."[11]

The grammatical form of the first person that characterizes the illocutionary, and which makes the "hereby" formulation possible, depends on the Reciprocity condition, and thus expresses a form of first-person authority that incorporates the point of view of another subjectivity. The understanding of the first-person position here is not arrived at by the Cartesian route of arriving at a notion of the "subjective" by a progressive reduction and interiorization of the scope of its authority (e.g., retreating from "how things are" to "how things *seem to me*"), such that "authority" means self-sufficiency with respect to a restricted, "internal" domain, but rather through an understanding of the mutual dependence of the pronouns

---

11 In his essay "Is There an Objective Spirit?" (1994, 117), Vincent Descombes makes this point by underscoring "the affinities between a sociological theory of spirit and a 'pragmatic' conception of language": "In terms of the classic distinction, there is an external relation between the individual and the person who takes on the role of her partner; but there is an internal relation between the activity which one of them undertakes (speaking to someone, selling a product, ordering) and another activity which is thereby necessarily called for on the part of someone else (listening, buying the product, obeying). Unless the second activity is carried out by someone, the first simply does not occur. The relation of the two is conceptual rather than physical (it is not enough to speak in order to create an audience). It is therefore an internal relation."

"I" and "you" in a situation of dialogue. In a classic study of the notion of
"person" in language (that is, the notion of first, second, and third persons as represented in grammar), Emile Benveniste puts the point in the
following terms.

> I use *I* only when I am speaking to someone who will be a *you* in my address.
> It is this condition of dialogue that is constitutive of *person*, for it implies that
> reciprocally *I* becomes *you* in the address of the one who in his turn designates
> himself as *I*. Here we see a principle whose consequences are to spread out
> in all directions. Language is possible only because each speaker sets himself
> up as a *subject* by referring to himself as *I* in his discourse. Because of this, *I*
> posits another person, the one who, being, as he is, completely exterior to
> "me," becomes my echo to whom I say *you* and who says *you* to me. This
> polarity of persons is the fundamental condition in language, of which the
> process of communication, in which we share, is only a mere pragmatic conse-
> quence. . . . Neither of the terms can be conceived of without the other; they
> are complementary . . . and, at the same time, they are reversible.[12]

In the present context, a way of spelling out what Benveniste means by
the "complementarity" or "reversibility" of "I" and "you" is to say that the
terms "speaker" and "audience" are not names of individuals, but names
for reciprocal roles occupied by individuals, and which depend on each
other for their meaning, roles between which the individuals alternate in
the course of a conversation. In speaking of the incorporation of the point
of view of the interlocutor in the speaker's confident declaration that she
is hereby warning or promising, the thought is that the first-person character of the illocutionary utterance and the role of self-consciousness in its
accomplishment can only be understood in terms of the complementarity
of the first- and second-person pronouns, the addressor and the addressee.
As often noted, a central aspect of the logic of the first person in these
and related contexts is that the speaker does not make such a statement
on the basis of identifying herself (perceptually or descriptively, etc.) or by
picking herself out from among others when she says, e.g., "I need something to drink," and so in this sense she does not identify the person who
is speaking in any way (as she would in using an ordinary referring expression such as a name or a demonstrative). In saying to her audience, "I
need something to drink" the speaker does not *tell* her audience *who* it is

---

12 "Subjectivity in Language," 224–25, in Benveniste [1966] 1971. See also "Relationships of
Person in the Verb" in the same volume.

that needs something to drink, since in a given case the speaker may not be in possession of any identifying information about herself and might not even know her own name. Perhaps all she knows is that she is thirsty, and if she is still recovering from a fainting spell, she is not in a position to say much of anything about *who* it is that is so thirsty. And yet, in the ordinary case, the audience does learn from the speaker's utterance who it is who needs a drink, for he either sees the speaker before him or is otherwise in possession of some identifying information about the person addressing him, the source of this utterance. The audience does need to know "who" it is that is speaking for the speech exchange to continue, for it to amount to anything, but the speaker's own use of the pronoun "I" (without any accompanying information like "I, RM, would like . . .") does not itself express any possession of this information. We might say: the utterance of "I" cannot function as a referring expression except insofar as it is tied up in a possible situation of dialogue with an addressee who (being exterior to that "I") does gain identifying information from the speaker's act of addressing the utterance to him, information that need not be in the possession of, and is in any case not appealed to by, the speaker herself who says "I." The speaker's use of "I" is indeed "identification-free" in Gareth Evans's sense,[13] and it does in such a context function as a referring expression, but it can only do so because its use in an illocution is bound up with a possible addressee who does tie the utterance to identifying information that enables him to pick out the speaker as one person from among others.

Further, as Benveniste points out, there can be no use of "I" that is not coupled with the speaker's ability to recognize herself over the course of the conversation as the self-same person who, after having employed the first person in the course of addressing her interlocutor ("I need something to drink") is in response addressed as "you" by that interlocutor. Even the person recovering from a fainting spell can appreciate that when the response to her first-person request is, "I'll go get you some water," the word "I" here refers to the person speaking to her and the word "you" refers to herself, the person whose thirst she just expressed with the word "I." What Benveniste calls the "polarity of persons" and their reciprocal dependence is given by the role of the grammatical differences of "person" within a conversation. Command of the first-person pronoun is equivalent to understanding its role in dialogue, which is to say, understanding that when I say,

---

13 Evans 1982, chap. 7, which is a refinement of Shoemaker's account (1968).

"Can you get me something to drink?" I am addressing someone whom I refer to as "you," and that this person addresses me in turn using the very same pronoun ("you"), and that the success of my speech act means that I recognize myself in this "you," and that I can convert this "you" addressed to me into the "I" that I started out with, thus continuing the exchange. This subjective recognition of oneself as the "you" being responded to means that the speaker acknowledges that the person whom her interlocutor picks out from among others by means of ordinary identifying information that she herself does *not* avail herself of and may not even possess, that this person is indeed herself, the person who spoke and who is now being addressed in turn. "I" and "you" are thus names of interchangeable roles within a situation of dialogue, and the speaker is only in a position to declare what she is "hereby" doing in an illocution by presuming the situation of dialogue, meaning that she is heard and understood by a subject she addresses as "you," and who says "I" when he addresses the speaker in turn as "you."

6.3 Speech as Production and Speech as Social Act

In ordinary informative verbal communication it is understood that the reason for belief provided by the speaker's utterance depends on the assumption that the speaker is aware of what she is doing and understands what she is saying. My regional accent may provide my audience with a reason to believe something about me without my having any understanding of how it does so, that it does so, or the meaning of the words I am speaking. But my *telling* my audience something must "provide a reason for belief" in a different sense because here if I don't understand the words I am saying, then I have made no assertion at all that might be believed or disbelieved. The previous discussion of the constitutive role of such understanding for ordinary illocutions like "telling" enables us to say that for speech acts like these the epistemic reason for belief (content) is *formally* dependent on the speaker's understanding of her illocution. That is, the meaning of saying that the *act description* is formally dependent on the agent's understanding is that, in the case of testimony, the *reason to believe* the content is formally dependent on the speaker's awareness and understanding of her act. And the completion of the illocution depends on this illocutionary understanding being shared by speaker and interlocutor. This sort of picture provides a way of understanding why it should matter to the description of the exchange that the audience is confronted with a self-conscious *act* of another person, why it matters to the epistemological story that the phenomenon in question is specifically an expression of mind, and not simply a phenomenon or state of affairs that prompts belief about something. The *epistemic reason* relative to the content of the utterance depends on its being an act that does not happen to be intentional in this particular instance, as with a perlocutionary effect like "annoying," but rather an act which is necessarily intentional, necessarily an expression of the speaker's understanding with respect to a particular content.

At the same time, many reconstructions of the epistemology of testimony split the roles of the consumers and producers of testimony in such a way as to make it hard to understand how it could matter epistemically that the putative source of knowledge for the consumer is someone's intentional act, one whose status as an illocutionary act is formally dependent on the speaker's shared understanding of it in those terms. From the consumer's point of view, we saw earlier that the Indicative model has trouble accounting for why it should matter epistemically, from the perspective of the recipient of testimony, that what he is confronted with is the intentional, self-conscious act of another person. For unconscious reflexes as well as deliberate actions have their own revealing, evidential significance, often superior to that of anything intentionally displayed. And in thinking about the speaker's role in terms of the production of an interpretable sign, it would seem that on a Gricean model of communication in which the meaning of the act is understood in terms of bringing one's audience to believe something, the role of the speaker's knowledge and understanding of what she is doing could only be an efficacious or enabling one, a way of intelligently directing one's action to the production of a desired result, but one which could in principle have been realized otherwise than by someone's self-conscious intentional action.

Insofar as we see the meaning of the speaker's act in terms of seeking to get her audience to believe something, then *this* description of the act in terms of a result achieved would be available independently of the act being intentional. Like "offending," it would be contingent to the verbal act of "getting someone to believe something" that in a given case it was a result achieved intentionally and with understanding or otherwise.

The description "bringing someone to believe that P" is specifically a description of an action in terms of a result achieved and hence is not formally dependent on the agent's awareness or understanding. Thus insofar as we understand the speech act of telling someone something in unilateral terms of seeking to produce a certain result in the mind of one's audience, we cannot explain why "telling" belongs on the list of "social acts of mind" along with "calling" and "contracting," even though it is clear that the description "telling" *is* formally dependent on the act being an intentional one, performed with understanding of its significance. On a unilateral understanding of the act of telling someone something, however, the knowledge of what one is doing could only be seen as playing an enabling and not a constitutive role in bringing off the result in question.

In his book *Traditional and Analytical Philosophy*, Ernst Tugendhat makes a criticism of the unilateral understanding of the meaning of assertion that enables us to relate the picture of the kind of *act* on the part of the speaker to the picture of the nature of the *sign* responded to on the part of the recipient, as these are represented in what we have been calling the Evidential or Indicative picture of testimony. In the lecture called "The Employment-Rule of an Assertoric Sentence. Argument with Grice and Searle," he argues for "abandoning the suggestion that we should relate the meaning of assertoric sentences to an intended effect and interpret their employment-rules as instrumental rules," and he does so by emphasizing the dialogic fact that "Two linguistic responses to a statement that are always possible are the utterances 'yes' and 'no'" (1982, 184). Whatever story we may tell about how the act of telling provides a reason to believe its content, it belongs to the nature of assertion that it provides room for a linguistic response of the same kind, another assertion affirming or denying what the first speaker has just affirmed or denied. This basic fact about the meaning of assertion in the context of a conversation is incompatible, Tugendhat argues, with a characterization of the act of assertion as aiming to produce a result (viz., a state of belief) in the mind of one's audience.

> If what the speaker is doing is to be interpreted as trying to bring something about then it remains unintelligible what it is that the hearer is contradicting or what it is that is denied or affirmed by the hearer. If we ask ourselves without preconceptions what is it that is denied by the hearer the answer is that clearly it is that which the speaker asserted. (185)

If it makes sense to respond with "yes" or "no" to a speaker's assertion, this must be because speaker and interlocutor share the recognition of a common content that is presented as true by the speaker and is either affirmed or denied by her interlocutor. As we've seen, insofar as the speaker's act is seen in terms of the production of a result, as with a perlocution like "offending," it will be a contingent matter whether that result is achieved intentionally or otherwise. A response of "yes" or "no," however, can only be understood as an act of shared understanding between two participants in a conversation, and the response of "yes" or "no" itself is not the external evidence that the speaker's action has either succeeded or failed at its aim of producing a belief, but is itself a countermove to the original utterance within the same conversation.

> And indeed this counter-utterance of the hearer is related to the speaker's utterance in precisely the same way that the speaker's utterance is related to the hearer's utterance; this is because, as we saw earlier, there is no absolute distinction between affirmative and negative statements. We can only say that the latter is the denial of the former. But then the former is equally the denial of the latter. This results in a far-reaching relativization of the distinction between speaker and hearer. If the hearer responds with "no" the distinction reduces to this: that the original speaker makes so to speak the first "move." Thus in so far as the relation between speaker and addressee is not a one-way street it corresponds neither to the stimulus-response schema nor to the Gricean conception of a purpose-related act. It is not just that the act of the hearer reacts upon the speaker or his act; rather both acts clearly relate—though of course in a way that has yet to be explained—to the same thing: the one denies what the other affirms. . . . And because all other possible responses by means of speech acts also presuppose one of these position-takings they too are not mere responses to the speaker's utterance. One can call all these speech-responses which presuppose the possibility of denial, including denial itself, answers instead of responses. (189–90)

There are two points from this passage that I would like to draw out and relate to each other. One is the criticism Tugendhat makes of the unilateral or "one-way" characterization of the act of the speaker that figures in so many neo-Gricean accounts of verbal communication, and the corresponding emphasis in Tugendhat on the "relativization of the distinction between speaker and hearer" (or what Benveniste calls their "reversibility"). The other point is that the responses of agreement or denial in a conversation cannot be understood as responses to an

utterance as occurrence, a phenomenon with the potential epistemic
interest of an indication or sign of something else, but as replies to the
statement made by the speaker, such that "the one denies what the other
affirms."

For Tugendhat, the fundamental distinction in thinking about speech
exchanges is that between conceiving of the meaning of an act such as
making a statement in terms of seeking to produce a result in the mind
of the audience, and conceiving of the act as one for which the interlocutor may respond with agreement or denial, with a "yes" or "no."
He claims these are incompatible perspectives, that regarding the addressee of an act of assertion as "the object of an intended effect" cannot
make sense of the addressee responding to the assertion by denying or
affirming what was said. For the hearer to be able to contradict the
very thing the speaker has asserted, there have to be the conditions for
describing the "common content" that is asserted by the one and denied
by the other. His larger argument is that any account of assertion in
terms of the production of a result cannot capture this central aspect
of the meaning of an act of assertion within a conversation. If we are
thinking of an act such as making a statement as the attempt of a speaker
to produce a result in the mind of some audience, then from the perspective of this audience we can only think of the speaker's statement as
an event which is the possible *occasion* for believing something, a possible
source of some true belief, and not as the very thing affirmed or denied
by the audience in turn. And indeed, putting it this way shows that in
thinking of the act of assertion in essentially productive, instrumental
terms, we are not thinking of the audience or hearer as necessarily an
interlocutor at all, for that notion has not been provided for by the model
of "seeking to produce a result." As far as being the intended object of a
certain effect goes, it can matter only accidentally whether that person
is a possible respondent to the original speaker or is someone who has
no part to play in the exchange but is merely the patient or recipient of
that action. (Arguably, it has not even been provided for that the "hearer"
is in a position to *understand* the effect that the speaker's words have on
him, so long as the desired belief is produced in the way specified.) The
Gricean picture is essentially unilateral, the "hearer" being conceived of
as the transitive object of the speaker's action, and not as a partner in a
conversational exchange.

If the speaker is conceiving of her own act as the production of a result, then she will be conceiving of the hearer as responding to her act as an event or state of affairs with a certain possible epistemic interest, possibly something directed to his attention, like Grice's example of the broken china left lying around, either deliberately or inadvertently. But while the broken china on the floor may be a good source of true beliefs about what happened, it is not something of the right logical type to be capable of truth or falsity itself, affirmation or denial. In this, a phenomenon like broken china or any other "state of affairs" belongs to a different logical category than does a statement or an assertion, for it belongs to what a statement is that the possibilities of truth or falsity belong to it essentially (leaving aside questions of vagueness or ambiguity). Neither the broken china nor the wrong kind of illocution (e.g., a question) can be denied or contradicted, believed or disbelieved.

Discussing testimony within the general area of epistemology places it within the context of responses to perception, memory, and other forms of evidence. These can be good or bad sources of belief depending on both the sources themselves and the epistemic subject's relation to them. But among things done with words, something needs to be a *statement* or assertion for it to play the role in conversation as something affirmed or denied, and thus a possible object of testimonial belief. It matters here that the possible object of belief, a statement, is something which itself may be affirmed or denied in turn by the interlocutor. Among different speech acts, a question, a request, or a command does not involve presenting some proposition as true, and hence is not a possible object of reply in the form of agreement or denial. Illocutionary acts of any different kind may well be the *sources* of true beliefs, as may an inarticulate cry, and we can tell various stories in which witnessing the asking of a question or the issuing of a command can be a reliable source of true beliefs for some audience or observer, but only something with the logical shape of a statement can be countered, affirmed, or denied. There must be a kind of grammatical fit between the kind of speech act and the responses to it of agreement or disagreement. These responses are responses to something that is *as such* a proposal for belief, in that what they respond to is not only a content with some truth value, but the affirmation of that content as true. Truth and falsity are the relevant dimensions of assessment for both statements *and* beliefs; that is how they are fitted to each other (the speaker's statement and the audience's belief). And, of course, a statement or claim presents some proposition *as* true, which provides the sense in which it is internal to a statement or a claim that it is offered for belief. All this is obvious enough, but it distinguishes the types of response possible for statements from those possible for other speech acts such as questions, requests, and commands. These do not admit of truth or falsity, and these are not *possible* direct objects of belief, any more than is an unstructured list of words, a person's regional accent, or some broken china on the floor. A different kind of illocution, as when a speaker asks a question or expresses a wish, can also be the *occasion* for believing something, can be the reliable *source* of belief about something, but not by being believed itself.

In this regard we can compare the situation of a Holmesian detective (or psychoanalyst or other interpreter) with that of an ordinary participant in a conversation. For the purposes of her forensic "deductions" it may make no difference whether the utterance she is confronting is a statement or a question or the recitation of an unstructured list of words. And in the situation where it is indeed someone's statement that the detective is concerned with, the knowledge that she takes away from this may concern a topic utterly unrelated to the topic of the person's statement (e.g., it may be the speaker's accent that confirms some unrelated suspicion of hers). In adopting this position to the speaker's utterance, in detaching the topic of her deductions from the topic of the speaker's statement, the detective places herself outside the situation of dialogue with the speaker, outside the responses of agreement or disagreement with what has been said. And if the detective asks this person a question, say about where he was last night, her point in doing so may not be to be informed about his whereabouts at all, but rather to learn about something quite different and unknown to him. In such a context the detective is not asking her question in the expectation of believing the speaker when he responds to her question, believing him because he has *answered* her question and thereby informed her. Her understanding of her own epistemic point in posing her question and the relevance to that point of the speaker's reply is otherwise, and is detached from the topic of the speaker's answer, or his own understanding of his response as reply to her question. We may think of such detachment as a permanent possibility in the course of speaking together, but the very meaning of questions and answers in conversation must be different from this. For in the defining practice of asking questions and giving answers to them the two acts are related in the following way: a question to someone concerning some topic seeks an answer from that person concerning that very topic, and the respondent's answer (when offered as informative and not a response of demurral) presents itself as settling that question, *telling* the first speaker the answer to her question, concerning that very topic. (Tugendhat: "both acts clearly relate . . . to the same thing: the one denies what the other affirms.") The inquirer addressing a question to someone asks him to adopt the role of informant, someone who can settle that question, an answer that can itself be doubted or accepted, responded to with a "no" or "yes" in turn.

There is no possibility for a shared understanding of the conversation, or the possibility of its continuation, without the assumption that the inquirer's question concerning T aims at an informative answer from the respondent concerning T, and where the assumption is instead that the respondent's answer cannot count as settling the question of T itself, or perhaps any other question, and could rather only play the same role as any inadvertently revealing gesture. Even the Holmesian detective needs an actual *reply* from the suspect to be the object of her forensic deductions, and for that her respondent must be able to understand his own role in the conversation as giving a potentially informative answer to the question asked, regarding the very topic of that question. The detective must at least present her question in the guise of seeking to be informed about its topic; otherwise the other person will not know how to respond to it, what role he is to play in the conversation, what the question he just heard calls for from him, or even what it might mean that this question is in some sense *addressed* to him and not just something uttered in his presence. Without understanding his role in the conversation at this level, he can't understand what conversational move he might be making in saying anything at all at this point. The bare responses of "yes" or "no" can't make sense unless understood as replies to the very topic of the question asked, as answers purporting to settle that question. Apart from the understanding of statements as answers to questions there is no possible object of testimonial belief, and the epistemic import of the answers given belongs to an illocutionary practice that is social-relational, and not to be modeled on either the "production of a result" (from the speaker's perspective) or the confrontation with a state of affairs (from the audience's perspective).

6.4 The Meaning of Mutuality

Tugendhat says that the understanding of the act of assertion must include the possibility of the responses of "yes" or "no" to what is claimed in the assertion. The assertion presents a certain content as true, and it is this content that is either affirmed or denied by the interlocutor. In a situation of discourse, this agreement or denial is expressed in a "counter-utterance" which is addressed to the original speaker and whose topic is the content of the original speaker's assertion, such that "the one denies what the other affirms." What he refers to as the "relativization of the distinction between speaker and hearer" is the same as what Benveniste refers to as the "reversibility" of "I" and "you" in the context of a conversation. The speaker asserting something as true to her interlocutor must understand her own act as one which invites and makes possible a "counter-utterance" from that person, one which addresses her as "you" and which affirms or contradicts her assertion. If we think of the meaning of the act unilaterally, in terms of one person (the speaker) seeking to produce a certain result (belief) in the mind of another person (the hearer), then it could only be an accidental matter that the same content is known by both parties to be at issue between them, as the object of a possible agreement or disagreement. The model of the production of belief in a hearer does not provide for the possibility of a "we," such that the two parties can say "we agree/disagree about P." For the belief in that content could indeed be successfully produced by means of the full Gricean mechanism, that is, by means of the hearer's recognition of the speaker's intention to produce in him that very belief, but without the first speaker having addressed her interlocutor and thus invited and made possible the "counter-utterance" of her addressee. In imagining the progressive refinement of the Gricean formula (from seeking to produce belief, to seeking to do so with one's intent recognized by one's audience, to seeking to do so *by means of* the audience's recognition of that very intention) we always already have in mind the familiar situation of conversation between two people who understand each other, so it can be easy to miss how the resultant formula assumes that understanding of what it is for two speakers to be in contact with each other but without actually providing the elements to characterize that form of contact. In an ordinary successful case of one person telling another, e.g., that the cat has escaped, the result is not simply that, whereas before only one of them knew that the cat had escaped, now they both do, but also that each knows of the other that he or she knows this. This formulation, however, is not sufficient to describe the manner of their shared knowledge, for again the situation of each knowing that the other knows about the cat could be realized in their total isolation from each other, and without either of them being in a position to address a "counter-utterance" to the other with regard to a shared content at issue between them. The knowledge each of them has about the situation of the cat, and the knowledge each of them has about the other's knowledge about the cat, could all still be privately held by each of them, as could the knowledge that the audience's knowledge is the result of the actions of the first speaker.

In an illocutionary act the speaker's practical knowledge of what particular act she is performing is a matter of her illocutionary authority to determine which overt commitment she is taking on with respect to her interlocutor, combined with the interlocutor's "uptake" of that utterance which is the condition of its completion. For the act of asserting or promising to take place the two parties have to both understand and "know together" what it is that they are doing, for this shared knowledge is the formal cause of the reality of the act of illocution itself. Their separately held knowledge and understanding will not constitute the completion of any illocution, even if this knowledge is iterated into higher levels such that they each know about the other's knowledge of their own knowledge and understanding. The illocutionary knowledge and understanding must be actually held in common such that the speaker's knowledge is the condition of the interlocutor's knowledge and vice versa. It is this structure that makes possible the sort of "counter-utterance" Tugendhat is referring to, so that the content that is affirmed by the speaker and denied by the interlocutor is a matter of common but opposed "position takings" by them, and not only a complex content entertained singly by each of them.[14]

The characterization of the awareness held in common between two people in a situation of dialogue has proven curiously resistant to philosophical explication.[15] It is generally agreed that an intersubjective encounter is not given merely by two people entertaining similar thoughts

14 "Moreover, the affirming, and likewise the questioning, doubting, etc., responses of the hearer refer back to the speaker's utterance in fundamentally the same way as denial, namely as different *position takings* to the same thing whose negation is asserted in the denial" (Tugendhat 1982, 190).

15 For some recent work on the logical form of the second person see Longworth 2013 and 2014, Martin 2014, Peacocke 2014, Rödl 2007, Salje 2017, and Thompson forthcoming.

about each other, but that each individual's thought must concern not only the other person, but also the other person's *thought* about oneself, including one's thought about the other person. What is called "mutual knowledge" is normally characterized by a succession of higher-order states that the two parties hold with regard to each other. So, not only does Person A know that Person B would like him to open the window, but Person B knows that Person A knows this, and likewise Person A knows all this about Person B, and so on. This idea has been adopted in the description of cooperative behavior generally by a number of theorists in game theory, philosophy of communication, developmental psychology, and primatology. Michael Tomasello has done some of the most interesting empirical and theoretical work synthesizing these different perspectives on human communication and summarizes part of his approach in *Origins of Human Communication*:

> We thus proposed that the basic cognitive skill of shared intentionality— recursive mindreading—arose as an adaptation for collaborative activity specifically (given an initial adaptation in the direction of tolerance and generosity with food), leading to the creation of joint attention and common ground. The combination of helpfulness and recursive mindreading led to mutual expectations of helpfulness and the Gricean communicative intention as a guide to relevance inferences.[16]

The very fact that "recursive mindreading" has become a favored term for describing the target notion of a communicative encounter is noteworthy in this connection. For mind reading, whether genuinely telepathic, or an ordinary skill based on tacitly picking up on such things as facial expressions or other behavioral cues from another person, is precisely a solitary activity that needn't have anything to do with two people being in actual contact with each other or responding *to* one another. Actual mind reading, whether literal or figurative, does not require for its practice that the communicative capacities of the other person are being solicited or engaged with at all. The person whose mind is being read, whose thoughts are detected, need not have any idea that this is happening, and indeed the unawareness of the other person, his unwittingness of the process, will often make the mind reader's task easier and more reliable in its results.

---

16 Tomasello 2008, 217–218. A related formulation toward the end of the book: "The basic cognitive skill of shared intentionality is recursive mindreading. When employed in certain social interactions, it generates joint goals and joint attention, which provide the common conceptual ground within which human communication most naturally occurs" (321).

We may get a better picture of how either "mind reading" or a succession of higher-order states fails to capture the situation of two people in a mutually self-aware encounter with each other by considering a case of failed mutuality, one where it is precisely the avoidance of mutuality that is the aim of one of the parties. In *Middlemarch* there is a scene between Dorothea Brooke and her husband, the scholarly and remote Mr. Casaubon, as they have begun to grow distant from each other. Casaubon is older, and his health, never the best, has taken a turn for the worse. He has developed a heart condition that Dr. Lydgate, who is a friend to both him and Dorothea, has told him is not curable and will likely prove fatal before long, although it is impossible to tell how much longer he may have to live. For various reasons he does not wish to confide this to his wife, but given that Lydgate is a friend to both of them, Casaubon is anxious to know just what Dorothea knows about his condition and his own knowledge of it. As it happens, Dorothea has recently met with Lydgate about funding for his hospital, and during their conversation the doctor spoke to her in very general terms about her husband's health issues. Toward the end of this chapter (44) she returns home to Casaubon, and Eliot says the following:

> Dorothea told him that she had seen Lydgate, and recited the gist of her conversation with him about the Hospital. Mr. Casaubon did not question her further, but he felt sure that she had wished to know what had passed between Lydgate and himself. "She knows that I know," said the ever-restless voice within; but that increase of tacit knowledge only thrust further off any confidence between them. (Eliot 1997, 414)

This scene occurs as the marriage of Dorothea and Casaubon is disintegrating from the limited intimacy that characterized it before to a settled mutual alienation. Eliot describes this scene as a failure of confidence between the two of them, but one that is nonetheless characterized by a kind of tacit knowledge they each hold of the other. Casaubon says to himself, "She knows that I know," meaning that he realizes that his wife Dorothea knows the general facts about his illness, as well as his own knowledge of this, all of which he has kept from her so far. For our purposes we can assume that she really does know, and that Casaubon really knows, and does not merely suspect, that she knows this. In the novel, he reacts to this realization with fear, and the resolution to continue to avoid confiding in her. From a certain point of view on communication, this may seem not just a regrettable response on his part, but an incomprehensible one. For if he really takes

Dorothea to already *know* about his illness and his own knowledge of it, then there is no longer any possibility of *keeping* this information from her, so what could the meaning of "withholding" even *be* in this context? They both know, and each knows that the other knows. There are no further secrets to reveal.

What would need to be added to this description in order to change it from one of a severe form of alienation between two people to something closer to "reciprocity" or "mutual recognition," the ordinary sort of openness that characterizes everyday interactions between people? It seems clear that it would not necessarily help to add further layers of tacit knowledge or intent, for we could easily imagine a different Casaubon as *wanting* Dorothea to know about his illness and his own knowledge of it, because he wants her care or pity, but imagine him as unable to bring himself to tell her, or perhaps not thinking that this knowledge should come from *him*. He just wants her to know somehow. And we may just as easily imagine Dorothea as a penetrating and astute "mind reader" of all the signs in his face, and voice, and other behavior, which enables her to see right away that her husband harbors this knowledge, that he cannot or will not ever confide in her, and that he nonetheless wants and needs her to know. All of this may be "immediately visible" to her, and not involve any labored inference on her part. And we may imagine further that Casaubon, for his part, knows perfectly well that, not only is his wife aware of all the facts of his "medical issues," but also that she knows that he knows about her own knowledge that he *wants* her to know about his illness, and that all *this* is revealed immediately in his own behavior. And yet, as Eliot says at the end of the passage, it is the very *increase* in tacit knowledge that further *distances* them from each other. We don't arrive at a mutual encounter here by adding more elements of the same kind.

6.5 Grice's Third Clause and the Role of Overtness

It is sometimes objected to Grice's approach to communication that it is overly intellectualistic, and burdens the "utterer" with a complex (potentially infinite) set of higher-order attitudes just in having a genuinely communicative intention, and burdens the hearer with a similarly complex inferential task in order to successfully interpret the utterer's action. For Grice's original formula for an utterer to mean something by X requires that she intend all of the following: (1) that her utterance X produce a particular response in her audience, (2) that the audience recognize her intention, and (3) that the audience's recognition of this intention should play a role (as a reason) in producing the response aimed at in (1).

It can seem that complex intentions and inferences of this sort cannot reasonably be ascribed either to young children or even to adult communicators in the rush of verbal and nonverbal communication that makes up daily life.[17] I think that these objections are responding to a genuine problem with the Gricean approach but that they do not locate the problem in the right place. There will inevitably be ways to deflect the worry about intellectualism or the proliferation of nested attitudes since the defender of a Gricean approach can always respond that such attitudes either don't have to be explicitly represented at all, or only at a subpersonal level, and that "inference" itself needn't refer to explicit mental operations that are represented in consciousness. Many writers on the subject are happy to build various forms of "metacognition" into the architecture of the mind prior to psychological maturity or any initiation into social forms of life, and which operate below the threshold of consciousness (Sperber and Wilson 2002). Granting all this suggests that the worry about "oversophistication" in the description is really the symptom of a deeper problem. Rather, it seems that *any* amount of "metacognition" or higher-order states could only be a more complex version of the kind of alienation from each other we see with Casaubon and Dorothea. To overcome this situation of mutual alienation, Casaubon (as our Gricean communicator) would have to overtly seek that *he himself* be recognized, not just that the facts be revealed or that his *intent*

17 In later work, Tomasello himself has downplayed the importance of "recursive mind reading": "In the original analyses of Schelling and Lewis coordinating in this way required some kind of mutual knowledge or recursive mind reading: for me to go, I have to expect you to expect me to expect you. . . . For both Schelling and Lewis, this process, while remarkable, did not cause alarm. Later commentators problematized this analysis, pointing out that an infinite back-and-forth of us thinking about one another's thinking could not actually be happening, or no decision could ever be made. Clark . . . proposed as a more realistic account, that humans simply recognize the 'common ground' they have with others. . . . Our position is that human individuals are attuned to the common ground they share with others, and this does not always involve recursive mind reading, but still, if necessary, they may decompose their common ground a few recursive layers deep to ask such things as what he thinks I think about his thinking" (2014, 38).

that they be revealed be recognized. The description of an intersubjective encounter would have to include at the beginning the idea of Casaubon expressing himself *to* Dorothea, and not simply making something known to her through either some complex inferential process, or something immediately discernible in his behavior.

Grice's account took the shape it did because he was trying to give a philosophical characterization of the difference between what he calls "natural" and "non-natural" meaning, and the difference between "deliberately and openly letting someone know" and "telling" and between "getting someone to think" and "telling" (Grice 1967, 44). It is for this reason that he invoked the controversial "third clause," according to which the utterer intends not only that her intention that her audience believe P be recognized by her audience, but that this recognition of her intention should itself play a role in her audience's coming to believe that P. Several recent writers defending a roughly neo-Gricean approach to both linguistic and nonlinguistic communication have suggested that we should simply drop the third clause altogether.[18] There are several motivations for this revision, among which are the desire to emphasize the continuum of cases from "showing" to "saying," and to show how something like a Gricean structure could in principle characterize the forms of nonverbal communication found among nonhuman animals.

However, if what we are seeking to understand is the specific form of intersubjectivity made possible by linguistic communication, then it is important to be clear about the reasons motivating Grice to push his analysis in the direction of the third clause and what the significance is of marking the distinction between "telling" and "deliberately and openly letting know." It is quite true that as providers and recipients of information from others we are sometimes rightly indifferent to just how the end of informing another person is achieved (e.g., when alerting someone that a car is coming) and we just take the simplest, most efficacious means to the end of conveying that information. In a given case it may not matter at all that the other person gets this information in virtue of *understanding* me at all, or even by taking me to understand what I am doing and what its epistemic import is. All that matters is that the person come to possess the information, one way or another. But it would be another matter entirely to claim that in the

18 See the papers by Stephen Neale (1992), Dan Sperber and Deirdre Wilson (2015), and Richard Moore (2016).

understanding of ordinary informative assertion it is incidental to its informative role that the speaker understands what she is saying and is seeking to be understood by the other person. The understanding of linguistic communication cannot do without the idea of a speaker *saying something*, and indeed saying something *to* another person whose recognition is the success of the speaker's illocutionary act. If this is the phenomenon we are seeking to understand, then a neo-Gricean analysis that eliminates reference to the role played by the recognition of the speaker's intention will fail to describe the target notion.

It is pointed out by Stephen Neale as well as Dan Sperber and Deirdre Wilson that in both verbal and nonverbal communication it can happen that the action of the utterer produces its informative effect on the audience by simply drawing his attention to something in the environment, where the redirection of the audience's attention does not depend in any way on his recognition or understanding of the utterer's intent. As Neale puts it, "some natural feature of the utterance in question makes it *completely obvious* that P" (1992, 548). When something is made completely obvious to an audience, the audience can be expected to gain the information directly from the source, without any epistemic dependence on the utterer once his attention has been directed that way. This can of course be accomplished by a wordless gesture, but linguistic examples have been offered as counterexamples to the requirement of the recognition of intention, such as saying, "I'm over here" to someone lost in the woods, or Neale's example of someone simultaneously demonstrating and saying, "I can speak in a squeaky voice." But, as Kent Bach points out, such cases are of doubtful relevance to the understanding of linguistic communication since in such cases the meaning or understanding of the words makes no difference to what the audience comes to learn. As he puts it, "the hearer could infer the speaker's whereabouts even if he said 'I am in Rangoon' or merely blew his nose" (1987, 149). We cannot understand the nature of verbal communication from consideration of cases where the content of what a speaker says is playing no role. In addition, a further difficulty with the idea of dropping Grice's third clause is that it becomes hard to see what would justify retaining the *second* clause once the third one is dropped. That is, there's no reason left to require (as part of the utterer's intention) that the audience *recognize* her intention, if the recognition of that intention is idle and not playing any role in the production of belief. Without the recognition of intention playing some actual role in realizing the aim of communication, there seems no principled motivation for the analysis to require such recognition as part of the utterer's intention in the first place. And of course if we do drop the second clause as well, then we've abandoned anything intersubjective in the notion of communication, and the picture really *is* one of just producing effects one way or another on the minds of others.

Sperber and Wilson in particular are motivated to drop Grice's third clause out of a desire to preserve what they see as the natural unity in a spectrum of cases of what they call "ostensive-inferential communication," which display a variety in both the extent to which the information in question is explicitly propositional or "coded" and the extent to which recognizing the intentions of the "utterer" is important to the conveyance of the information. This broad family will include nonverbal showing, either very broadly ostensive (gesturing to the scene before one) or more specific (pointing to a bandage on one's leg in response to an invitation to play squash), as well as a range of cases of nonliteral or nonpropositional verbal communication, including irony, metaphor, and the varieties of conversational implicature. Along this spectrum there will be a great range of degrees of dependence on the utterer's intention as well as degrees of definiteness in the utterer's intention itself. As they see it, Grice's third clause was an attempt to specify a form of communication that is not itself a natural kind but only a case that falls at the far end of the communicative spectrum from showing to (explicit, propositional) saying. But they argue that the fundamental neo-Gricean notion of communication is captured by the first two clauses alone: the utterer intends (1) that her utterance X produce a particular response in her audience, and (2) that the audience recognize her intention (Sperber and Wilson 2015).

There is no doubt that there is such a spectrum of cases of communicative behavior, and since the publication of *Relevance* (1986), Sperber and Wilson have demonstrated its importance in thinking about communication generally. In the current context we can see them as arguing that there is no good reason for the theory of communication to seek a definition that will satisfy the intuitions driving the refinements of the original Gricean formula as though it were a natural theoretical kind, when what those intuitions are tracking is really just one sort of case lying at the far end of the showing/saying spectrum. Some philosophers might dig in their heels here and say that the cases toward the "showing" end of the spectrum simply aren't cases of communication in the first place, but that position seems to me hard to sustain.[19] I don't see how we can deny that there is a family of cases, from the various nonverbal ways of making something manifest to another person, to metaphor and conversational implicature, which display a range of forms and degrees of dependence on the recognition of the utterer's intentions, that this family is broadly "communicative," and that outright "telling" belongs within this family. Indeed we shouldn't have to deny that in our use of the example of Casaubon (imagining him doing something to let his knowledge of his medical condition be known) he is communicating something to Dorothea, after a fashion, even when he wishes to avoid acknowledgment, and wishes for his intention in revealing this to play no more of a role in getting his message across than it does in Grice's example of a husband leaving the china that his daughter has broken lying in full view when his wife gets home.

There are, however, two ambiguities to consider in the idea of a form of communication that makes no appeal to the idea that it is part of the utterer's intention that the audience grasp what is to be communicated in part by his recognition of her (the utterer's) intention. There is an ambiguity in the *kind* of role played by this recognition, and an ambiguity as to *what* it is that is communicated. In a given case, the utterer may not intend that the recognition of her intention should play any role in contributing to the *convincingness* of her "utterance" (taking that term broadly, to include actions of various kinds). But in a case where she *does* intend that her intention *be* recognized by her audience (that is, the first two clauses of Grice's original definition) then it would be quite another thing to consider that the recognition of her intention should play no role in *directing the attention* of her audience so that he will pick out the right features of her act and the environment in which it takes place. In this dimension of the dependence of communication on the recognition of the utterer's intention this recognition is not playing the role of providing a *reason* for believing what is being communicated, but it is playing the role of directing the audience's attention in the desired way (after which the audience may "see for himself"). Thus if we were really to drop Grice's third clause altogether, we would have to eliminate the audience's reliance on what he takes to be the

19 This seems to be the view of Kent Bach, for instance: "However not every case of acting with the intention of making something known, even when it is clearly overt, is an act of communication. For if the audience's recognition of the intention is inessential to its fulfilment, the utterance is not communicative" (1987, 149).

utterer's intention for picking out the right features in the environment to attend to. It would then be quite unclear what basis there could be for retaining the second clause of the utterer's intention, that there be recognition of intention at all.

To say this is not to deny that there can *be* cases where there is recognition of intention but where it plays no role in getting the message across, and perhaps Grice's "broken china" example is such a case (the context and the salience could be just good enough for the target audience to "get the message"). But it would remain unclear what reason there could be for including just this (the first two clauses but not the third) in the scope of the *utterer's intention*. We would have to imagine the utterer's thought as something like, "I want him to see for himself, and in such a way that his recognizing my intention to draw his attention to this something need play no role in actually drawing his attention just there. However I do mean for him to recognize *that* I mean to draw his attention there. Without that recognition my communicative intention will have failed." It's hard to see what sort of intention this would even be, especially since, given that the issue here is the direction of someone's attention and not epistemic support for a content, it will be difficult or impossible for the utterer ever to be sure that the recognition of her intention really did play no role at all in directing the attention of her audience in just the desired way. Given that her intention was recognized by her audience, and given how variously our gestures may be interpreted, the idea that this recognition played some such role in the successful case would after all be the most natural assumption to make.

A second ambiguity in eliminating Grice's third clause concerns *what* it is that is communicated. When U shows a photograph to A (let's abbreviate for now), what A learns from the photograph may not depend in any way on his recognition of U's intentions in showing him the photograph. But A does learn from U's showing him the photograph that they now *both* know about the photograph and most likely that they both see what it is that is captured in the photograph. This establishment of their *shared* awareness may well be the whole point of the exchange, the whole point of what U does. If U is intentionally showing something to A, then U herself is *aware* that she is doing so, and normally this very awareness of what she is doing in showing it to A will itself be part of what U wishes to communicate to A. She means to communicate both what is in the photograph and her awareness of that to A (as well as her awareness that she is *showing* this to A). In being recognized as intentional, U's gesture does not only communicate the awareness of what is shown, but makes the thing shown and U's act of showing it both a matter of shared knowledge between them. That is, it establishes all this as "mutually manifest" between them in Sperber and Wilson's sense.

But if A does *not* believe that U is aware of what her gesture has revealed to him, if the gesture was unconscious and unintentional, as in the case where he notices something from picking up on her unconscious shifting glance toward someone in the room, then what A picks up on here is *not* "mutually manifest" between them, not a matter of their joint attention or shared awareness. It is when A recognizes that U's ostensive gesture is intentional that A can be sure that U herself is aware of what she is doing and what she is ostending. Without A's recognition that U's gesture is intentional (and thus self-aware) A will have no reason to think that what is indicated by U's gesture is something that they are now *both* aware of, something "mutually manifest." In this way, mutual manifestness depends on the fact that A recognizes U's gesture as intentional (second clause), and that this recognition plays the role of confirming for A that what U's gesture ostends is now "mutually manifest" between them (third clause). Hence if we are really to eliminate a genuine role played by A's recognition of the intentional character of U's gesture, we will be unable to describe the conditions for mutual manifestness itself and there will be no reason left to think of the situation as a communicative one. Dropping the third clause would mean that the recognition of U's intention plays no role in either bringing A to pick out the right features of the environment or in making what is shown "mutually manifest" between U and A. And with this there would remain little or no reason to retain the second clause, that U's intention be recognized by A, in the definition of the utterer's intention.

6.6 Strawson and Avowability

Sperber and Wilson ask what intuitions about a target notion are really driving the progressive refinements of the Gricean definition as it moves from the first two clauses to the controversial third clause and beyond, in Grice's own later work and in that of philosophers taking their bearings from him. And they ask further whether, even if the analysis could be satisfactorily completed, we would have good theoretical reason to think that the target notion represents a genuine conceptual unity, one that matters to the understanding of linguistic communication. In "Intention and Convention in Speech Acts," P. F. Strawson takes seriously the identification of some notion of "telling" as being the notion that Grice is seeking to identify (1971, 156), and he employs certain features of Grice's analysis to shed light on Austin's distinction between the illocutionary and the perlocutionary. He arrives at a formulation that I think points to something crucial in the target notion aimed at by both Austin's distinction and Grice's (between "natural" and "non-natural" meaning), and which I think enables us to accommodate what is right in Sperber and Wilson's insistence on a spectrum of cases of "ostensive-inferential" communication, and yet still maintain that the notion being tracked by the progressive refinements of the Gricean definition is indeed a fundamental one, albeit one that cannot be given the kind of reductive analysis Grice himself was pursuing.

At one point Strawson tests whether a roughly Gricean model can explain why "warning" will count as an illocution in Austin's sense but that two other cases, "showing off" and "insinuating," will not. In the first case, he notes that while with the illocution of "warning" the audience's recognition of the speaker's intention will normally contribute to the audience being "put on guard" (the aim of warning), by contrast insofar as "showing off" aims at *impressing* one's audience, the recognition of this intention will normally *not* contribute to and may positively interfere with the realization of this aim.[20] By now this is a familiar point, and part of the explanation for why there is no explicit first-person illocution of the form "I hereby impress you." Strawson then says,

> Insinuating fails, for a different reason, to be a type of illocutionary act. An essential feature of the intentions which make up the illocutionary complex is their overtness. They have, one might say, essential avowability. This is, in one respect, a logically embarrassing feature. (163)

A person's intention is not "overt" in the sense intended here just in virtue of being obvious to the parties in question. Rather, as the identification with "avowability" implies, a person's intention is overt with respect to an audience when it is unrestrictedly open between them in the conversation, and that very openness is part of the intention itself. When a person chooses to merely insinuate but not say that, e.g., her interlocutor is a liar, her intention

---

20 Modulo cases like sheer "effrontery," as Strawson notes in a footnote credit to Brian McGuinness.

may be obvious enough to her audience, but in merely insinuating this she is not willing to express that intention *to* her interlocutor. The communicative intention remains unacknowledged. What is "logically embarrassing" in the idea of "essential avowability" is that, understood in the Gricean terms that Strawson adopts here, "the way seems open to a regressive series of intentions that intentions should be recognized" with no obvious way to arrive at a "complete and rounded-off set of conditions." Strawson himself says that he does not see anything necessarily objectionable in this, and indeed there is nothing objectionable in the notion itself of the "essentially avowable," but the embarrassment he mentions does show that this notion cannot be captured in a series of intentions, however large, that the individual parties entertain with respect to each other. At no level of the series will we have closed off the possibility that what the person is aiming at is that her intention (or her intention that this intention be recognized by her audience, etc.) work upon the mind of the other person, rather than that they recognize each other mutually and overtly. Hence the cycle of various attempts to close off the loop in Grice's third clause, and the recommendation by Sperber and Wilson among others that we get along without it.

Strawson relies on the notion of "essential avowability" throughout the remainder of the essay, as the touchstone for identifying the form of the communication that he takes both Grice and Austin, in their different ways, to be seeking to capture.[21] At the same time, he leaves the notion somewhat undeveloped for reasons that I believe are not accidental. For Strawson himself never actually departs from a unilateral perspective on communication that seems inextricable from the Gricean project (and which is not part of Austin's perspective on the illocutionary). This comes out in his explanation of why "insinuation" should not count as an "essentially avowable" form of communication. In the case of "showing off" we saw why the person in question does *not* want her intention to play a role in the reception by her audience, because it would be more than likely to play a negative role and thwart the aim of impressing. Not only does she not wish her intention to play a role, she more than likely does not wish the intention to impress to be recognized at all.[22] Strawson says that "insinuation"

---

21 "[I]n this understanding the notion of wholly overt or essentially avowable intention plays an essential part" (Strawson 1971, 165). The notion is explicitly appealed to in the remaining pages of the essay as he sums up his account.

22 Jon Elster discusses some paradoxes in the idea of "trying to impress" under the heading of "states that are essentially by-products" in his book *Sour Grapes* (1983).

fails the test of "avowability" for a different reason. He says, "The whole point of insinuation is that the audience is to *suspect*, but no more than suspect, the intention, for example, to disclose a certain belief. The intention one has in insinuating is essentially non-avowable" (163). The difference from "showing off" is supposed to be that in that case Grice's second clause could apply but not the third, but we have seen reason to doubt this. More importantly, however, insinuation does *not* do its work with no recognition of intention at all, and Strawson's emphasis on the difference between merely "suspecting" the intention and being more certain about it places the emphasis in the wrong place. "Unavowability" does not concern the difference between the audience merely suspecting the speaker's intention and being more sure about it. When someone insinuates but does not say that her interlocutor is a liar, that person may be as certain as can be of the speaker's intentions, yet they may remain unavowable between them, as in the case of open hypocrisy. The unavowability of insinuation lies elsewhere.

As in its ordinary linguistic sense of "avowing" a motive or aim, to avow (as with "admit") is a first-personal act in which the speaker does not only make something known, but opens her assertion to the response and address of the other person. A communicative act is "avowable" when its address to another person is something that could be made explicit, when the speaker could say what she is "hereby" doing, expressing the self-consciousness of her act to an interlocutor addressed as "you." The person insinuating but not saying that her interlocutor is a liar may be making her message perfectly clear, but in holding back from outright saying she does not present her interlocutor with that statement to reply to. To address an interlocutor as "you" is to enter into the space of a conversation within which one's statement creates the possibility of what Tugendhat calls a "counter-utterance," that is, where a possibility of a reply of the same kind (an agreement or denial) has been provided for. As Strawson suggests, the true target notion that is guiding the refinements of the Gricean formula is the form of communication that is "essentially avowable," but this cannot be captured from an essentially unilateral perspective on communication in terms of various ways of "producing a result" on the mind of an audience. In this model there is no provision for an interlocutor who is in a position to address the original speaker about what she has said, taking a position with respect to a content and an act that is an object of shared recognition. In the same way that what is called "mutual knowledge" ("she knows that he knows that she knows" etc.) can obtain between two people without any actual encounter between them, we can have the fulfillment of the Gricean conditions of "non-natural communication" without there being any possibility of the audience addressing the speaker in turn and saying "yes" or "no" to what she has said. Rather, there can only be further refinements of the earlier stages of doing something with the intent of producing some result in the mind of one's audience, which efforts the target audience may be well aware of without that altering the unilateral nature of the act. By contrast, communication that is "essentially avowable" provides for the possibility of an interlocutor who, having been addressed as "you," can in turn address the original speaker using that same pronoun and contradict or affirm what she has said. The upshot of what Strawson calls the "logically embarrassing" character of the notion of "essential avowability" is that it cannot be modeled on a series of higher-order thoughts that the subject has about the other and the other's thoughts about her, which is to say that it cannot be modeled as the structure of a unilateral act, but has to be understood from the beginning as an act with the "reversibility" of "I" and "you" described by Benveniste. The target notion that drives the progressive refinements of the Gricean formula is that of communication that is "essentially avowable," and this notion is indeed central to Austin's distinction between "perlocution" and "illocution." Grice's third clause as well as the later revisions of this clause are part of the attempt to capture this notion while retaining a unilateral perspective on communication. Insofar as avowability is central to the notion of illocution, it is central to the notion of *saying something* in the sense of making a claim or statement with one's words, and in this we have a concept that is indeed fundamental to linguistic communication, even while it is true that not all linguistic communication (let alone nonverbal communication) takes this form. So while it is true that this concept cannot be captured with the materials Grice is working with, this does not provide a reason for dropping the third clause and making do with a notion of verbal communication that remains within the basic Gricean framework but seeks to make do with only the first two conditions.

At the same time, to claim that the notion of "essentially avowable" communication captures both what the progressive refinements of the Gricean formula are aiming at, as well as something fundamental to Austin's distinction between the perlocutionary and the illocutionary, is not to say that there is necessarily anything defective in instances of communication, verbal and nonverbal, that don't take this form. The spectrum of cases that

Sperber and Wilson and others draw our attention to need not be seen as so many approximations to "genuine communication." For the present purposes we can distinguish five kinds of case where communication falls outside of full avowability.

1. In Strawson's case of insinuation, there may be a definite content the speaker wishes to get across, but the message is inadmissible for one reason or another, or its believability would be interfered with by an overt statement.

2. In the case of "showing off," the content the person wishes to communicate may not be anything definite but rather a rough sense of her own impressiveness, and the communication would be interfered with by the recognition of this as her intention.

3. In the case of figurative speech (metaphor and other tropes), as well as in certain jokes, etc., the content may be indefinite but not in any way inadmissible. In some such cases perhaps the message could be spelled out, but doing so would spoil the joke or flatten the metaphor. In other such cases, the whole point will be to communicate something inadmissible, unavowable (whether more or less definite), and to do so in a way that preserves the speaker's deniability.

4. In Sperber and Wilson's case of two people arriving at the seaside (1986, 55), the content ostended by one person to another is essentially indefinite, a diffuse impression of the whole scene, but there is nothing "inadmissible" in the person's desire to communicate something by her gesture. There just isn't a definite proposition in the offing to be expressed in the explicit, "essentially avowable" form, but as with poetic metaphor or certain jokes, the context of this dimension of communication can be the opposite of any failure of intimacy (Cohen 1978).

5. The motive of "tact" will normally depend on a specific context, and there may be reasons to communicate only indirectly something which in another context could be said outright. In a context requiring tact the concern is not that overtness would interfere with the convincingness of what is communicated, but rather that the outright statement would have other unwanted consequences (for instance, it might be important for someone to communicate something to another person but without drawing attention to the fact that she knows what is communicated).

In short, the forms of communication that exhibit "avowability" to only a partial degree need not be seen as defective in any way, or as failed approximations to what I am claiming is the form of communication Grice was trying to capture. In a given instance they may or they may not be, and that will depend on such things as the difference between, for instance, the "motives for metaphor" (Wallace Stevens) in poetry or contexts of intimacy, and the reliance on various tropes of indirection in political contexts where the avoidance of avowability is in the service of deniability and other strategies of manipulation.[23] At the same time this does not mean that the "essentially avowable," the concept of outright saying, has no more central theoretical interest than that of a set of cases at one far end of this spectrum, without any conceptual unity of its own. For this concept characterizes the specific form of overtness in intersubjectivity that the institution of language makes possible, the form of intersubjective acts constituted by shared recognition. The concept of the "essentially avowable" is fundamental to the understanding of the illocutionary, and thus is fundamental to understanding the acts of claiming or telling someone something, without which there is no such thing as human testimony.

6.7 The Perspective of the Conversation

In our revision of the story in *Middlemarch*, we were imagining a Casaubon who wants his wife to know about his illness and his fears about it, but who cannot or does not want to face her about it. There could be many reasons for this. He does not want to invite a response from her, or he does not want to make it appear as though he is *appealing* to her in any way, that he is asking for some sort of response from her, or he does not want to expose himself to further inquiries from her, or to any open display of pity or concern. Or he does not want the facts about his illness to be "common ground" in any conversation between them, such that each of them will now be entitled to assume this truth in their overt dealings with each other. Or he wants to find a way to let her know, perhaps a way that involves his saying something, and perhaps even in a way that involves her recognizing

---

23 I explore these issues at greater length in "Seeing and Believing: Metaphor, Image and Force" (1989) and in "Artifice and Persuasion: The Work of Metaphor in Aristotle's *Rhetoric*" (1995), reprinted as chaps. 2–3 of *The Philosophical Imagination* (2017).

his intention, but he does not want to "talk about it" with her; that is, he doesn't want to face her about it because that would involve being faced *by* her about it. He would like to install the correct belief in Dorothea's mind, but he does not want a conversational partner. His informative interests here are purely unilateral. He wants to produce a certain belief in his audience, and he has come to the conclusion that something like the full Gricean mechanism is the best means to accomplish this. If Dorothea understands Casaubon's attempts to bring her to know about his illness and his fears in the same unilateral way as we are imagining that he understands it, then her ability to "get the message" will indeed depend entirely on her skills as a mind reader and an interpreter of the evidence. That is the position she will have been relegated to, since she is not a participant in a conversation with him. It is only in communication that is "essentially avowable" in Strawson's sense that the people in question would have any use for a second-person pronoun or a first-person plural, a "you" or a "we," to address each other and express their presence to each other in the conversation. By contrast, the full Gricean calculation we imagined being rehearsed by Casaubon in his desire to let Dorothea know about his condition can be fully laid out without any use of the second person, since the very conception of "informing" that he is operating with is a unilateral one in terms of acting upon the beliefs of another person.[24]

The meaning of the "essential avowability" of the illocutionary is that the speaker addresses her interlocutor and explicitly assumes the responsibility for the particular illocutionary force of her utterance, which in the case of claiming or asserting includes avowing responsibility for *what* it is that is being claimed and why. The speaker has to be assumed to know how she is committing herself in speech and with respect to what content for her utterance to be so much as a candidate for a testimonial reason for belief. This understanding of the speaker's role does not belong to the speaker alone but must be shared with her interlocutor for the illocution itself to

---

24 The criticism here of the higher-order picture (or "mutual knowledge") as an account of what it is for two people to encounter each as addressor and addressee is of a piece with my earlier criticism of the "higher order" account of "conscious belief" in *Authority and Estrangement* (2001). In the same way that a second-order belief is just another belief about a different topic, and hence could just as well be an unconscious belief as any other one (and hence not a belief that I could speak for with the first person), so two people could have iterated levels of beliefs about each other and each other's beliefs without their having encountered each other, without their being in a position to address each other as "you."

be accomplished, and both must see the question of which illocution is at issue to be decisive for the kind of reason for belief that her utterance is to be. That is, while in a given case it may be possible for an audience to derive some information from the speaker's utterance independently of the kind of reason-giving she takes herself to be involved in, as when we draw some conclusion from the speaker's wordless exclamation, this is quite different from the kind of giving a reason for belief that the speaker presents herself as doing when she *tells* her audience something. The speaker's perspective on how her act of telling counts as a reason for believing what she says is that her speech provides a reason to her audience precisely because it is *that* illocution, that she is actually claiming something as true, and not asking a question or reciting the words with no illocutionary force at all.

This speaker's perspective on her role in determining the illocutionary status of her utterance is at one and the same time an expression of her practical self-knowledge as a speaker and her incorporation of the perspective of her interlocutor. For the speaker's understanding of the determining role she plays in whether and how her utterance counts as a reason for belief includes the fact that this is not simply an understanding of her role that is shared with her interlocutor, but is an assumption of responsibility in speech that her interlocutor expects and demands of her as a condition of understanding her and his own part in the conversation. The interlocutor would have no way to respond if he didn't take the speaker to be the very person who answers the question whether she is asking or telling, whether she is really claiming or just making a conjecture, and whether the way her audience is inclined to understand her meaning is indeed how she means to be understood. The interlocutor needs to know these things if there is to be any possibility of the continuation of the conversation, and it is part of the participants' shared understanding of the practice that the source of such knowledge is the speaker's reflective understanding of how she means to express or commit herself here. The speaker's first-person knowledge of what she means and how she is staking herself in her utterance is thus not a private or individual matter but is itself the speaker's incorporation of a demand from the perspective of her interlocutor, to be able and willing to overtly express the illocution she is assuming responsibility for. In this way, a further dimension of the "essential avowability" of the illocutionary is expressed in the interchangeability of the roles of speaker and hearer, the fact that each role incorporates an understanding of the other, which is the condition for the continuation of the conversation. This emerges from their shared role in constituting the illocution (as discussed in the previous chapter), the fact that the illocution of "telling" or "claiming" consists in their shared understanding of the act and their reciprocal roles in its realization. The mutuality in the exchange does not consist simply in each participant having the illocution as a common object of attention, but rather in the fact that the speaker's understanding of her role in the illocution incorporates an understanding of the reciprocal role of her interlocutor.

The possibility of the continuation of the conversation requires that both parties not only understand themselves as occupying the role of speaker and audience in turn, but that the speaker understands her own perspective in the exchange in terms of an expectation of first-person avowability of the illocution stemming from the perspective of her interlocutor. The very form of illocutionary authority, how it is that a speaker knows, e.g., that she is telling and not asking, advising about the possibility of a ride to work but not promising one, must be understood not individually but as part of the shared understanding of the practice, as a bilateral and not a unilateral understanding and authority. The possibility of the continuation of the conversation, if only in the minimal form of a response of "no" or "yes" to the speaker's assertion, is given by the reciprocal understanding of the roles of speaker and interlocutor in terms of each other. The very deployment of episodic examples in the philosophical discussion of communication tends to obscure this interdependence, since such discussions typically proceed by way of examination of single-sentence examples of one person saying or doing something before some audience, which is then tacitly understood to be the end of what happens as far as communication is concerned. But the audience cannot respond epistemically to the speaker's utterance if he has no idea what, if any, illocution is thereby performed; and their shared understanding of this act must be understood by each of them as containing the possibility of occupying both roles in turn. The possibility of the continuation of the conversation in reply, denial, agreement, etc. (what Tugendhat calls the "relativization of the distinction between speaker and hearer") is demanded by the intelligibility of the illocution itself. "Essential avowability" means that the speaker's role in constituting her utterance as a reason to believe something is being openly acknowledged, and with it the possibility of reply for the interlocutor (a possibility that is closed off or evaded in the context of "insinuation").[25] What is avowed by the speaker is thus not only the particular content and force of her utterance, but also the possibility of reply or counterassertion.

The interlocutor's expectation of the speaker to be in a position to determine and declare her illocution is at the same time the interlocutor's deferral to the speaker to fulfill a role which he, the interlocutor, cannot occupy in her place. But of course it is not up to the speaker alone to determine that actual accomplishment of her illocution. Her interlocutor must play his part, must hear, recognize, and understand her for the actual success of the illocution, and here the speaker must defer to her interlocutor and cannot take over that role for herself. Given this structure of dependencies, how should we understand the surface grammar of the speaker's utterance when she says something like, "I hereby refuse, warn, apologize, deny . . . ," which has the appearance of a first-person statement of fact? That is, given that the truth of what is apparently claimed here depends not only on the speaker herself but on everything included under the conditions of "uptake" for the success of the illocution, where the speaker must defer to the other participant in the exchange, it would seem that in making the first-person declaration of her illocution she is speaking beyond what she is in a position to know, or at least not in any first-personal manner. Let's see if we can take the appearance of a claim being made at face value and see what it may tell us about the form of knowledge it may express.[26] The speaker has the practical authority to determine her commitments in speech, and she communicates this to her addressee by way of declaring a particular illocution. Insofar as she is entitled to assume that she has communicated this practical illocutionary knowledge to her audience, she is in a position to say to her addressee, "Now you, in virtue of the fact that I have communicated this to you, my reflective knowledge of how I am declaring myself to you in this very utterance, you are thus in a position to know that I *do* in fact perform the very illocution named in my utterance. You are in a position to

25 In "Seeing and Believing" ([1989] 2017), I discuss "praeteritio" (or "apophasis") and related rhetorical devices which put an idea forward while simultaneously disavowing it, and thus denying the possibility of counterassertion.

26 I realize that Austin (1962, 3 and 100) and many following him may see this assumption as a form of the "descriptive fallacy," but I think that that criticism is strained and not required by the understanding of such utterances as acts, and closes off a host of questions which should interest us.

know this because it is your very recognition of the illocutionary meaning of my act (and my standing to perform it) that is its condition of realization, that makes it the case that I do refuse, warn, apologize, or deny. And for my part, I know as speaker that your uptake, your recognition of my expression of this reflective knowledge of my illocution, is sufficient for its success in these circumstances. Hence insofar as I am entitled to the assumption that you hear and understand me, I can say with confidence and in one breath 'I refuse, apologize . . .'" Accomplishment needing nothing further to happen (McDowell), the speaker can thus say that she *thereby* does the thing in question.

In this way we can understand the "hereby" of illocution as including implicit reference to the addressee's recognition and uptake. The reflexivity of "hereby" does not refer simply to the speaker's utterance but to the assumption of shared awareness and understanding with the addressee. And indeed, we can see in the "hereby" the expression of the simultaneity of the speaker and addressee's knowledge of the accomplishment of the speech act, the truth expressed in saying "I hereby promise, refuse . . ." That is, the speaker's entitlement to say outright, "I promise, I do apologize, I'm telling you . . . ," her entitlement to say that this is indeed what she is (hereby) doing, is understood to be dependent on her addressee hearing, understanding, and recognizing her, and to include that understanding in her expression itself. And her interlocutor for his part is only entitled to take her to be speaking knowledgably (in saying "I promise you, I warn you . . .") on the assumption that she is aware that *he* has heard and understood her. The "hereby" expresses not only the simultaneity of their knowledge of what the speaker claims in naming her illocution, but also the fact that this knowledge itself is mutual or intersubjective and not only held in common, for what they each know here is dependent on the knowledge of the other. The speaker can only know what she is doing insofar as she acknowledges the dependence of that knowledge on her interlocutor's recognition and uptake of her illocutionary self-understanding of her act. And for his part the interlocutor's recognition and uptake of the utterance is dependent on his entitlement to assume that the speaker knows what she is doing, is appropriately exercising her illocutionary authority, and understands the meaning of her speech act. The distinction of roles in the accomplishment of a single social act means that each participant's knowledge is grounded in deference to the other; it is for the speaker to determine how she means to commit herself in the exchange, what illocution is at issue, and this role cannot be taken over by her interlocutor; while at the same time the speaker must defer to her interlocutor for the actual accomplishment of her act. The possibility of "hereby" as the mark of the illocutionary signals the formal dependence of acts of this kind on the participants' shared knowledge and understanding of it, a form of knowledge which involves each incorporating the perspective of the other, and where each participant's knowledge is only possible on the assumption of the other participant's knowledge, and their shared recognition of this very dependence.

7

The Self and Its Society

One of course speaks, in a certain sense, even in soliloquy, and it is certainly possible to think of oneself as speaking, and even as speaking to oneself, as, e.g., when someone says to himself: "You have gone wrong, you can't go on like that." But in the genuine sense of communication, there is no speech in such cases, nor does one tell oneself anything: one merely conceives of oneself as speaking and communicating.

—Husserl, Logical Investigations (1900)

7.1 Thinking as the "Soul's Conversation with Itself"

In considering Reid's characterization of the "social acts of mind" as those "which necessarily imply social intercourse with some other intelligent being who bears a part in them," the specific weight of his reference to "some other" intelligent being raises questions that have been mostly implicit in the discussion so far. There is the fact that, as Stanley Cavell puts it, "We speak of standing in various relations to our selves, e.g., of hating and loving ourselves, of being disgusted with or proud of ourselves, of knowing and believing in ourselves, of finding and losing ourselves. And these are relations in which we can stand to others."[1] The fact of relations to ourselves that are also forms of relation in which we may stand to other people raises questions of the relative primacy of either the social or the individual

---

1 Cavell 1979, 384. I take it that the splitting of the first instance of the word "ourselves" in this passage is meant to be a way of signaling the philosophical risks involved in conceiving of such self-relations as relations a person may have to a "self" as something distinct from the single person. In any case, the distinction between persons and "selves" is questioned later in this chapter.

case for understanding such relations, as well as questions of whether and when the coherence of certain relations and acts is undone when the idea of a "social relation" is applied to the case of a single individual. In the context of the current discussion, if the acts of illocution involve the interplay of distinct roles for the completion of the act, is there a principled reason why the roles of speaker and interlocutor must always be occupied by distinct individuals? Each of us is an "intelligent being" who not only may act upon and enter into relations with him- or herself, but may often enough be enjoined to do such things as take charge of oneself or treat oneself with greater self-respect. In cases like these and others, philosophers find it very natural to describe the person as adopting both roles in a relation that normally involves two or more people, as when the person ashamed of herself may be described as occupying the roles of both judge and person judged. Since a person may correct herself, prevent herself from doing something, blame herself for what happened, and alternate between self-trust and self-doubt, there may seem no reason to limit the forms of relation to others that may properly be applied to oneself, including the social acts of commanding and obeying, telling and believing, giving and receiving.[2]

There is also a venerable tradition in philosophy, beginning with Plato, encouraging us to think of the person as in fact a kind of community composed of person-like agencies who interact with each other much as ordinary distinct individuals do. A human being is an organism, of course, composed of the functional unity of different organs and tissues, each with its role to play, and in thinking of the person as such many thinkers have found it compelling to describe the person as composed, not of physical

---

2 In the course of writing this book I have been instructed by connections between certain themes here and some of the recent work of Vincent Descombes. In various works, he proposes a class of what he calls "sociological verbs" (which include those for Reid's "social acts of mind") on the analogy with Wittgenstein's treatment of "psychological verbs":

"Just as psychological verbs are defined by the asymmetry between the first-person and the third-person (in the indicative present), sociological verbs will be defined by the asymmetry between their ordinary transitive use and their reflexive use. I can give the book to somebody else, but I cannot give the book to myself (the grammatical reflection to be considered here is not between the giver and the given object but between the giver and the intended beneficiary of the gift). In the same way, it is clear that I can exhort myself to do something or blame myself for having done it, but it is doubtful whether I can literally give orders to myself or condemn myself for not having done what I was ordered to do (unless I hold from a legitimate source the required authority to command or to judge myself)" (Descombes, 2004a, 286).

This thought is developed much further in his *Le complément de sujet* (2004), chapter 38, "Philosophie des verbes sociologiques," and in the essay "Heritez de vous-même!," reprinted as chapter 4 in Descombes 2014b.

organs, but of agencies or quasi-persons who also each have their roles to
play and which in healthy conditions compose a kind of political unity of
the self. Since genuine political relations like bargaining or claiming a right
can only obtain between actual persons with individual lives and destinies,
there are doubtless limits to how far the analogy can be taken literally. The
individual organs of the body may be said to each have its job to do and
to need to work together for the continuance of the life of the body and
thus for their own individual continuance, but the individual organs do not
have lives of their own which they might choose to pursue apart from the
particular body they belong to, nor can their interests be set against those of
the organism as a whole. Nonetheless the idea of the person as composed
of interacting parts, on analogy with an organism, may be thought to lend
support to the idea that there is already enough "otherness" within a single
individual to satisfy Reid's conditions for a social act which requires "some
other intelligent being who bears a part" in it, and that relations like those
between command and obedience or between duties and rights can have
unproblematic application with respect to a single individual in relation to
him- or herself.

The picture of a single individual as engaging in discourse with herself is also a Platonic one, and here the image does not appear to rest on
the division of the self into parts, but rather aims to describe the activity
of thinking itself, concerning a single person taken as a whole. In the
Theaetetus, Socrates offers a definition of thought as "the talk which the
soul has with itself about any subject which it considers," and argues for a
strict parallelism between the forms of speech in affirming, denying, asking
a question and giving an answer, and the forms of thought within a single
individual.

> The soul, as the image presents itself to me, when it thinks, is merely conversing
> with itself, asking itself questions and answering, affirming and denying. When
> it has arrived at a decision, whether slowly or with a sudden bound, and is
> at last agreed, and is not in doubt, we call that its opinion; and so I define
> forming an opinion as talking and opinion as talk which has been held, not
> with someone else, nor yet aloud, but in silence with oneself. (190a)

Here we are not given a picture of the interaction of agent-like "parts" of
the soul but rather a picture of the soul in solitary conversation with itself.
There is not one role (e.g., asking a question) given to one part of the soul
and another role (e.g., answering a question) given to another part of the

soul, but rather a single intelligence occupying both roles. In itself there need be nothing paradoxical in the idea of a single individual bearing relations to herself, and we do not need to divide the person into parts in order to describe someone as, for example, proud of herself, or her own worst enemy. But in thinking of the soul as in conversation with itself we will nonetheless want to understand how it is that the soul can ask itself a question and think of itself as posing that question to someone in possession of the answer. If it is the same person who is asking the question and who is assumed to possess the answer, there would appear to be no need for speech whether silent or out loud. The question would be pointless or merely rhetorical. Admittedly, the scenario of deliberation does not require that we see it as one of posing to oneself a question to which one is already in possession of the answer, but rather as posing the question to someone who is *in a position*, upon reflection, to deliver the answer, and that person may well be oneself. The posing of the question is thus not to be seen as requesting the answer from an informant with the requisite knowledge, but instead the posing of the question is that which prompts the reflection on the subject which culminates in the arrival of the soul's knowledge of the answer. The soul is not relating to itself in the mode of inquirer to informant or respondent but is rather inciting itself to reflection by posing questions and counterconsiderations to itself. This is a perfectly possible solitary activity, but there are difficulties in seeing it as an account of thinking itself. For this way of understanding the "discursive" model of solitary thought seems to rest on an assumed understanding of the activity of reflection itself; for instance, thinking things over in response to a question, which was the activity that the model of internal conversation was supposed to explicate. If thinking is to be seen as "merely conversing with itself, asking itself questions and answering," we will still be in need of a different characterization of the forms of thought that go into *responding* to someone's question and the effort to come up with a satisfying answer, not to mention the thought involved in framing a relevant question in the first place and posing it to oneself. Even a conversation with no one but oneself must be understood in terms of a prior conception of the various forms of thought, responsiveness, and understanding that make any conversation more than the pronouncing of words.

It is a few pages after discussing the forms and limits of various relations to oneself, and remarking on the strains on that idea with respect to such forms as envy and apology, that Cavell (1979, 386) remarks on the difficulties in the idea of believing oneself (as noted in 2.7). In the ensuing discussion he distinguishes between believing what someone says, believing it *because* she said so, and believing *her*, which involves a particular form of dependence on the speaker. The idea of dependence is also part of the explanation for Anscombe's similar claim that the notion of believing *someone* that P has no reflexive form. She immediately goes on to say, "Since one can tell oneself things, that may seem odd. We shall see why it is so later" (1979, 144).

The concession is indeed striking, since one might think that there could be no point in telling oneself anything if there were never any possibility of believing oneself (and the speaker would always be aware that she could never be believed). Unless, of course, what we call "telling oneself something" is not at all the same thing as telling another person something, and the appearance of the same kind of act being addressed sometimes to another person and sometimes to oneself is an illusion. But in that case the concession is really no concession at all. On Anscombe's account the dependence in question rests on distinctions similar to Cavell's, such that believing someone is not simply believing what she says but believing it "on the strength of" her saying it (145). This is not itself sufficient to rule out cases of "double bluffing," in which a person believes what the speaker says because he takes her to be lying but to believe the contrary of the truth (151), and Anscombe leaves off the essay with the question why we should speak of believing the person only when we take the speaker to be both knowledgeable and truthful in intent, and whether circumscribing the idea of "belief with a personal object" in this way is a merely terminological feature of the ordinary case (that is, ordinary informing of another person and not "double bluffing"). Though she does not say so, this worry is to a significant extent dependent on the philosophical concentration on examples of single utterances outside the context of a continuing conversation. For we may think of ourselves as believing or disbelieving the speaker when we are in conversation with each other and there is the mutually understood possibility of replying to someone's assertion with "yes" or "no," where that expresses agreement or disagreement with *what the person said* and not private assent to something else (contrary to) the proposition affirmed. When the interlocutor is relating to the speaker's statement in the manner of "double bluffing," there is no possibility of replying to the speaker as though the two of them are talking about the same thing. Continuing the conversation would require the possibility of the interlocutor expressing agreement or disagreement with the proposition asserted to the speaker herself, addressing her in the second person and, e.g., asking her to respond to the challenge of her original assertion. But if the interlocutor takes the situation to be one where the speaker is either not knowledgeable or not sincere in what she says, but nonetheless one where her utterance can serve indirectly as an indication of some truth (perhaps, but not necessarily, the one asserted), then a challenge to the statement actually addressed to him will not be to the point, since either the interlocutor has already satisfied himself as to the epistemic import of the speaker's assertion or he cannot take further responses to his challenge to be relevant to what he wants to know. The possibility of believing the speaker (and not just the proposition affirmed) requires a mutually acknowledged dependence of the interlocutor on the speaker herself, and not merely the unilateral or unacknowledged inferential reliance on what she has done. The nature of this dependence on the person as such is left open by Anscombe and Cavell, but it is what we need to clarify in order understand the role of "otherness" that the idea of a "social act of mind" requires.

Zeno Vendler develops the distinction between what he calls a "weak sense of 'saying something'" which involves the mere utterance of a word or phrase, whether or not in a language one understands, and the "full" sense of saying something involving understanding and meaning what one says, in order to underscore the logical differences between thinking something and saying something (in the "full" sense) (1972, 53–54). In the course of this he makes some arguments against the equation of "thinking" or "judging" with a kind of "saying to oneself," one of which takes the following form.

> The illocutionary aspect leads to another trouble. How can I say—even mentally—something to myself? If I say—really say—to you, "He must have done it," I claim your belief. But if my realization that he must have done it actually consists in my saying to myself, "He must have done it," then how can I claim my own belief in something which I already realize in making that very claim? Thus I cannot say something to myself in the full sense of say. Is it then enough if that sentence merely crosses my mind? This cannot be, since the wildest sentences may cross my mind without my realizing anything. "No"—my opponent argues—"you must *assent* to it; 'this is it,' you must feel." Thus I must *recognize* it as the one I need, must *realize* that it contains my realization—and the infinite regress is on its way. (66–67)

The thought here is rather compressed, but the idea is that "saying" in the full, illocutionary sense requires more than the mental pronunciation of the words, but something like "assent" to the proposition expressed by those words. The point is thus restricted to forms of "saying" related to communicative speech acts like "telling" or "informing," and excludes other uses of words, either silently or aloud, where they serve not to communicate but simply to formulate one's thought, consider some possibility, etc. There is no "claiming of belief" when one silently repeats a series of numbers to oneself in the course of counting cigarettes, or when one mentally rehearses the steps in some complex task and runs through the different possible outcomes. And the "saying" involved in ordinary argument need not even involve presenting the proposition as true to one's interlocutor, but only presenting it as a consideration or as a possible rebuttal. If, however, we are considering the analogy of judging with mentally affirming to oneself, then Vendler's point would seem to be that my realization that "He must have done it" cannot be described as my mentally affirming that proposition to myself unless I understand my own (internal) words as expressing genuine assent to that claim in question. When he says, "how can I claim my own belief in something which I already realize in making that very claim?" he seems to be assuming that an utterance only counts as "saying" in the full sense if the speaker *believes* it ("something I already realize in making the claim"). And then the argument would be that telling oneself something is not so much impossible as pointless. Of course, in genuine interlocution a person may speak insincerely and "claim belief" of another speaker without herself believing what she is saying. What is required for the speech act of assertion is not actual belief but presenting one's statement as true. Then it seems that the suggestion would be that my mental assertion is pointless in another way, not because I already believe it, but because, being both speaker and audience, I cannot fail to know that I don't believe my own statement, and hence repeating it to myself can accomplish nothing. The description of the regress mentioned at the end plays on the ambiguity between the "realization" that "he must have done it," that is, the original thought in question, and the realization involved in "assent" to a sentence as being the one needed to express that thought. Once it is agreed that a mere train of words running through one's head cannot constitute a judgment about anything without a further mental act of "assent," then it would seem that we will need further silent words to be the act of assent itself, since that was really the cognitive act the original metaphor was meant to capture.

One might agree that, on pain of regress, thought and judgment cannot themselves be conceived of as forms of talking to oneself, since the inner speech itself would have to be expressive of thought in the sense of being "spoken" with understanding and not a mere silent mouthing of words. But not all talking, either to oneself or to others, is a matter of "saying" in Vendler's sense of "claiming belief" from one's interlocutor. We say things and talk with others when we reason and deliberate with each other, alongside countless other things we do together in words that have nothing to do with either deliberating or "claiming belief." Indeed much of what Reid describes as "solitary" acts of mind have their equivalents in acts that we perform together with others. Under this heading he includes remembering, reasoning, deliberating, and forming purposes, all of which are activities we can and do perform in talking with others as well (cf. Laden 2012). The question is not whether solitary acts of mind may also have social forms but rather to what extent the genuinely social acts of mind may have their equivalents in the case of silent or solitary speech, whether it is possible to substitute oneself for the missing conversational partner in performing acts like "testifying a fact" or "making a promise." But even in the case of internal monologue which is in the service of formulating and working out a problem for oneself, or rehearsing what one wants to say to someone else, or in exhorting oneself to do better, or cursing one's fate, in all of these the words that are part of one's internal monologue will have to already be part of one's understanding to do their job in deliberating or exhorting. Taking seriously the metaphor of thought itself as inner conversation means acknowledging the condition on ordinary discourse between two people, that if they are actually in conversation with each other, whether deliberating together or engaged in social acts like promising or making a request, they must *understand* what they are saying, and this understanding cannot itself be figured in terms of further levels of internal sayings.

7.2 Talking to Oneself, to Others, to No One

Common sense, after all, recommends that the purpose of speech is to convey thoughts to others; and a self-talker necessarily conveys them to someone who already knows them. To interrogate, inform, beseech, persuade, threaten, or command oneself is to push against oneself, or at best to get to where one already is, in either case with small chance of achieving movement. To say something to someone who can't hear it seems equally footless.[3]

What do we imagine talking to oneself to be? In the context of the "private language argument," after the discussion of the diary example, Wittgenstein asks, "Then did the man who made the entry in the calendar make a note of *nothing whatsoever?*—Don't consider it a matter of course that a person is making a note of something when he makes a mark—say in a calendar" (1956, § 260). Then he adds parenthetically at the end: "(One can talk to oneself.—If a person speaks when no one else is present, does that mean that he is speaking to himself?)." The implied answer to his question is no. However we are to understand the phenomenon of "talking to oneself," it will not be sufficient for me to be talking *to* myself or anyone else that I be speaking when no one else is around. At the very least, I must be *addressing* my words to the person in question to be talking to him, and that fact itself is one that presumes a wider practice of speaking and responding to the speech of others. The act of speaking must take place within the context of a set of practices for it to have the significance of asserting something or telling someone something, just as the mark made in a calendar by the "private diarist" only has the significance of a *note* of something (e.g., the recurrence of a certain sensation) given the wider grammar of sensation-language, the existence and use of calendars, and the practice of keeping notes and reminders. In a related context in his earlier "Notes for Lectures on 'Private Experience' and 'Sense Data,'" Wittgenstein says, "When one says 'I talk to myself' one generally means just that one speaks and is the only person listening."[4] Again, the suggestion is that speaking while alone, either aloud or silently, is not itself sufficient to count as speaking *to* anyone at all. Leaving aside Wittgenstein's larger point about privacy here, these remarks allow us to distinguish several different possibilities.

(a) I am talking aloud while alone, and I am the only one listening to myself.

---

3 Goffman 1978, "Response Cries," 789. The article contains valuable analyses of the varieties of what he calls "self-talk."
4 Wittgenstein 1993, 208. Later he asks, "Can't I say something to nobody, neither to anybody else *nor* to myself? What is the criterion of saying it to myself?" (258).

(b) I am alone but talking aloud distractedly, unaware of myself, and *no one* is listening, not even myself.

(c) I am talking aloud to an absent person, or someone long gone, or an imaginary friend.

(d) I am talking aloud with other people around, but to no one in particular, to whoever may hear.

(e) I am talking aloud, but not talking *to* anyone, for I am "thinking aloud" in the sense of articulating a thought, laying out the possibilities of some course of action, etc., and this externalization helps me make my thought clear and explicit. Thinking aloud need not be seen as *addressing* oneself any more than ordinary silent thought does.

(f) In a silent internal monologue I explicitly formulate the steps of my thought in words, or I find that the words come naturally to me and seem the right expression for what I want to say.

(g) I am hearing a voice within and hearkening to it, perhaps certain of its meaning, perhaps seeking to interpret what it means. Here I don't take myself to be doing the (silent) talking.

(h) I am talking aloud and blaming myself for what happened, or telling myself that I have done enough (Cavell 1979, 391).

(i) In a silent internal monologue I am telling myself that I am to blame for what happened, or that I have done enough.

Just as it is not sufficient to be speaking to someone that I be talking while they are in earshot, so it is not sufficient for talking to myself, whether silently or aloud, that I be talking in my own presence, so to speak. Just as addressing another person requires more than that he can hear what I am saying, so it seems the same condition should apply to either form of talking to oneself. In a typical case, when I wish to talk to someone, I will need to *address* that person somehow, to call him or otherwise attract his attention. This will normally mean, however, that I am already thinking of that person, have already called him to my own attention and now seek to draw his attention to *me*. If so, then how can I call myself to my own attention if that requires the same act of having a particular person in mind that precedes the overt act of seeking to attract the attention of another person when I address him and tell him something? Perhaps one will think that this just shows how much easier things are in discourse with oneself, since here we save a step, and merely thinking of gaining one's own audience ensures one's own success. In ordinary discourse I may employ the second person in saying, "You're standing on my foot" to someone on a crowded bus, but fail to attract the attention of the person who is actually on my foot and instead gain the response of the wrong person, who protests his innocence. If this suggests that the use of the second person addressed to oneself is immune to such errors, as the first person is often understood to be, then this very parallel should cast doubt on the idea that there is any genuine addressing going on in such cases.

The cases described in (a) mark Wittgenstein's point that speaking while one is the only one listening is not by itself an analogue to talking *to* another person, with the place of the other person here taken up by oneself. As with the case of two or more individuals, more would need to be added to the description for it to be a case of a person talking to someone (perhaps herself). The case described in (b) adds the reminder that even Wittgenstein's assumption that I am the only one listening is not in fact always fulfilled when we talk out loud with no one else around. (There seems no reason to doubt that this same possibility of distracted, unheeded monologue is possible in the case of silent, internal monologue as well, which adds a further wrinkle to the picture of thought or judgment as a kind of internal dialogue. What if the soul described by Socrates poses questions to itself but fails to hearken to itself, out of its own internal earshot, as it were?) When I talk to an absent friend (c), or to someone no longer alive, I am clearly only talking to someone in an attenuated or figurative sense. That is not at all to say that such apostrophe is senseless or cannot be a serious act. But it cannot be the same as, for example, a genuine confession to the wronged person or the expression of gratitude there was never time for while the person was still alive, for here there is no possibility of response (or the risk of rebuke rather than the hoped-for or imagined response from the other person), and in the imagined dialogue the speaker would have to be playing both roles. A person can be talking aloud in the street, or in a lecture hall, where no particular person is being addressed (d), and even where there is only the slimmest chance that anyone is indeed listening. Here one's words are still *addressed*, however, and to actual, potentially responding people, and thus not like the previous three cases (a, b, c). Addressing in speech need not pick out a particular individual. In such situations the anxiety or irritation that no one may in fact be listening is sometimes expressed with words like, "I hope I'm not just talking to myself up here," but again, the mere absence of an attentive audience on the outside does not by itself ensure that one is addressing, let alone reaching, an audience on the inside. Nor does the intended addressee of one's words change from the outside audience to oneself just upon the discovery that one isn't reaching one's intended audience.

The activity of articulating a thought in words spoken aloud (c) can be part of speech addressed to another person, but it need not be. Even when this activity is carried out in the company of other people, the role of others in such discourse can vary from mere witnesses to active interlocutors. The activity of articulating one's thought in words, formulating a plan, following through an argument, etc., can be done either silently, or out loud but alone, or as part of a conversation with others. This is not far from the picture described in the *Theaetetus*, and it is presumably this kind of activity that Christine Korsgaard has in mind when she says that "thinking is just talking to yourself, and talking is just thinking in the company of others" (2009, xiii). But if the point is to highlight the parallel between cases like (e) and the articulation of thought that can take place in silent internal monologue (f), we should note that what matters to the activity described in cases like (f) is the explicitness of the verbal formulation and not the fact that those words are addressed to anyone at all, either oneself or another. Even hearkening to one's own silent verbal articulation, so as to be able to write it down later, is not the same as addressing those words to oneself or anyone else.

So when philosophers and others refer to "talking to oneself," especially when that is taken to be on analogy with solitary thought and judgment, it is usually what we may call the "articulative" sense of talking that people have in mind, as in (e), out loud, or (f), silently. But what is the force of the word "just" in Korsgaard's claim that thinking is "just" talking to oneself, and that talking with others is "just" thinking aloud in the company of others, and what picture of talking and thinking is being challenged in these formulations? In the context of her book *Self-Constitution*, as well as other work, it is clear that two related targets are a picture of thought and reasoning as essentially private activities that take place in a sphere independent of and inaccessible to the public world, and a basically instrumental picture of talking as the attempt to have an impact on the private mental lives of others. Against this she defends a picture according to which someone thinking to him- or herself, especially when doing so in explicitly verbal thought, is already inhabiting a public space of reasons, as one does in the give and take of ordinary conversation with others. And in such conversation with others the participants think of both their own contributions and the ones addressed to them as activities governed by norms of truth and rationality understood as public and shareable, and not as so many efforts to have an effect on the beliefs of one's interlocutor or resist the impact that others are seeking to have on one's own beliefs.[5] The picture of social acts of mind developed in this book, in particular the general relation between the criticism of the Unilateral model of the meaning of speech acts like telling, and the criticism of the Indicative model of the significance for the interlocutor of the speaker's utterance, is an elaboration of a related perspective on thought and speech. But in Korsgaard this is part of a larger Kantian point to the effect that relations with others and relations with oneself are ideally modeled on each other, that the fairness and truthfulness we wish to embody in our lives with others are to be understood as the kinds of relations in which we stand to ourselves, or cannot help standing toward ourselves,[6] and that the social aspect of such forms of relation can be absorbed within an understanding of how a single person relates to him- or herself. As she puts it toward the end of the book, "Every person interacts with others as he interacts with himself, and in this the good person is no different. A person who cannot keep a promise to himself cannot keep a promise to another. . . . Inward and outward justice go together" (206). In one way this can be seen as responding to the same demand for parity in how we treat and think of others and how we treat and think of ourselves that is given expression in Thomas Nagel's "Impersonal Principle": "To regard oneself in every respect as merely one person among others, one must be able to regard oneself in every respect impersonally" (Nagel 1970, 102).

In *Authority and Estrangement* (2001) I argue that the demand for impersonality cannot be legitimate if it is understood to require the effacement of the asymmetries, both practical and epistemic, between, for example, a person's relation to her own desires and preferences and the desires and preferences of others (Moran 2001, secs. 5.2, 5.5). Even though I acknowledge that I am "merely one person among others," it doesn't follow from this that in a situation of conflict and compromise with others, for

---

5 See her criticism of Sidgwick on the prohibition against lying, at the end of which she reiterates the claim that "Thinking, after all, is just talking to yourself" (2009, 196–97).

6 In a footnote she defines what she calls the "Platinum Rule": "Do unto others as you cannot help but do unto yourself" (2009, 183 n. 3).

example, I am entitled to take my own desires or preferences into consideration just as I do those of other people. For with regard to other people I can be obliged to *defer* to their desires and preferences, even when I find them misguided, even when I believe they would regret their choices if they saw things as I do. Such deference makes no sense with regard to my own desires and preferences. To recognize my own preference as misguided or misinformed is itself to call that preference into question, if not to abandon it outright. I might continue to feel the pull of the rejected preference, I might even feel that it is hopeless to fight against it and that I should plan on it getting the better of me at the moment of choice, but none of this is deferring to *myself*, but rather acquiescing to something that I *don't* take to represent myself or my own view of what is really preferable. To defer to the preferences of others even when we disagree with them is a form of respecting the other person, seeing her choices as rightfully "up to her"; to treat one's own preferences as fixed and to be accommodated even when misguided is to retreat from seeing them as up to oneself in the relevant sense, and will normally be a form of perverse obstinacy or bad faith. From the first-person point of view I may impose a sacrifice on myself that I am not in a position to impose on others. The self-other asymmetries that govern thought and action are themselves part of moral life and not something that the moral point of view can coherently seek to overcome. We lose sight of this when we think of the first-person point of view purely as a source of egocentric privilege, favoring or making an exception of oneself.

There are versions of Nagel's "Impersonal Principle" in both utilitarianism ("Everybody to count for one, nobody for more than one") and in Kant, but in the passages above Korsgaard is responding to a version of the demand in Kant that expresses itself not in the impersonal point of view itself ("The View from Nowhere") but rather in the internalization within oneself of two distinct points of view of an intersubjective relation, on the one hand, and the externalization toward others of the person's point of view on herself ("Do unto others as you cannot help but do unto yourself"), on the other. Insofar as normativity is grounded in autonomy, the person is understood as a self-legislator, bound only by a law that she gives herself. Our duties to other people are to be understood as grounded in our fundamental duty to ourselves. The external relation between lawgiver and subject of the law is represented within the person in the form of the distinction between two "selves," the empirical and the noumenal, and the possible relations they stand toward one another. As with Nagel's Impersonal Principle, however, the tendency is toward an ideal overcoming of the specific differences in the possibilities and the necessities in our relations to ourselves and our relations to others. Here as well, there are limits on the coherence of either taking a fully impersonal view on oneself or internalizing both parts of a social or interpersonal relation. For not all the forms of doing unto others have correlates in our relations to ourselves. A person may be pleased or displeased with herself, but cannot be said to envy herself or be jealous of herself; one may laugh at oneself, but the idea of insulting oneself strains coherence, especially if we are to include, as it seems we should, the reaction of hurt and indignation to the insult, or the possible confrontation with the insulter and the demand for retraction. We sometimes say that a person should or will thank herself later for something she's about to do, but without understanding that to include room for an ordinary reciprocal response to the thanks of the form, "You're quite welcome, you would have done the same for me." We sometimes speak of "inviting oneself along" to some occasion, but when we do we don't include the possibility of surprise and delight that I, of all people, should have been invited, or the regrettable necessity of politely declining the invitation this time, or the social obligation of returning the invitation before long. I can ask myself a question, either silently or aloud, and answer my own question, but I cannot ask myself as an informant to confirm my own suspicion, or swear to myself that what I say is true this time, asking myself to accept my own offer of trust. And when I do "tell myself I have done enough," I surely cannot respond to this assurance with the relief that I would when the other person I am trying to help tells me I have done enough. Here one's own assurance cannot substitute for the one needed, the one that must come from another. In all of these cases it seems that the scenario of possible relations to oneself borrows only parts of the relevant concepts, whose primary application is in their other-directed, other-dependent applications, and as a result although the same word may be used to describe a certain real possibility in self-relation, it cannot mean the same thing as it does in its social context. There is such a thing as self-respect, but insofar as respecting other people includes forms of deferral to them, stepping aside for them, self-respect cannot be a version of that deference somehow directed toward oneself.

7.3 Supplying the Missing Interlocutor

In the passage above Korsgaard says, "A person who cannot keep a promise to himself cannot keep a promise to another," and the possibility of promising to oneself, or self-obligation in general, has been controversial since before Kant made self-legislation the cornerstone of his moral philosophy. Hobbes's argument for the sovereignty of the Commonwealth rests on the denial that the one imposing an obligation and the one subject to that obligation can be one and the same person, since if the power to bind and the power to release are in the same hands, then no one is bound.

> No one can give anything to himself, because he is already assumed to have what he can give to himself. Nor can one be obligated to oneself; for since the obligated and the obligating party would be the same, and the obligating party may release the obligated, obligation to oneself would be meaningless, because he can release himself at his own discretion, and anyone who can do this is in fact free.[7]

On this view the concepts of duty or obligation would seem to be paradigms for the forms of relation that require a genuine distinctness of persons, for the forms of dependence or deference that characterize such relations can have no application to a selfsame individual. A promise is a free act in which the promisor relinquishes a part of her freedom to a different person, who then has the power to demand fulfilment of the promise or to release the promisor from the obligation should the promisee no longer wish its fulfillment. If the promiser could always release herself from her promise, then no obligation would have been created by the promise in the first place. When Hobbes speaks of the "discretion" with which the person can always release herself from the obligation, he is stressing that the ideas of promise and obligation require the ordinary dependence on or deference to a will that is not one's own, an independent freedom and subjectivity. By contrast, when we speak in ordinary life of forms of obligation to oneself, it is precisely this discretion of the person imposing obligation that is missing from the picture. When we tell someone, "You owe it to yourself" to do something, we can mean many things, such as that he really should do it, that doing so should take precedence over other competing concerns, or that he'll regret it if he fails to do it, but normally the very point of the language of such an

---

7 *The Citizen*, 6.14., in Hobbes 1998. The same point is made in *Leviathan* 26.6.

intervention is to stress that this course of action is not something merely optional for the person, but is rather something not to be avoided, and that we thus do not take ourselves to be addressing at once the creditor and the debtor of this "owing" such that the creditor may at her discretion cancel the debt at any time. To say to someone, "You owe it to yourself" to do something, is specifically *not* to say, "Of course, you might just as well not do it, since you might in this case decline to collect on what is otherwise rightfully owed to you. You are creditor as well as debtor here, after all." Here again, we take fragments of this social normative structure and apply them to oneself as a single person, and thus without the separation and independence of the two parties that is integral to the primary notion.

In his discussion of the idea of duties to oneself, Kant also begins with the insistence on the distinctness of persons for the ordinary idea of duty and obligation, and echoes the language in Hobbes to make this point. In the *Metaphysics of Morals*, he begins the section on duties to oneself with the assertion that "the concept of duty to oneself contains (at first glance) a contradiction."

> If the I that imposes obligation is taken in the same sense as the I that is put under obligation, a duty to oneself is a self-contradictory concept. For the concept of duty contains the concept of being passively constrained (I am bound). But if the duty is a duty to myself, I think of myself as binding and so as actively constraining (I, the same subject, am imposing obligation). . . . One can also bring this contradiction to light by pointing out that the one imposing obligation [*auctor obligationis*] could always release the one put under obligation [*subiectum obligationis*] from the obligation [*terminus obligationis*], so that (if both are one and the same subject) he would not be bound at all to a duty he lays upon himself. This involves a contradiction. (Kant 1996, 6:417, p. 543)

Since for Kant there can be no duties at all unless there can be duties to oneself, the solution to this antimony will be sought in the distinction between distinct *aspects* of the person, different *faculties*, or different "selves" which are recognized from the perspective of practical reason. He prepares for this thought with the substantivization of the first-person pronoun "I," to which philosophy has become so accustomed in the centuries since Kant, and says that there must be more than one "I" in question to resolve the apparent contradiction in the idea of duties to oneself. Since the original antinomy results from the application of a concept whose home is in the normative relation between distinct individual freedoms to a form of relation a person may bear to him- or herself, the solution is to be sought in some form of duality, "a doubled self" (Kant 1996, 6:439, p. 560n), that can reproduce the dependence of the person under obligation on the person imposing the obligation. And for these purposes it is important to be clear about the differences as well as similarities between, on the one hand, ordinary human beings and their possible relations to each other, and on the other hand the "faculties," "aspects," and "selves" and their possible relations to each other (or to the person as a whole). Since the original antinomy of obligations to oneself derives from the *identity* of the *auctor obligationis* and the *subiectum obligationis*, where such relations of obligation normally require the *difference* or distinctness between the person's occupying these two roles, the challenge is to describe the conditions for the application of a concept like duty (or promise, or telling as informing) where there is a relation of identity between the occupants of the two roles, but nonetheless enough of a distinction or difference between them to allow for the forms of deference and dependence that the concept seems to require.

In the continuation of the passage Kant appeals to the distinction between the "two attributes" under which a person views herself, as a "sensible being" and as an "intelligible being," the latter aspect being something which is "cognized only in morally practical relations." Given that the original antinomy rests on the challenge to installing within one and the same person a form of relation whose concept is grounded in the separation of powers of distinct individuals, it is not surprising that the language in Kant's account should register a tension between describing a possible relation a person bears simply to herself as such (as in, for example, restraining oneself or defending oneself) and a possible relation a person may bear to something *other* than herself, that is, to a different "self," to a part or aspect of herself, or to something "inside" herself. The simple reflexive form of description in "She defended herself as best she could" expresses a relation the person bears to herself as such, and not a relation to some part of herself or something within herself. In such a purely reflexive self-relation there is no duality between agent and patient (one defending, and the other being defended), and no need to describe a kind of separation of powers within the person in order to avoid contradiction. But Kant recognizes that normative acts like entitling or imposing an obligation do require a duality of some sort, and hence oblige the philosopher to find a way to distinguish the obligating party and the one obligated. The opening of the passage above says that we encounter contradiction if we take the "I" imposing obligation in the same sense as the "I" put under obligation, and the "solution" of the antimony in section 3 appeals to the thought that the person conscious of duty to herself views herself under "two attributes," as a "sensible being" and as an "intelligible being," which distinction of attributes is further nominalized in referring to this as the difference between *homo phaenomenon* and *homo noumenon*. Since what will be crucial for resolving this tension is whether the duality we arrive at can reproduce the kinds of relations between the *auctor obligationis* and the *subiectum obligationis*, it may be natural to think that the point of this division is to argue that the "sensible being" and the "intelligible being" can be seen in some sense as distinct individuals who can reproduce between them the relation of the one imposing obligation and the one obligated. In this way perhaps, the person as phenomenon could be obligated to the person as noumenon, without being in a position to unilaterally release herself from that obligation, since the empirical person is indeed being obligated by someone other than herself. But while Kant does indeed soon return to the language of division to resolve the original antimony, what he immediately goes on to say is that "*the same human being* thought in terms of his personality, that is, as a being endowed with inner freedom (*homo noumenon*), is regarded as a being that can be put under obligation and, indeed, *under obligation to himself* (to the humanity in his own person)" (emphases added). In the shift to the language affirming identity over difference, the original tension reasserts itself since either it is now simply assumed as a capacity of the *homo noumenon's* relation to itself that it somehow avoids the original antimony and can be both obligator and obligated without falling into contradiction, or (returning to the language of difference) the relation to something *other* to itself (the "humanity in his own person") provides sufficient distance between the two parties such that the *homo noumenon* is not in fact occupying both roles at once but is indeed obligated to something or someone other than itself, something within itself. Either approach to the original contradiction is problematic, for it is either claimed without explanation that the *homo noumenon* does not in fact fall into contradiction when it places itself under obligation to itself, or we are referred to something genuinely other to the person to serve as *auctor obligationis*, but something that is not itself a person and thus without the capacities and forms of authority that would be required for a genuine person to place another under obligation. This applies to the language of "internalization" as much as it does to the language of "doubling": what is "incorporated" within the person is either a part or aspect of the person, or simply the person herself seen from the perspective of some role or value. If we are thinking of the person herself, then we have moved no further from Kant's original antinomy, and if we are thinking of parts or aspects of the person, they are not such as to stand in social normative relations with each other such as commanding or obligating, which are possible only for whole persons.

It may be said that Kant's apparent reference to different "selves" and their relations does not require anything resembling a multiplicity of persons, but is rather a way of representing conflicts of values or of roles that a person may occupy. The "substantive" language describing the characters *homo phaenomenon* and *homo noumenon* or *auctor obligationis* and *subiectum obligationis* would be seen as a dispensable way of representing contrasting claims of different aspects or values of one and the same person. But if that were Kant's meaning, there would be no antinomy to solve and no need to speak of a "doubling" of the person, or of different "I's." Instead we would be describing the ordinary forms of conflict of aims or values that an undivided human being confronts in life. To describe such conflict in terms of a doubling of the self suggests that we can best understand a single, *undivided* self in terms of some single univocal value, something not in potential conflict with other values, since once we do have a conflict of values we will need to appeal to an additional "self" to play the part of the conflicting value. But that is the wrong way to count "selves," and indeed, this is one place where the very language of different "selves" causes trouble. A person, a human being, is someone who occupies different roles and can experience conflicts of values. And we do not individuate persons in terms of single, univocal values; a particular human being is someone who embodies many different roles and values and is not identical with any particular one of them.

The language of different "selves" encourages equivocation on this point. Either we are shifting between talk of persons (actual individuals) who *have* aims and values, and talk about the aims and values themselves; or we are favoring a form of expression such that that each value can be seen as "offering attractions" or "making demands" in much the same way that an actual living individual can make demands, and that such conflict can be understood the way we understand conflict between people. But the meaning of this latter form of expression (i.e., a value making particular demands) is difficult to distinguish from the purely formal claim that different aims

and values provide the person with different motivating reasons for potentially incompatible actions, which is after all the role of differing values, and
doesn't itself provide reason to divide the person into different "selves." And
indeed if different roles and values did need to be represented as different
"selves," then any ordinary person would have to be seen as inhabited by
a multitude of "selves," which only makes more urgent the need to *distinguish* "selves" from anything like persons or human beings, in order for it to
be possible to describe how an ordinary human being can "contain" them.
And once this distinction between ordinary persons and "selves" *is* made,
then it will turn out that the "selves" were just stand-ins for the values or
roles themselves. In this way "selves" turn out to be of quite a different logical type from ordinary persons, and cannot interact the way persons do,
since unlike persons, "selves" cannot *occupy* roles or *pursue* values, for they
are simply these roles and values themselves under a different guise.[8]

When Kant returns to this problem in his description of the conscience,
he describes it as a kind of "internal court," whose role as a judging and
obligating agency within the person requires at one stroke its distinctness
from the person as such and its identity with the person.

> Every human being has a conscience and finds himself observed, threatened,
> and, in general, kept in awe (respect coupled with fear) by an internal judge.
> (1996, 6:438, p. 560)

Kant stresses what is paradoxical in the very idea of conscience as both
representing a form of first-person consciousness and a form of alienation, relating to this voice as that of a being *other than oneself*, when he says
that this conscience "is peculiar in that, although its business is a business
of a human being with himself, one constrained by his reason sees himself
constrained to carry it on as at the bidding of *another person*" (560, emphasis
in original). And the reason for this emphasis on alienation is precisely the

---

8 I am grateful to Béatrice Longuenesse for discussion of this section and for trying to set me
straight. I should emphasize that I don't see Kant as having a settled position here, for in
the passages discussed here I see him as acknowledging that the relations of obligation he is
describing require distinct persons in relation to each other, and that only living persons can
perform acts like imposing obligations or releasing others from obligation. But the project of
grounding obligation generally in autonomy and self-legislation leads him to seek to install
the right kind of "otherness" within one and the same person, which project encounters the
problem that within one and the same person there may be many things (e.g., conflicting aims
or values), but nothing with the status of another person to whom one might be in a relation
of obligation.

sort of separation of powers that is required by the juridical model favored
by Kant:

> For the affair here is that of trying a case [*causa*] before a court. But to think of
> a human being who is accused by his conscience as one and the same person
> as the judge is an absurd way of representing a court, since then the pros-
> ecutor would always lose.—For all duties a human being's conscience will,
> accordingly, have to think of someone other than himself (i.e., other than the
> human being as such) as the judge of his actions, if conscience is not to be in
> contradiction with itself. (560)

The idea that "the prosecutor would always lose" is a version of the
Hobbesian problem Kant identifies in the original antinomy: "the one imposing obligation [*auctor obligationis*] could always release the one put under
obligation." The prosecutor would always lose because the person on the
dock, as both judge and accused, could always dismiss the charges as not
applying in this case.

As if to drive home the paradox in the form of moral psychology he is
asking us to imagine here, Kant adds in a note to this paragraph:

> A human being who accuses and judges himself in conscience must think of
> a dual personality in himself, a doubled self which, on the one hand, has to
> stand trembling at the bar of a court that is yet entrusted to him, but which, on
> the other hand, itself administers the office of judge that it holds by innate au-
> thority. This requires clarification, if reason is not to fall into self-contradiction.

The person accused stands trembling before an authority whose power
is beyond appeal, fearful of its judgment yet knowing she has no choice
but to submit to whatever the sentence turns out to be. The very posture
of submission, of "respect coupled with fear," stresses the otherness of the
power delivering judgment upon her, and yet all the while and in that same
posture the person must recognize that this is no alien power at all but is an
authority that she must acknowledge as entirely her own. The hearkening
to one's conscience is to be seen as an exercise in autonomy, not heter-
onomy. The self is doubled, at least enough for the separation of powers required of a court that is not a sham, but at the same time the self is one and
identical with the whole proceeding. What it trembles before at the bar it
must recognize as nothing other than itself, and yet that recognition should
not bring the relief that follows the realization that one had been startled
by nothing more than one's own reflection, but rather a renewed sense of

"respect coupled with fear." In Kant and elsewhere the voice of conscience has to represent itself as both something *other* to oneself, and as one's true or more authentic self.

However, when we interpret the language of "selves" so as to preserve the separation of powers Kant sees as necessary to resolving the original antinomy, and think of them no longer as parts or aspects but as actual moral beings who exist in relations of obligation and subordination to each other, we should be able to ask how these two "selves" came to be in such a relation to each other, how it is that one of them came to be in a position to obligate or submit to the judgment of the other. In the ordinary case of a promise between two empirical people, there will be a story to tell as to how the obligation was first generated, and how the two parties must understand their interaction such that one of them is now obligated to perform what is stated in the promise. These two individuals will have interacted with each other in various ways, or will live under a certain political regime that will account for how and whether they stand in these particular relations to each other. The relation of authority between the empirical self and the noumenal self is not like this, however, and there is no question, for instance, that the empirical self might legitimately challenge the authority of the noumenal self or someday liberate herself from its authority altogether, perhaps transferring her allegiance to a different noumenal self or to some like-minded group of empirical selves who are forming a community elsewhere. These "selves" have to be conceived of as person-like in order to enter into relations of authority and obligation, just as they would have to be for one of them to owe money to the other or dissolve their partnership. However, insofar as they are indeed person-like and genuinely distinct from each other, their particular normative relations must have a history that accounts for them and the possibility of a different development in the future. And in the case of the idea of conscience as an internal court we would have to find room for the full normative structure of actual relations of judgment and accusation between people, which include the possibilities of appeal, retraction, and counteraccusation. The conscience as an agency that can *only* "observe, threaten and keep in awe" is by that very one-dimensionality not a being one can enter into social or moral relations with.[9]

---

9 Naturally, insofar as this picture of the conscience is a development of the monotheistic image of God, the unilaterality of the relation is not accidental to it.

7.4 And Who Shall I Say Is Calling?

The very language of different "selves" obscures the difference that matters here, between a plurality of persons who perform acts which constitute the making of a promise or the imposing of an obligation, and "parts" or "aspects" of a person which, while we can describe them as in conflict or in harmony with each other, are not such as to enter into the normative relations like promising and obligating, which are reserved for ordinary persons who can also relate to each other in different ways. When we speak of one's ambition as being in conflict with one's fear of failure, or of a struggle within oneself between vanity and courage, we are not describing the scene of possible normative relations, since one part or faculty of a person cannot command or promise another part (or the whole person), any more than the person's left hand can do so. A part of a person or a "self" within the person cannot give an assurance to another part or "self" any more than it can cast a vote or pay back a debt. When the word "self" belongs to the ordinary reflexive form of words like "oneself" or "herself," then it expresses a relation of identity and not a relation between two different people or two different parts of a single person. The idea of different "selves" is really an oxymoron, since the word "self" is here the fragment of another word ("himself," "herself") whose purpose is precisely to express identity and not difference. Within such identity we can describe such conditions as being frustrated with oneself or such actions as defending oneself, where this involves no self-division or multiplication of selves, but rather the ordinary reflexive form in which we maintain the sense of speaking of one and the same undivided person (cf. Descombes 2004, esp. chaps. 12–13).

The language of different "selves" composing a person is sometimes applied to the temporal aspect of human existence, and this may be thought to afford the requisite "difference-in-identity" to allow us to internalize within one person the forms of interpersonal relatedness that make up our lives with other people. So, for instance, a promise to oneself is sometimes described as a commitment to one's "future self," and the act of informing oneself by "testifying a fact" (Reid) may be made out in terms of communication with one's future self. In "Language and Communication" Michael Dummett argues that "the use of language for self-addressed utterances, whether silent or aloud, is an imitation of its use in linguistic interchange, and involves nothing essentially different," and appeals to the idea of temporal selves in asking rhetorically, "Could we not save the thesis that language is primarily an instrument of communication by regarding the people in Wittgenstein's fantasy as communicating with themselves? Is not someone writing in his private diary communicating with his future self? If so, is not someone soliloquizing communicating with his present self?" (Dummett 1993a, 185). As to this last question, we have already seen that by itself soliloquy need not count as addressing anyone at all, neither one-self nor another nor some other version of oneself. On a given occasion a speaker may not be seeking any audience at all, and is not provided with an audience with herself simply in virtue of the absence of any other one in her vicinity. And while it is perfectly true that someone writing in her diary may then read what she has written at a future date and thereby learn something or at least be reminded of it, what happens here is not a self-directed version of a dialogue between two people, precisely because there cannot be any encounter or any reciprocity between the two "parties" in the exchange (see Haase 2014, 5). If we allow ourselves to speak of present and future selves as though they were persons who can enter into relations of promisor and promisee or teller and person told, then the elaboration of the analogy will have to take seriously the metaphysical consequences of their temporal distinctness from each other, which means that they can never enter into the give and take of genuine interlocutors. The present self can do something like make an entry in a diary with the intention of leaving a trace that will be encountered by the future self, but the present self can never hope for a reply from the future self, nor can the future self bring any considerations to bear on the past self. By the nature of the case the temporal "parts" of a person can never encounter one another, for the existence of the one excludes the existence of the other. While the person reading her diary entry later may go so far as to address her "past self" with the second-person pronoun and ask, "What could you have been thinking here?" there cannot be what Benveniste calls the reversibility of "I" and "you" such that in a situation of dialogue the two parties shift between the one speaking as "I" and the one being addressed as "you." The "you" here could only be rhetorical, since it is spoken without the reciprocal possibility of the person addressed as "you" replying in her own voice by saying "I" and addressing the first speaker as "you." Instead, the idea of communica-tion between different temporal stages of a person can only be represented unilaterally. The present self can produce the effect of belief on its future self, but there can be no conversation between them since from the per-spective of one "self" the other partner has to be forever silent, out of reach.

And the idea of trying to reconstruct a notion of commitment out of the relations between temporal stages of a person would founder on the fact that there can be no relations of commitment between entities whose existence is not just transitory, but indexed to particular times such that they cannot in principle be present to each other. The forms of commitment (and the possibility of follow-through) that are enacted in promising and telling are only possible between whole persons who exist *in* time, are identifiable across times, and can be present to each other in the same time.

In the passage above, Dummett moves indifferently from the case of someone writing a reminder for himself in a diary to the idea of soliloquy as "communicating with his present self," but the ordinary possibility of writing a reminder for oneself later is not what is at issue in Anscombe's denial that the verb "believe" with a personal object can be reflexive, or Cavell's similar claim about "believing myself." What is important to these claims is precisely the first-person reflexive form, which is exhibited in the form of illocution itself but not in the case of reading one's own entry in a diary. We have seen that it is essential to an illocutionary act that it is performed intentionally and in self-conscious understanding of its import as one sort of speech act rather than another. In this the illocutionary differs from the perlocutionary aspect of speech, whose effects may be intentional or not, known to the speaker or not, and which knowledge may be for the speaker a matter of ordinary observation. By contrast, for the speaker to constitute her utterance as an assertion rather than a question or supposition is for her to commit herself explicitly in speech, where the sense of "herself" is precisely the reflexive (cf. Anscombe [1975] 1981 and Geach 1957). "Committing herself" in this way is not a transitive act performed upon herself (or her "self"), but is rather the exercise of a form of practical agency by an undivided person. As such it is the manifestation of a form of self-consciousness whose expression is a first-person thought understood "reflexively," where that means that the identity between the thinker (or speaker) and the topic of the thought (the person whose illocution is in question) is not accidental but defines the form of thought itself. Here, unlike various possible cases of mistaken identity in other contexts, the speaker could not fail to appreciate the identity between herself and the producer of the utterance. Insofar as she is making an assertion or other illocution, she is aware that "she herself" is doing so, and knows this first-personally. By contrast, with regard to other things one's discourse may be provoking (perlocutionarily or otherwise), one may need to determine that it is in fact oneself and not another person in the conversation who is responsible.

When a speaker makes an assertion or a promise, her reflexive self-consciousness of her act is expressed in the fact that there is no question for her whose act of assertion is in question, no question for her of identifying who the source of the utterance is. If in her speech she took it to be possible for her to misidentify herself as the person speaking, if her consciousness of herself were "as object" and not "as subject" (Wittgenstein 1958, 66–74), then neither she nor her audience could understand her as being in the course of making an assertion or a promise. For her audience, perhaps at the other end of a telephone line, the question "Who is this speaking now?" may be the beginning of establishing communication, but for the speaker herself this could only be the confession of a kind of dissociation suspending the possibility of ordinary conversation itself. This absence of identification in the first-person consciousness of the speaker is related to another aspect of its reflexivity. The speaker's knowledge of the illocutionary status of her utterance (e.g., whether serious or not, whether an assertion or a mere conjecture) is practical as well as institutional. That is, for her to know whether she is making an assertion rather than a mere conjecture is for her to know how she means to commit herself or decline to commit herself in her speech act. This is essentially first-personal awareness as well. For the speaker to be in doubt as to whether she is producing her utterance as an assertion or as mere conjecture can only mean that she has not yet settled the status of her claim here, and hence her utterance can't count fully as one or the other, either for herself or for her audience.

Any uncertainty the speaker herself may entertain about how she means her utterance to count as a reason is a ground for uncertainty as to whether her utterance *has* any definite illocutionary status. To say, "I'm fairly sure that I'm promising you a ride to work, but I could be wrong" would be to undermine the possibility that this utterance could count as a promise of a ride to work, nor could the audience treat it as one. The self-consciousness expressed in the speaker's speech act, her certainty or uncertainty about how it is to count in the conversation, is not separate from the reality of the illocution itself, but is a constituent element of it. The speaker's own expression of uncertainty will mean the hedging or qualification of the commitments undertaken in speech, rather than a theoretical question about an illocution whose identity is already constituted. The speaker's resolution of such uncertainty is not a matter of the discovery of a truth about

her own illocution, a discovery which might in principle be made by another person as well as herself, but is rather the resolution of her practical
commitments in speech, an essentially first-person expression of her autonomy. It is a question for the speaker to answer for herself, and her interlocutor is dependent on her resolution in order to know how to respond
to what she has said.

In confronting a page from my diary, I am in a quite different relation to
what I find there. Here I do indeed need to identify the person who is the
source of that entry, and I realize that it is perfectly possible that I could be
mistaken as to who actually wrote it. Even if I am the writer of those words
and know it, my knowledge here is not "identification-free" in Evans's sense,
and is not an expression of the reflexive self-consciousness of my act at the
time of writing the entry. In the act of writing, there was no room for the
thought, "I see under my hand these words appearing. Someone is writing
a note here which looks like a reminder about a doctor's appointment, but
who? And is it an actual doctor's appointment in question or could this
writing be an experiment in fiction?" In reading the entry, if I thought that
there was for the writer, in the act of writing those words, an open question
as to whose words they were and what their significance might be, I could
not, reading them now, relate to them as a possible form of testimony at all.
But as reader of my own words written earlier, my possible uncertainty as
to whether I am indeed the author of that diary entry does not suggest any
alienated state of mind on the part of the person who wrote it. Likewise,
any uncertainty I may have now as to the particular illocutionary status of
the entry (as reminder, as experiment in fiction) implies no indeterminacy
in the speech act itself, and is compatible with the assumption that the
utterance indeed has a definite illocutionary status as serious utterance or
not, assertion or conjecture, etc. As reader of the diary, I may have a thought
of the form, "Here I'm not sure whether this represents any actual claim
of mine or whether I'm just sketching something out." Whether as interlocutor to another person's discourse or as reader of my own diary entry,
I take myself to be presented with an utterance that is either serious or
nonserious, having a definite illocutionary status or not, questions I need
to learn the answer to if I am to know how to respond to it. I take these
questions to have been settled (or not) by the writer, independently of me
now. My uncertainty here as reader regarding the status of what I take to be
my own words does not undermine the status of the original diary entry
as being a committed claim or assertion, or something else. But insofar as

I imagine the original writer as wondering how these words should count, then I can only see the status of the illocution itself as unsettled, and any possible claim expressed by the entry as held in suspense. But if this were a genuinely reflexive case, then the two forms of thought would have to be one and the same, for we would be describing one consciousness, one thought, and in that case I could not relate to those words as testimony from anyone.

When, as in Dummett's example, a person leaves a note for herself in a diary, she is relying on the same institution of diaries, calendars, and notes that she does in reading anyone else's diary, and she is counting on herself to recognize all this when she comes to read her note to herself later. But when she does, her relation to her own words is indeed "essentially different" from what she has to assume it was at the time of writing if the inscription she reads is to count as an informative reminder, for if she is to be informed she has to rely on the identity of an illocution already constituted. This can be seen as "communicating with one's future self" only if we reify "temporal selves" and accept a form of "communication" that is essentially nonreciprocal, and where the separation of powers between the illocutionary authority of the speaker/writer and the recognition of the hearer/reader is preserved. But it is this very separation which prevents its application to the idea of "communicating with one's present self" or "believing oneself" understood reflexively, as the description of a single self-conscious thought.

7.5 Last Words

We learn from others not only in what we pick up on by observing them and interpreting their behavior, but also when another person openly teaches us or tells us something true. Knowledge is transferred between people not only as a byproduct of their behavior but also, and primarily, by its overt communication, where it is essential to the process that the parties take the transmission of knowledge to be precisely what they are engaged in, and take their mutual understanding in the act of discourse to be the very form of the communication of knowledge. In claiming something as true, a speaker purports by her speech to put her interlocutor in a position to know the same thing. It is not accidental to the ideas of reasons and knowledge that they can be communicated overtly between persons in this way, but is part of the publicity of reasons and the objectivity of truth.

For one person to overtly present herself in speech as providing her interlocutor with a reason, whether in assertion, promise, or apology, involves the two parties in a relation of distinct but reciprocally related roles. For the overt communication of reasons in speech requires the speaker to be recognized as having not only the ability to produce a well-formed utterance, but the authority to constitute her utterance as one form of commitment, one form of declaration, rather than another one or none at all. No one else speaks for the speaker here, and this illocutionary moment is the condition for the utterance having the status of a claim or proposal for belief. The speaker exerts one kind of agency or "authoring" (Hobbes) in the vocal or written production of the utterance, and she exerts another kind of agency in the determination of her utterance as specific form of commitment, a particular illocutionary form. The speaker's "authorship" in the production of her utterance is in one aspect no different from the agency she exercises in producing certain sounds or moving her hand to write the words on a page. In principle, another person could move her hand across the page to write those same words, and she could do so with another person's hand. But she exercises a different form of agency in the circumscription of her commitments when she declares that she is hereby only suggesting but not promising, or conjecturing but not asserting. And here the agency she exercises is one that her interlocutor has to defer to in order to be a partner in the exchange. It is possible to move another person's hand to form the words of an apology or a declaration of love, but one cannot in this way make those words count in the desired way, for the determination of the illocution is beyond the direct reach of anyone but the speaker.

The interlocutor has to defer to the speaker here in order to know what manner of reason is being proposed, and thus to understand his own role in the exchange. There is no circumventing this dependence or usurping the speaker's specific role, for it is the condition of there being something with the status of a reason of the sort associated with an assertion or other illocution. Here the interlocutor is essentially dependent on the speaker for the specific form of reason-giving that is to be at issue between them, as he is not so dependent in his private interpretation of the meaning of her unconscious gestures. Correlatively, since the speaker is not simply acting so as to have some influence on the beliefs of her interlocutor, but is proposing a reason by way of openly making herself answerable to him in specific ways, she has to defer to the interlocutor for the recognition of her role in determining the form of reason to be communicated. Without the recognition and the taking up of this proposal the speaker hasn't accomplished anything in speech, and this dependence is no more surpassable than is the interlocutor's dependence on her illocution. This interdependence of forms of deferral is the structure of the ordinary forms of reason-giving in speech. The constitutive role of shared understanding, and the polarity of roles in the accomplishment of the act, are essential to the distinction between social acts of mind and the various other ways in which people may make a difference to the beliefs and expectations of others.

Bibliography

Alston, William P. 2000. *Illocutionary Acts and Sentence-Meaning*. Ithaca, NY: Cornell University Press.

Anscombe, G. E. M. (1963) 1981. "The Two Kinds of Error in Action." In *Ethics, Religion and Politics: Collected Philosophical Papers*, 3, 3–9. Minneapolis: University of Minnesota Press.

———. (1969) 1981. "On Promising and Its Justice, and Whether It Need Be Respected *in Foro Interno*." In *Ethics, Religion and Politics: Collected Philosophical Papers*, 3, 10–21. Minneapolis: University of Minnesota Press.

———. (1975) 1981. "The First Person." In *Metaphysics and the Philosophy of Mind: Collected Philosophical Papers*, 2, 21–36. Minneapolis: University of Minnesota Press.

———. (1957) 1976. *Intention*. Ithaca, NY: Cornell University Press.

———. (1978) 1981. "Rules, Rights and Promises." In *Ethics, Religion and Politics: Collected Philosophical Papers*, 3, 97–103. Minneapolis: University of Minnesota Press.

———. 1979. "What Is It to Believe Someone?" In *Rationality and Religious Belief*, edited by C. F. Delaney, 141–51. Notre Dame: University of Notre Dame Press.

Aristotle. 1984a. *Nicomachean Ethics*. In *The Complete Works of Aristotle: The Revised Oxford Translation*, vol. 2, edited by Jonathan Barnes. Princeton, NJ: Princeton University Press.

Aristotle. 1984b. *Politics*. In *The Complete Works of Aristotle: The Revised Oxford translation*, vol. 2, edited by Jonathan Barnes. Princeton, NJ: Princeton University Press.

Austin, J. L. 1962. *How to Do Things with Words*. Cambridge, MA: Harvard University Press.

———. 1979. "Other Minds." In *Philosophical Papers*, edited by J. O. Urmson and G. J. Warnock, 76–116. 3rd ed. Oxford: Oxford University Press.

Bach, Kent. 1987. "On Communicative Intentions: A Reply to Recanati." *Mind and Language* 2, no. 2.

Bach, Kent, and Robert Harnish. 1979. *Linguistic Communication and Speech Acts*. Cambridge, MA: The MIT Press.

Benveniste, Emile. (1966) 1971. *Problems in General Linguistics*. Translated by Mary Elizabeth Meek. Miami: University of Miami Press.

Biletzki, Anat. 1997. *Talking Wolves: Thomas Hobbes on the Language of Politics and the Politics of Language*. Dordrecht: Kluwer.

Brandom, Robert. 1983. "Asserting." *Nous* 17, no. 4: 637–50.

———. 1994. *Making It Explicit*. Cambridge, MA: Harvard University Press.

Brown, Jessica, and Herman Cappelen, eds. 2011. *Assertion: New Philosophical Essays*. Oxford: Oxford University Press.

Burge, Tyler. 1993. "Content Preservation." *Philosophical Review* 102, no. 4: 457:88.

Carson, Thomas. 2006. "The Definition of Lying." *Nous* 40, no. 2: 284–306.

Cavell, Stanley. 1979. *The Claim of Reason*. Oxford: Oxford University Press.

———. 2006. "Performative and Passionate Utterance." In *Philosophy the Day after Tomorrow*, 155–91. Cambridge, MA: Harvard University Press.

Coady, C. A. J. 1992. *Testimony: A Philosophical Study*. Oxford: Oxford University Press.

Cohen, Ted. 1978. "Metaphor and the Cultivation of Intimacy." *Critical Inquiry* 5, no. 1: 3–12.

Craig, Edward. 1990. *Knowledge and the State of Nature*. Oxford: Clarendon Press.

Darwall, Stephen. 2006. *The Second-Person Standpoint: Morality, Respect, and Accountability*. Cambridge, MA: Harvard University Press.

Descombes, Vincent. 1994. "Is There an Objective Spirit?" In *Philosophy in an Age of Pluralism: The Philosophy of Charles Taylor in Question*, edited by James Tully and Daniel Weinstock, 96–119. Cambridge: Cambridge University Press.

———. 2004a. "Replies to Taylor, Rorty, Brandom and Haugeland." Symposium on *The Mind's Provisions* (Princeton, NJ: Princeton University Press, 2001), in *Inquiry* 47, no. 3: 267–88.

———. 2004b. *Le complément de sujet*. Paris: Gallimard.

———. 2014a. *The Institutions of Meaning*. Cambridge, MA: Harvard University Press.

———. 2014b. *Le parler de soi*. Paris: Gallimard.

Dummett, Michael. 1993a. "Language and Communication." In *The Seas of Language*, 166–87. Oxford: Oxford University Press.

———. 1993b. "Testimony and Memory." In *The Seas of Language*, 411–28. Oxford: Oxford University Press.

Eliot, George. 1997. *Middlemarch*. Oxford World's Classics. Oxford: Oxford University Press.

Elster, Jon. 1983. *Sour Grapes*. Cambridge: Cambridge University Press.

Evans, Gareth. 1982. *The Varieties of Reference*. Oxford: Oxford University Press.

Feinberg, Joel. 1970. "The Nature and Value of Rights." *Journal of Value Inquiry* 4: 243–60.

Ford, Anton. 2011. "Action and Generality." In *Essays on Anscombe's "Intention"*, edited by Anton Ford, Jennifer Hornsby, and Frederick Stoutland, 76–104. Cambridge, MA: Harvard University Press.

Fricker, Elizabeth. 2006. "Second-Hand Knowledge." *Philosophy and Phenomenological Research* 73, no. 3: 592–618.

Fricker, Miranda. 2007. *Epistemic Injustice: Power and the Ethics of Knowing*. Oxford: Oxford University Press.

Geach, Peter. 1957. "On Beliefs about Oneself." *Analysis* 18, no. 1: 23–24.

Goffman, Erving. 1959. *The Presentation of Self in Everyday Life.* New York: Anchor Books.

———. 1978. "Response Cries." *Language* 54, no. 4: 787–815.

Green, Mitchell. 2007. *Self-Expression.* Oxford: Oxford University Press.

Grice, H. P. (1957) 1967. "Meaning." In *Philosophy of Logic,* edited by P. F. Strawson, 39–48. Oxford: Oxford University Press. Originally published in *Philosophical Review* 66 (1957): 377–88.

Haase, Matthias. 2014. "Am I You?" In "The You Turn," special issue edited by Naomi Eilan, *Philosophical Explorations* 17, no. 3: 358–71.

Hobbes, Thomas. (1651) 1994. *Leviathan.* Edited by Edwin Curley. Indianapolis: Hackett.

———. (1647) 1998. *On the Citizen.* Edited and translated by Richard Tuck and Michael Silverthorne. Cambridge: Cambridge University Press.

Holton, Richard. 1994. "Deciding to Trust, Coming to Believe." *Australasian Journal of Philosophy* 72: 63–76.

Hornsby, Jennifer. 1994. "Illocution and Its Significance." In *Foundations of Speech-Act Theory: Philosophical and Linguistic Perspectives,* edited by Savas L. Tsohatzidis, 187–207. New York: Routledge.

Hume, David. (1748) 1977. "On Miracles." In *An Enquiry Concerning Human Understanding.* Indianapolis: Hackett.

———. (1751) 1983. *An Enquiry Concerning the Principles of Morals.* Indianapolis: Hackett.

Husserl, Edmund. (1900) 1970. *Logical Investigations.* Vol. 1. Translated by J. N. Findlay. New York: Routledge.

Kant, Immanuel. (1797) 1996. *The Metaphysics of Morals.* In *Practical Philosophy. The Cambridge Edition of the Works of Immanuel Kant,* 353–604. Edited by Allen Wood, translated by Mary J. Gregor. Cambridge: Cambridge University Press.

Korsgaard, Christine. 2009. *Self-Constitution: Agency, Identity, and Integrity.* Oxford: Oxford University Press.

Kukla, Rebecca, and Mark Lance. 2009. *"Yo" and "Lo": The Pragmatic Topography of the Space of Reasons.* Cambridge, MA: Harvard University Press.

Lackey, Jennifer. 2008. *Learning from Words: Testimony as a Source of Knowledge.* Oxford: Oxford University Press.

Laden, Anthony. 2012. *Reasoning: A Social Picture.* Oxford: Oxford University Press.

Lavin, Douglas. 2008. Review of Stephen Darwall, *The Second Person Standpoint: Morality, Respect, and Accountability. Notre Dame Philosophical Reviews.* http://ndpr.nd.edu/news/the-second-person-standpoint-morality-respect-and-accountability/.

Lawlor, Krista. 2013. *Assurance: An Austinian View of Knowledge and Knowledge Claims.* Oxford: Oxford University Press.

Leite, Adam. 2004. "On Justifying and Being Justified." *Philosophical Issues* (a supplement to *Nous*), vol. 14, *Epistemology,* pp. 219–53.

Locke, John. (1690) 1975. *Essay Concerning Human Understanding.* Edited by Peter Nidditch. Oxford: Clarendon Press.

Longworth, Guy. 2013. "Sharing Thoughts about Oneself." *Proceedings of the Aristotelian Society* 113: 57–81.

———. 2014. "You and Me." In "The You Turn," special issue edited by Naomi Eilan, *Philosophical Explorations* 17, no. 3: 289–303.

MacDowell, D. M. 1986. *The Law in Classical Athens.* Ithaca, NY: Cornell University Press.

MacFarlane, John. 2011. "What Is Assertion?" In *Assertion: New Philosophical Essays*, edited by Jessica Brown and Herman Cappelen, 79–96. Oxford: Oxford University Press.

Martin, M. G. F. 2014. "In the Eye of Another: Comments on Christopher Peacocke's 'Interpersonal Self-Consciousness.'" *Philosophical Studies* 170, no. 1: 25–38.

Marušić, Berislav. 2015. *Evidence and Agency: Norms of Belief for Promising and Resolving.* Oxford: Oxford University Press.

McDowell, John. (1980) 1998. "Meaning, Communication, and Knowledge." In *Meaning, Knowledge, and Reality*, 29–50. Cambridge, MA: Harvard University Press.

McMyler, Ben. 2011. *Testimony, Trust, and Authority.* Oxford: Oxford University Press.

Mellor, D. H. 1977–78. "Conscious Belief." *Proceedings of the Aristotelian Society* 78: 87–101.

———. 1991. "Consciousness and Degrees of Belief." In *Prospects for Pragmatism: Essays in Memory of F. P. Ramsey*, edited by D. H. Mellor, 30–60. Cambridge: Cambridge University Press

Millikan, Ruth. 2004. *Varieties of Meaning.* Cambridge, MA: MIT Press.

Moore, Richard. 2017. "Gricean Communication and Cognitive Development." *Philosophical Quarterly* 67, no. 267: 303–26.

Moran, Richard. 2001. *Authority and Estrangement: An Essay on Self-Knowledge.* Princeton, NJ: Princeton University Press.

———. (1989) 2017. "Seeing and Believing: Metaphor, Image, and Force." In *The Philosophical Imagination: Selected Essays*, 26–48. Oxford: Oxford University Press. Originally published in *Critical Inquiry* 16, no. 1: 87–112.

———. (1995) 2017. "Artifice and Persuasion: The Work of Metaphor in the Rhetoric." In *The Philosophical Imagination: Selected Essays*, 49–60. Oxford: Oxford University Press. Originally published in *Essays on Aristotle's Rhetoric*, edited by Amelie O. Rorty (Berkeley: University of California Press, 1995), 385–98.

———. (2004) 2017. "Anscombe on 'Practical Knowledge'." In *The Philosophical Imagination: Selected Essays*, 219–39. Oxford: Oxford University Press. Originally published in *Agency and Action*, edited by J. Hyman and H. Steward, Royal Institute of Philosophy Supplement 55 (Cambridge: Cambridge University Press), 43–68.

———. 2017. *The Philosophical Imagination: Selected Essays.* Oxford: Oxford University Press.

Nagel, Thomas. 1970. *The Possibility of Altruism.* Princeton, NJ: Princeton University Press.

Neale, Stephen. 1992. "Paul Grice and the Philosophy of Language." Review of Paul Grice, *Studies in the Ways of Words* (Cambridge, MA: Harvard University Press, 1989). *Linguistics and Philosophy* 15, no. 5: 509–59.

Nietzsche, Friedrich. (1886) 1966. *Beyond Good and Evil.* Translated by Walter Kaufmann. New York: Random House.

Owens, David. 2000. *Reason without Freedom.* New York: Routledge.

———. 2006. "Testimony and Assertion." *Philosophical Studies* 130, no. 1: 105–29.

Pascal, Blaise. (1670) 1995. *Pensées.* Translated by A. J. Krailsheimer. New York: Penguin.

Peacocke, Christopher. 2014. *The Mirror of the World: Subjects, Consciousness, and Self-Consciousness.* Oxford: Oxford University Press.

Peirce, C. S. 1934. *Belief and Judgment.* Cambridge, MA: Harvard University Press.

Pettit, Philip. 2008. *Made from Words: Hobbes on Language, Mind and Politics.* Princeton, NJ: Princeton University Press.

Plato. 1997. *Theaetetus.* In *Complete Works,* edited by John Cooper, associate editor D. S. Hutchinson, translated by M. J. Levett, revised by Myles Burnyeat. Indianapolis: Hackett.

Plotinus. 1956. *Enneads.* Translated by Stephen MacKenna. London: Faber & Faber.

Proust, Marcel. (1913) 1998. *Swann's Way.* Translated by C. K. Scott Moncrieff and Terence Kilmartin. New York: Modern Library.

Quine, W. V. O., and J. S. Ullian. 1970. *The Web of Belief.* New York: Random House.

Raz, Joseph. 1972. "Voluntary Obligations and Normative Powers." *Aristotelian Society Supplementary Volume* 46, no. 1: 79–102.

———. 1999. *Practical Reason and Norms.* Oxford: Oxford University Press.

Reid, Thomas. 1764. *An Inquiry into the Human Mind, on the Principles of Common Sense.* Edinburgh: Printed for A. Millar, London, and A. Kincaid & J. Bell, Edinburgh.

———. (1788) 2010. *Essays on the Active Powers of Man.* Edited by Knud Haakonssen and James A. Harris. Edinburgh: Edinburgh University Press.

Reinach, Adolph. (1913) 1983. *The Apriori Foundations of Civil Law.* Translated by John F. Crosby. Irving, TX: International Academy of Philosophy Press. Originally published in *Alethia: An International Journal of Philosophy.*

Ricoeur, Paul. 1970. *Freud and Philosophy: An Essay on Interpretation.* Translated by Denis Savage. New Haven: Yale University Press.

Rödl, Sebastian. 2007. *Self-Consciousness.* Cambridge, MA: Harvard University Press.

Ross, Angus. 1986. "Why Do We Believe What We Are Told?" *Ratio* 28, no. 1: 69–88.

Rumfitt, Ian. 2005. "Meaning and Understanding." In *The Oxford Handbook of Contemporary Philosophy,* edited by Frank Jackson and Michael Smith, 427–53. Oxford: Oxford University Press.

Salje, Léa. 2017. "Thinking About You." *Mind* 126: 817–840.

Saul, Jennifer. 2012. *Lying, Misleading, and What Is Said.* Oxford: Oxford University Press.

Searle, John. 1969. *Speech Acts: An Essay in the Philosophy of Language*. Cambridge: Cambridge University Press.

Schapiro, Tamar. 2001. "Three Conceptions of Action in Moral Theory." *Nous* 35, no. 1: 93–117.

Schmitt, Frederick. 2010. "The Assurance View of Testimony." In *Social Epistemology*, edited by A. Haddock, A. Millar, and D. Pritchard, 216–41. Oxford: Oxford University Press.

Shell, Marc. 1978. *The Economy of Literature*. Baltimore: Johns Hopkins University Press.

Shoemaker, Sydney. 1968. "Self-Reference and Self-Awareness." *Journal of Philosophy* 65, no. 19: 555–67.

Sperber, Dan, and Wilson, Deirdre. 1986. *Relevance*. Cambridge, MA: Harvard University Press.

———. 2002. "Pragmatics, Modularity and Mind-Reading." *Mind and Language* 17, nos. 1–2: 3–23.

———. 2015. "Beyond Speaker's Meaning." *Croatian Journal of Philosophy* 15, no. 44: 117–49.

Stone, Martin. 1996. "On the Idea of Private Law." *Canadian Journal of Law and Jurisprudence* 9, no. 2: 235–77.

———. 2001. "The Significance of Doing and Suffering." In *Philosophy and the Law of Torts*, edited by Gerald J. Postema, 131–82. Cambridge: Cambridge University Press.

Strawson, P. F. (1964) 1971. "Intention and Convention in Speech Acts." In *The Philosophy of Language*, edited by John Searle, 23–38. Oxford: Oxford University Press.

Thompson, Michael. 2004. "What Is It to Wrong Someone? A Puzzle about Justice." In *Reason and Value: Themes from The Moral Philosophy of Joseph Raz*, edited by R. Jay Wallace, Philip Pettit, Samuel Scheffler, and Michael Smith, 333–84. Oxford: Oxford University Press.

———. Forthcoming. "You and I: Some Puzzles about 'Mutual Recognition.'"

Tomasello, Michael. 1999. *The Cultural Origins of Human Cognition*. Cambridge, MA: Harvard University Press.

———. 2008. *Origins of Human Communication*. Jean Nicod Lectures. Cambridge, MA: MIT Press.

———. 2014. *A Natural History of Human Thinking*. Cambridge, MA: Harvard University Press.

Traiger, Saul. 1993. "Humean Testimony." *Pacific Philosophical Quarterly* 4, no. 2: 135–49.

Trilling, Lionel. 1971. *Sincerity and Authenticity*. Cambridge, MA: Harvard University Press.

Tugendhat, Ernst. 1982. *Traditional and Analytical Philosophy: Lectures on the Philosophy of Language*. Translated by P. A. Gorner. Cambridge: Cambridge University Press.

Vendler, Zeno. 1972. *Res Cogitans: An Essay in Rational Psychology.* Ithaca, NY: Cornell University Press.

Wallace, R. Jay. 2007. "Reasons, Relations, and Commands: Reflections on Darwall." *Ethics* 118, no. 1: 24–36.

Walton, Kendall. 1984. "Transparent Pictures: On the Nature of Photographic Realism." *Critical Inquiry* 11, no. 2: 246–77.

Wanderer, Jeremy. 2010. "Inhabiting the Space of Reasoning." *Analysis* 70, no. 2: 367–78.

———. 2013. "Testimony and the Interpersonal." *International Journal of Philosophical Studies* 21, no. 1: 92–110.

———. 2014. "Alethic Holdings." *Philosophical Topics* 42, no. 1: 63–84.

Watson, Gary. 2004. "Asserting and Promising." *Philosophical Studies* 117, nos. 1–2: 57–77.

Weinrib, Ernest. 1995. *The Idea of Private Law.* Cambridge, MA: Harvard University Press.

Welbourne, Michael. 1986. *The Community of Knowledge.* Aberdeen: Aberdeen University Press.

Williams, Bernard. 1973. "Morality and the Emotions." In *Problems of the Self,* 207–29. Cambridge: Cambridge University Press.

———. 2002. *Truth and Truthfulness: An Essay in Genealogy.* Princeton, NJ: Princeton University Press.

Williamson, Timothy. 2000. *Knowledge and Its Limits.* Oxford: Oxford University Press.

Wittgenstein, Ludwig. 1956. *Philosophical Investigations.* Translated by G. E. M. Anscombe. Oxford: Blackwell.

———. 1958. *The Blue and Brown Books.* Oxford: Blackwell.

———. 1980. *Remarks on the Philosophy of Psychology.* Vol. 1. Translated by G. E. M. Anscombe. Oxford: Blackwell.

———. 1993. "Notes for Lectures on 'Private Experience' and 'Sense Data.'" In *Philosophical Occasions, 1912–1951,* edited by James C. Klagge and Alfred Nordmann, 202–88. Indianapolis: Hackett.

Index of Names

Alston, William, 130, 133
Anscombe, G. E. M., 25n13, 59n13,
    65n18, 74, 79–80, 145–149, 151, 153n8,
    194–195, 215
Antonioni, Michelangelo, 50
Aristotle, 8–9
Arnold, Matthew, 91
Augustine, ix
Austin, J. L., 31–32, 34, 60, 74n23, 108n6,
    119n9, 129, 134, 137, 153, 178–179,
    181, 187n26

Bach, Kent, 136n15, 173, 175n19
Benveniste, Emile, 156–157, 161, 166,
    181, 214
Biletzki, Anat, 9n4
Brandom, Robert, 13n6, 64n17,
    119n9, 123
Burge, Tyler, 18n11, 39

Carson, Thomas, 81n1
Cavell, Stanley, 7n2, 12n5, 65n18, 134n12,
    154n10, 190, 193–195, 199, 215
Coady, C. A. J., 37, 39–40, 61–62n14
Cohen, Ted, 182
Craig, Edward, 18–19, 20n12, 79,
    93n11, 126n5

Darwall, Stephen, 73n22, 122–128, 131n9
Descombes, Vincent, 16n10, 155n11,
    191n2, 213
Dummett, Michael, 213–215, 218

Eliot, George, 169–170
Elster, Jon, 179n22
Evans, Gareth, 157, 217

Feinberg, Joel, 7–8, 122
Ford, Anton, 150n6

Fricker, Elizabeth, 139n18
Fricker, Miranda, 8n3, 143n19

Geach, Peter, 215
Goffman, Erving, 85, 197–198
Green, Mitchell, 100
Grice, H. P., 52–56, 59–61, 97–101, 103–104,
    119n9, 159–163, 166, 170–181, 183
Grotius, Hugo, ix

Haase, Matthias, 214
Harnish, Robert, 136n15
Hobbes, Thomas, ix, 9–11, 14, 15, 205–206
Holton, Richard, 62n15
Hornsby, Jennifer, 135, 136n14,
    143n19, 151
Hume, David, ix, 37, 47, 108–109, 110n7,
    111–112, 113, 114
Husserl, Edmund, 22, 190

Kant, Immanuel, 202–203, 205–212
Korsgaard, Christine, 201–203, 205
Kukla, Rebecca, 13n6, 125n4

Lackey, Jennifer, 19–20, 138n17
Laden, Anthony, 134n12, 197
Lance, Mark, 13n6, 125n4
Lavin, Douglas, 124n3
Lawlor, Krista, 44n7
Leite, Adam, 73n21
Lewinsohn, Jed, 110n7
Locke, John, 36n1
Longuenesse, Béatrice, 210n8
Longworth, Guy, 167n15

MacDowell, D. M., 8n3
MacFarlane, John, 75n24, 123n2
Martin, M. G. F., 167n15
Marušić, Berislav, 126n5

McDowell, John, 98, 100–102, 119, 154n9, 188
McMyler, Benjamin, 126n5
Mellor, D. H., 91
Millikan, Ruth, 17, 100n3
Moore, Richard, 172n18
Moran, Richard, xi–xii, 147n4, 183n23, 184n24, 202

Nagel, Thomas, 202–204
Neale, Stephen, 172n18, 173
Nietzsche, Friedrich, 87n5

Owens, David, 85n4, 87n6, 138n17

Pascal, Blaise, 14
Peacocke, Christopher, 167n15
Peirce, C. S., 123, 138, 139
Pettit, Philip, 9n4
Plato, 191–192
Plotinus, 76–77, 82, 120
Proust, Marcel, 92n10

Quine, W. V. O., 17

Raz, Joseph, 131, 152
Reid, Thomas, 1–5, 28, 34, 96, 102n4, 111n8, 120, 132n10, 141, 146, 155, 190, 191n2, 192, 197
Reinach, Adolf, 152
Rödl, Sebastian, 167n15
Ross, Angus, 45–49, 54n12, 56, 61, 63–64, 68
Rumfitt, Ian, 98n2

Salje, Léa, 167n15
Saul, Jennifer, 81n1

Schapiro, Tamar, 133n11
Schmitt, Frederick, 138n17
Searle, John, 107, 123, 135
Shell, Marc, 12n5
Shoemaker, Sydney, 157n13
Socrates, 80, 192, 200
Sperber, Dan, 171, 172n18, 173–174, 177–179, 182
Stevens, Wallace, 183
Stone, Martin, 73n22, 123n1
Strawson, P. F., xii, 98n2, 100, 119n9, 177–184

Thompson, Michael, 73n22, 123n1, 125, 167n15
Tomasello, Michael, 144n20, 168, 171n17
Tugendhat, Ernst, 160–162, 165, 166–167, 180, 186

Ullian, J. S., 17

Vendler, Zeno, 12, 111, 195–197

Wallace, R. Jay, 124n3
Walton, Kendall, 49–50
Wanderer, Jeremy, 13n6, 126n4, 127n5
Watson, Gary, 67n20
Weinrib, Ernest, 73n22, 123n1
Welbourne, Michael, 46n9, 97n1
Wilde, Oscar, 148
Williams, Bernard, 63n16, 78–80, 82–85, 89–92, 137n16
Williamson, Timothy, 66n19, 78
Wilson, Deirdre, 171, 172n18, 173–174, 177–179, 182
Wittgenstein, Ludwig, ix, 45n8, 198, 200, 216

Index of Subjects

a priori warrant, 40
accountability. *See* responsibility
address, 3, 86, 88, 100, 119–120, 122,
    156–158, 165, 166, 180–181, 184
    self-address, 198–202, 213–214
agency
    productive, 27, 30, 97, 99–100, 104, 116,
      159–163, 165
    two forms of, 130–133, 215, 219
agreement and disagreement, 34, 72,
    116–119, 160–167, 181, 194
animals, non-human, 9, 11
apologizing, 28, 62, 74–75, 85–86
assertion, 24–25, 31, 45n8, 61, 69–71,
    78–83, 107–110, 123, 130,
    160–163, 166
    vs. telling, 38, 46–47, 78–82, 89
assurance, 44–45, 51, 61, 68–72
authority, 10–11, 15, 124–134, 143, 208,
    211–212
    illocutionary, 51, 58–59, 65–66, 72–73,
      94, 128–134, 142–143, 152–153,
      185–189, 215, 219
avowability, xii, 177–187

believing the speaker, 19, 38, 40–41,
    59–60, 65, 74, 79–80, 126n5, 194–195
    believing oneself (reflexive), 65, 190,
      194, 213–218

commitment, 33, 65, 72, 123–124, 130,
    138–139, 142, 215
conscience, 210–212
consumer's point of view, 20–21, 159
counter-utterance, 160–167, 180, 187

dependence, 15
    and deference, xii, 34, 126, 187–189,
      203–207, 217, 219–220

on the person as such, 42–45, 49, 52,
    54, 60, 68, 73n21, 79–80, 86, 103, 133,
    171–172, 194–195, 219
    reciprocal, 154, 185–189
detective, 23–24, 164–165
disharmony, 69–75, 164–165
double-bluffing, 59–60, 70–72, 194–195
duties to oneself. *See* obligations to
    oneself

encounter, 13, 36, 60, 104, 108, 114, 117,
    120, 168–170, 172, 181, 184, 214
entitlement, 4, 13n6, 16, 18n11, 37, 39n4,
    64n17, 73, 116, 123–124, 142
epistemology, 17–21
evidence, 37–38, 40–52, 54–56, 61,
    63–64, 69, 94
expression, 2–5, 9–10, 26, 35, 74
    "direct," 83–84, 87
    personal vs. impersonal, 85–88,
      88–89n7, 93, 107–108, 110, 128, 172

the first person, 18, 21, 153–157, 187–189
freedom, 43–45, 49, 51, 69, 130, 133, 141,
    206. *See also* agency

guarantee. *See* assurance

higher-order attitudes, xii, 114–115, 120,
    167–170, 171, 184n24

"I" and "You," 22, 155–158, 161–162, 166,
    180–181, 184, 187–189, 200
illocution, 31–35, 60, 107n5, 129–137, 143
    vs. perlocution, 32, 129–134, 135–137,
      149, 153–154, 178, 181, 215
    reflexivity of, 215–218
    role of "hereby" in, 60, 66, 75, 134, 136,
      153–155, 178, 180, 188, 215

illocution (*cont.*)
  uptake of, 34, 134, 141, 153, 167,
    187–189
  See also authority: illocutionary; in-
    stitution: as context for illocution;
    understanding: formal dependence
    of illocution on
implying and insinuating, 178–180,
  182, 187
Indicative model, 23–31, 35, 43, 96–97,
  105, 140, 159–160, 202
informant vs. 'source,' 18–20, 79–80,
  93n11, 126n5, 193
institution, 101–102, 198
  as context for illocution, 143, 149, 218
  language as, 6, 12–15
insulting. *See* offending
internalization, 203–204, 208–209
intersubjectivity, 5, 35, 133, 166–170, 183,
  185–189, 219–220

knowledge
  constitutive role of, 30–33, 94–95, 103,
    106, 111–112, 146, 150, 217–218
  "mutual knowledge" as higher-order
    notion, 114–115, 120, 167–170,
    180–181
  practical, 33–34, 111–112, 142, 146–148,
    185, 216–217
  transmission of, 5, 38, 97, 142, 218
  of what one is doing, two forms of, 33,
    110–112, 142, 150

lying, 42–43, 87–88
  and sincerity, 81n1, 82–83, 107, 114

Manifest condition, 108–109, 112–113,
  115, 140–141
metaphor, 174, 175, 182–183
mind reading, xii, 23, 28, 43, 76–77, 96,
  120, 168–170, 184
monologue vs. dialogue, 156–158,
  160–162, 164–165, 186, 194
Moore's Paradox, 45n8, 112–119
mutual manifestness, 177

natural vs. non-natural meaning, 46,
  52–63, 109–110, 172, 178, 181

normative power, 30, 131–134, 141,
  152–153

obligations to oneself, 203, 205–210, 212
offending, 134, 136, 145, 148–149, 204
other minds, 22–23, 26
overhearing, 67–68, 138–139
overtness, 28–29, 114–115, 119–120, 137,
  178–181, 183. *See also* avowability

perception, 17–18, 49, 100–104
perspective
  incorporation of, 34, 143–144, 155–156,
    185–189
  of the participants, 20–21, 73, 141–144
photographs, 47–51, 54–55, 60, 64, 126,
  141–142, 176
praeteritio, 187n25
promising, 4, 34–35, 62, 67–71, 106–110,
  131–133, 212
  vs. asserting, 67, 75n24, 138–139, 141
  oneself, 205, 207

questions, 98, 102, 106, 115, 118, 163–165,
  192–193

Reciprocity condition, 135–137, 151–152,
  154–155
recognition, 7–8, 35, 112, 134–137
  of intention, 54–57, 59–61, 172–177
  mutual, 61, 149–152, 166–170
reply, 34, 118–119, 186–187. *See also*
  counter-utterance
respect and self-respect, 191, 203, 204
responsibility, 34, 44–45, 48, 51, 58,
  61, 64, 67–69, 72–75, 85–86, 95,
  130–134, 139
retraction, 65, 75, 212
rights, 7–8, 122, 132

saying vs. showing, 50–51, 53–55, 99, 101,
  140–141, 172–176
the second person, 184, 195, 200
  second-personal normativity, 73n22,
    120, 122–128, 131
self-consciousness (reflexive), 103, 180,
  215–216
self-legislation, 203, 206–210

self-presentation, 34, 57–58, 60, 65, 91,
    101, 113, 115–117, 128, 140. *See also*
    sincerity: Sincerity condition
selves vs. persons
    within the person, 190–192, 203–204,
        206–213
    temporal stages, 213–218
signs, 13, 17, 23–26, 31, 52
    two kinds of, 109–110
sincerity, 76–95, 116–117, 120, 196
    Sincerity condition, 105, 106–107,
        109–110, 112–116
    See also lying: and sincerity
social acts of mind, 1–5, 28, 34–35, 96,
    101, 112, 151–152, 190–191, 219–220
speech acts, 31–32, 34, 58, 75, 101,
    107–108, 129–137, 143

tact, 182
talking
    to oneself, 192, 197–201, 213–214
    in one's sleep, 24–25, 48, 61, 62, 106
    vs. saying something, 6–7, 24, 173,
        195–197
telepathy. *See* mind reading

telling, 24–25, 31–33, 38, 40, 47, 54–56,
    71–74, 79–80, 82, 89–90, 105–110,
    158–165. *See also* assertion: vs.
    telling
thinking aloud, 199, 201–202
true, presenting as, 27, 33, 51, 58, 62–63,
    72, 116–121, 163–165, 196

understanding
    formal dependence of illocution on,
        147–152, 158, 160, 189
    self-understanding, 22, 32, 94, 101,
        146–153
    shared, 21–22, 33–34, 60, 112, 116, 144,
        149–152, 155, 159, 166, 185–186,
        188–189
    Understanding condition, 105–106,
        109–113, 115, 140
    See also knowledge
unilateral model, 20, 99–100, 104, 112,
    116, 119, 143, 160–165, 179, 180–184,
    202, 212n9, 214

Yes and No. *See* agreement and
    disagreement

Lightning Source UK Ltd.
Milton Keynes UK
UKHW011428180319
339375UK00002B/207/P